Research Prompts

800+ Student-Centered Research Challenges

Second Edition

Kevin L. Potter

Potter Analytics LLC   Los Angeles

Research Prompts
800+ Student-Centered Research Challenges

Copyright © 2018 by Kevin L. Potter

Cover Design by Kevin L. Potter

Potter Analytics LLC
400 Continental Blvd.
6th Floor
El Segundo, CA 90245
www.potteranalytics.com

ISBN-13: 978-0-692-98532-8

Table of Contents

Chapter 25 — 577

Appendix A — 601

Appendix B — 605

Index — 613

Introduction

Research Prompts are a set of challenges that use research tasks such as a combination of open-ended questions, closed-ended problems, and cognition-sparking scenarios to guide students through various levels of thinking based on Bloom's Taxonomy. This book addresses two problems. The first problem is most modern students have access to the majority of closed-ended questions through internet resources; while, the second problem is many students depend heavily on the search capabilities of search engines versus working in tandem with their own questioning abilities.

Correct answers to closed-ended questions are stepping stones to deeper knowledge. However, in reality, many students are not getting the full value of their research, because they may gather the data to complete their assignments. Yet, they forget the information, because it does not appear to have value or relevance beyond an academic exercise. Besides, students realize that the answers to these types of questions are almost instantly available by way of the Internet. In the past, educators had to battle the statement by students "Are we ever going to use this?" Now, teachers have to contend with "Why do I have to remember (recall) all of this information! It's already on the internet and I almost always have the internet!" These thoughts actually are quite logical if you only wish to recall knowledge like a calculator or spell-check device. But when comprehension, application, analysis, and synthesis are necessary, this logic falls short. With student-centric Research Prompts, students are pushed to value the answers to many research challenges. In many cases, a student must recall and comprehend the previous information to complete the next research challenge. Furthermore, student-centered challenges provide incentives for students to take interest in their assignments, while practicing critical thinking, creative problem-solving and research skills.

Secondly, in this age of information, the Internet has delivered the ability to gain immediate answers to most closed-ended questions, but, in addition to this revolutionary feat, the Internet has brought about the ability to predict users' questions. Now to an adult, this may seem like a beneficial feature, but for edu-cators specifically teaching digital citizenship, this feature can inhibit the questioning process. Plus, the ability to question is one of humanity's greatest tools; moreover, the ability to question is in use when tran-scending through recalling, comprehending, applying, analyzing, synthesizing, and evaluating knowledge. Therefore, the majority of Research Prompts are de-signed to be search-engine-resistant, not search-engine-proof. For example, students must explain and defend their answers to questions that cannot be fulfilled with a short fill-in-the-blank answer. Some of the research tasks may seem strangely simple; whereas, some of the research tasks may seem per-plexingly challenging, but in general, the research tasks of this book usually require creative problem solving, critical thinking, and research skills.

Guiding students to additional opportunities that encourage them to question as much as possible is the strategy of student-centered, Research Prompts. Although, the quest for Higher-Order Thinking, also known as Analysis, Synthesis, and Evaluation, is not always a smooth journey, but questions tend to be there throughout the trek for knowledge. All in all, even though students have immediate access to the answers of most closed-ended questions, Research Prompts drive students to be questioners whether on the Internet or at a library through challenges that can spark curiosity and ultimately more questioning.

XII

Road Rules for Research Prompts

1. **Challenges can potentially be overcome with time, effort, and thought**. This road rule is a reminder to students that these research challenges can be overcome with time, effort and most importantly thought.
2. **It is okay to be curious.** This road rule is a declaration to the benefits of curiosity. It is curiosity that is the compelling soul of questioning. Even though, many multicellular organisms exhibit curiosity from lab rats to civil cats; it is humans that can thoroughly exercise the ability to question and take advantage of current and future results. Therefore, remind students of the benefits of curiosity.
3. **Gathering answers are not necessarily understanding answers.** This book frequently requires research to complete each challenge. Each challenge usually depends on the previous challenge. However, the majority of the research challenges requires creative questioning and critical thinking, as well. Comprehension is paramount to completing the first or second challenge of a Research Prompt, so remind students to take the time to comprehend the data that they gather.
4. **Thinking about thinking** is the last road rule. Thinking about thinking also known as metacognition helps build cognitive strategies and mental planning when faced with challenges in the classroom or the "real world". By observing their own internal thought processes, students through creative thinking, critical thinking and research skills gain invaluable lessons. Therefore, practicing metacognition when challenged

by Research Prompts, will help students gain "know-how", "tricks of the trade", or tacit knowledge.

Research Prompts Format:

Each chapter of this book is divided into five sections. Furthermore, each section contains a collection of related research challenges. The sections of each chapter have a major and minor theme. The benefits of each section are listed below.

Section 1:

Translating and communicating the expressions of ideas in the form of images, words, or both represents the goal of Section 1. For instance, locating or creating expressive images has become a requirement across the board from journalists to bloggers to business people to research scientists. The Internet has become a visual medium. It is not just text any more. Whether individuals are seeking funding from investors, explaining a new scientific concept, or reporting novel information; images help tell the story. Furthermore, students must defend their visual expressions. Thus, Section 1 has opportunities for students to demonstrate their understanding through multiple mediums.

Section 2:

The main goal of Section 2 is to spark thinking that nudges students to consider alternative solutions and additional possiblities when there appears to be only one answer. These types of problems are presented, so students can practice thinking outside-the-box. Thinking inside the box could loosely be considered convergent thinking. For example, $8 + 8 = 16$, always. Whereas, "thinking outside the box", which could loosely be considered divergent thinking, looks for alternative answers. There are numerous alternatives to "$8 + 8 =$"; however, students should attempt to figure it out on their own, initially. To recap, the research challenges of Section 2 help students practice the skill of discovering alternative answers.

Section 3:

In this section, students immerse themselves in a topic. Students have the ability to choose literary works or create literary works such as quotations, poems, biographical statements, and more. These challenges provide students the opportunity to demonstrate not just understanding but higher-order thinking skills.

Section 4:

This section provides challenges that focuses on evaluation and synthesis through the examination of wise sayings from various cultures. In addition, students practice composing multimedia scenarios through posters and evaluating alternative solutions to semi-difficult to hard problems. Similar to the other sections, the challenges in this section require time and thought.

Section 5:

This section dedicates itself to examining the nature of organizations and the impact of their services and products. Students will spend time and energy analyzing, creating(Synthesizing), and evaluating in an effort to nurture their higher order thinking skills. As with most of the challenges in each section, students have an opportunity to explore their own interests which may inspire them to dig deeper and think longer about their chosen subject.

Using Bloom's Taxonomy While Nurturing Research Skills:

In an effort to inspire metacognition, thinking about thinking, students will notice Research Prompts are followed by one of six words in parentheses. These words are **Knowledge**, **Comprehension**, **Application**, **Analysis**, **Synthesis**, and **Evaluation**. Even though, Knowledge, Comprehension, and Application, are known as Low Order Thinking Skills, these skills are normally important for learners to grasp High Order Thinking Skills. For instance, knowing rules, terms, and facts will ultimately assist students with comprehending the game of chess. Furthermore, you could have the rules to the game chess memorized, but comprehending the advantages and disadvantages per move is another level of thinking called Comprehension.

Using the same example with chess, a new player can learn the advantages and disadvantages over time while playing chess. However, through practice and thinking, a new player can exhibit the ability to apply different strategies that can be learned from failed experimentation or successful actions from previous games. This is Application in action. Application is an important bridge between Low Order Thinking Skills and High Order Thinking Skills.

Analysis is the skill of examining situations for cause and effect. Still, using chess as an example, a player learning chess should eventually start wondering about their opponent. Chess is a game of defense and offense; therefore, analyzing your opponent's strategy whether simple or complex is a part of the game. Furthermore, a new player could draw connections and parallels between other less-complex games such as Checkers and Tic-Tac-Toe. For instance, a new chess player who is an experienced checker player, may be more willing to sacrifice a knight, rook, or bishop for a tactical advantage than a non-checker player.

Synthesizing and Evaluating are the last two High Order Thinking Skills. Even if a new player gains experience and formulates their own 'new' tactics in chess, this is extremely healthy in the realm of higher order thinking skills; unfortunately, the vast majority of strategies in chess have been claimed and named. This example applies in learning and life. Many of the hypothesis, theories, strategies, and ideas during a person's educational journey are not original; however, they are normally necessary to construct new knowledge. So, don't be discouraged that you did not originate the concept of Metacognition(Psychology & Educational Psychology), Mores(Sociology), or the Distributive Property(Mathematics).

Finally, Evaluation is the highest order of thinking based on Bloom's Taxonomy. Evaluation helps chess players by judging their own skills based on assessments. For example, a chess player may think that he or she is the best chess player at their Middle School or the greatest chess strategist in town. Whether a chess player has realistic or unrealistic ideas about their tactical skills in chess, the chess player must be able to support and defend their statements. In other words, the thought must be tested and defended over time. Another example would be a student concluding that "Chess is a game of mistakes, the person who makes the least mistakes wins." The only problem is some chess players would disagree with this conclusion. At this point, the student would have to defend their point with supporting evidence and logical examples. So, whether it is an internal argument or external debate, evaluation assists with the growth of a student's cognitive abilities.

Lastly, when it comes to metacognition, the Research Prompt approach provides research scenarios that drive students to question and think before, during, and after search engine resistance challenges. From a metacognitive perspective, a student could ask the following questions when working on a math assignment.

Example: Metacognition and Improper Fractions	
Knowledge (recall)	Do I remember the definition of improper fractions?
Comprehension	Do I understand the definition (concept) of improper fractions?
Application	Am I able to apply my understanding of improper fractions to complete my assignment?
Analysis	Am I able to identify the difference among proper fractions, improper fractions, and mixed fractions? Is there a pattern?
Synthesis	Am I able to organize a chart of fractions that are used in other fields like a quart of milk or a quarter of a dollar?
Evaluation	Is there a better method for converting fractions to another form such as decimals?

Convert Research Challenges into Games

Do you want your students to be even more engaged with the research challenges provided in this book? Here are **seven** techniques to transform research challenges into games.

Gaming Modification 1a:
Forecast Game (Predict the most common answer)

Rules: Students have 5 to 10 minutes to brainstorm and list as many answers as possible based on the research challenge. For instance, name stories that have a talking wolf? *Little Red Riding Hood* and *The Neverending Story* are two examples with wolves. Next, each student predicts the most frequently chosen answer among the class. Then, the teacher tallies the answers. The student(s) who predict the most popular answer wins. Teachers can modify this game to fit their class size and schedule.

Gaming Modification 1b:
The Most Unique Answers (Vote on Unique Answers)

Rules: Students have 5 to 15 minutes to brainstorm and think of a unique answer to a research challenge. However, each student is competing to come up with the most unique answer for the class to win. For instance, there are 19 students and 1 teacher in the classroom. *"How many individuals are in the classroom room?"* This could potentially stump many students, because the obvious answer is 20. Is there more than one answer that can be provided? Yes. The purpose of research challenges is to provide perspective. Another answer is 00010100 which is binary for 20. This game focuses on exploring **divergent** answers to research challenges. Feel free to modify.

Gaming Modification 2:
The Roundup (Gather as many answers as possible)

Rules: Students have 5 to 15 minutes to brainstorm and gather as many answers as possible to a research challenge. Students can work in groups. Student(s) with the most correct answers win. For example, 6 hours equals...

- 21,600 seconds
- 360 minutes
- 1/4th of a day
- 21,600,000 milliseconds, etc

A more complex research challenge would be "*How much did the first cellphone weigh?*" Then, provide as many answers as possible?

Game Modification 3a:
Art Show Game Contest

Rules: Create an illustration, chart, or diagram that expresses the answer(s) to a research challenge.

Game Modification 3b:
Artistic Scavenger Hunt Contest

Rules: Students have 5 to 15 minutes to gather diagrams, charts, and/or illustrations from other sources.

Game Modification 4:
The Analogy Competition

Rules: Create a simple analogy that explains a process, cycle, or set of instructions. The analogy can be verbally expressive, visually crafted, audio-enhanced, computer-generated or a physical construction. The goal is simplicity; therefore, the class votes on the best "simple" analogy. Feel free to modify.

Game Modification 5:
Tricks of the Trade(for confusing words)

Rules: The Teacher randomly selects a word from a research challenge(or the list below). Students share and compete for great ways to remember difficult or confusing vocabulary. For example:

How do you remember the difference between *horizontal* versus *vertical*? My hint is horizon.
Fiction Versus *Non-fiction*. My hint is science fiction.

Small List of Potentially Confusing Words

scent/cent	lessen/lesson	hole/whole	waive/wave
rain/reign/rein	board/bored	desert / dessert	your/you're
infamous/ famous	discrete/ discreet	among / between	confuse / confess
affect/effect	ball/bawl	its/it's	hair/hare
clothes/close	later/latter	night/knight	alone/lonely
idol/idle	hyphen/dash	levee/levy	aisle/isle
assure/ ensure / insure	empathy / sympathy / apathy	immigrate / emigrate	breath /breathe
farther / further	historic / historical	hanger / hangar	principal/prin- ciple
brake/break	lead/led	loose/lose	imply/infer
grate/great	know/no	since/sense	forego/forgo
rise/raise	either/neither	suit/suite	either/ether
too/to	then/than	witch/which	buy/by/bye
stationary/sta- tionery	allusion/ illusion	adverse/ averse	meddle /metal/ medal
fair/fare	aloud/allowed	pail/pale	mail/male
hoard/horde	parcel/partial	borne/born	assent/ascent
whether/ weather	veracious/ voracious	convex/ concave	perpetuate/ perpetrate
suit/suite	sweat/sweet	racket/raquet	here/hear
assent/ascent	are/our	bear/bare	pour/pore/poor

Game Modification 6:
Language Detective (Why do they call it that?)

Rules: Students are to discover, breakdown and digest the meaning of a selected word. The student(s) with the best explanation(s). For instance,
Geometry: Geo and metry(meter)....
Longitude: longitudo....
Latitude:....
Corona:....

The teacher selects vocabulary from their subject. For instance, a math classroom might use the word *PERCENT*.

Language Detective Examples by Subject		
Subject	**Example #1**	**Example #2**
Math	Fraction	Volume
Algebra	Algebra	Absolute Value
Geometry	Tangent	Radius
Language Arts	Preposition	Metaphor
History	Archeology	Pyramid
Geography	Pennisula	Eurasia
Biology	Prokaryote	Ribosome
Chemistry	Atom	Titanium
Physics	Velocity	Vector
Literature	Prose	Novel
World Languages	Tiempo (Spanish)	Tempus (Latin)
Computer Science	Binary	Algorithm
Art	Romanticism	Realism
Business	Investment	Finance
Music	Melody	Harmony

Game Modification 7:
The Great Debate Combo Game:

(Similar to the Most Unique Answer Game)
Rules: Students have 5 to 15 minutes to brainstorm
as many answers as possible to a research challenge.
Once the time for brainstorming has elapsed, must
provide a **scenario** that gives context or perspective.
The **scenario** can be simple/vague or detailed. For
instance, the scenario could be as simple as stating
Math Class or a *French Class*.

Before students debate each other over their "better"
answer. The teacher must select a set of criteria such
as
> 1.) Appropriateness -
>> Is the answer appropriate to the
>> scenario
> 2.) Originality/Uniqueness -
>> Is the answer original or unique in relation
>> to the answers provided by other students
> 3.) Advantageous/Innovative -
>> Is the answer advantageous or innovative
>> to the scenario
> 4.) Convenient/Efficient -
>> Is the answer convenient or efficient to
>> the scenario
> 5.) Reliable/Standardized
>> Is the answer reliable and standard to
>> the scenario

Last, provide 3-5 minutes for students to figure out
which of their answers fit the criteria, if any. Next,
the teacher must ask the class who has the best answer. Then, students must debate and defend their
answer. The winner is determined by the class, but
the teacher referees. So, whoever provides the best

answer first, is the winner of the game.

Since this game modification is a little more complex, I will provide two step-by-step examples.

Step 1: The Problem or Challenge
The teacher provides a problem such as a research challenge. For example, **2 + 5 =**

Step 2: The Brainstorming Session
2+5=

a.) 7 (number in decimal form)
b.) VII (number in Roman Numerals)
c.) 0111(number in Binary form)
d.) Seven (number in text form)
e.) 3+4 (answer distributed)
f.) $7.00 (currency format)
g.) and more divergent answers

Step 3: The Decision Phase
The teacher sets the **scenario** along with the **Criteria**. *See Table Example 1.*

Example 1: 2+5 =		
Scenario / Situation	Criteria #1	Student's Answer
Basic Math Class	Effective	7
On a Cell Phone Keypad	Reliable	7
Market	Convenience	$7.00
Grammar	Effective	Seven
In Algebra Class	Advantageous	3+4
Computer Class	Unique	0111
Spanish Class	Effective	Siete

Step 4: The Debate Phase
The teacher asks the class for the best answer based on the scenario and situation. Then, the teacher moderates the debate for the better/best answer.

Another Example:
Step 1: The Problem or Challenge
The teacher provides a problem such as a research challenge. **What is the height of Mount Everest?**

Step 2: The Brainstorming Session
What is the height of Mount Everest?

a.) 29,029 feet   e.) 8.848 kilometers
b.) 9,676 yards   f.) 348,346 feet
c.) 5.5 miles   g.) 29,029 rulers (12")
d.) 8,848 meters   h.)116 Jumbo Jets
              i.) 40,352 Apple iPads (4th Gen)

Step 3: The Decision Phase
The Teacher sets the scenario along with the criteria. *See Table Example 2.*

Example 2: What is the height of Mt. Everest?			
Scenario / Situation	Criteria #1	Criteria #2	Student's Answer
Math Class	Appropriate	Reliable	29,029 feet
Management	Unique	Innovative	40,352 iPads (4th Gen.)
Geography	Appropriate	Efficient	5.5 Miles

Step 4: The Debate Phase
Let students debate based on the criteria.

In conclusion, feel free to modify this game for your classroom environment.

Chapter 1

Connections to
Common Core State Standards:

CCSS.ELA-LITERACY.WHST.6-8.6
Use technology, including the Internet, to produce and publish writing and present the relationships between information and ideas clearly and efficiently.(2010)

CCSS.ELA-LITERACY.WHST.6-8.7
Conduct short research projects to answer a question(including a self-generated question), drawing on several sources and generating additional related, focused questions that allow for multiple avenues of exploration.(2010)

CCSS.ELA-LITERACY.WHST.6-8.8
Gather relevant information from multiple print and digital sources, using search terms effectively; assess the credibility and accuracy of each source; and quote or paraphrase the data and conclusions of others while avoiding plagiarism and following a standard form of citation.(2010)

CCSS.ELA-LITERACY.WHST.6-8.9
Draw evidence from informational texts to support analysis, reflection, and research.(2010)

Connections to
Common Core State Standards:
<u>(continued)</u>

CCSS.ELA-LITERACY.WHST.6-8.10
Write routinely over extended time frames(time for revision and reflection) and shorter time frames(a single sitting or a day or two) for a range of discipline-specific tasks, purposes, and audiences.(2010)

CCSS.ELA-LITERACY.RH.6-8.1
Cite specific textual evidence to support analysis of primary and secondary sources.(2010)

CCSS.ELA-LITERACY.RH.6-8.4
Determine the meaning of words and phrases as they are used in a text, including vocabulary specific to domains related to history/social studies.(2010)

CCSS.ELA-LITERACY.RH.6-8.7
Integrate visual information(e.g., in charts, graphs, photographs, videos, or maps) with other information in print and digital text.(2010)

CCSS.ELA-LITERACY.RST.6-8.1
Cite specific textual evidence to support analysis of science and technical texts.(2010)

CCSS.ELA-LITERACY.RST.6-8.2
Determine the central ideas or conclusions of a text; provide an accurate summary of the text distinct from prior knowledge or opinions.(2010)

CCSS.ELA-LITERACY.RST.6-8.
Distinguish among facts, reasoned judgment based on research findings, and speculation in text.(2010)

Chapter 1
Section 1

Exploration of the Idiom:

Method in One's Madness

Common Core State Standards:
- CCSS.ELA-LITERACY.WHST.6-8.8
- CCSS.ELA-LITERACY.WHST.6-8.10
- CCSS.ELA-LITERACY.RH.6-8.4
- CCSS.ELA-LITERACY.RH.6-8.7

Learning Objectives:
A. Understand the figurative meaning of idioms
B. Comprehend the problematic issues with literal translations of idioms
C. Expand personal creative boundaries through visualization and problem solving

Method in One's Madness

Instructions:
Place your answers to each challenge into a journal or folder

Challenge One:
Translate "Method in One's Madness" **into your own words**.(Comprehension)

Challenge Two:
Create two separate sentences using the idiom "Method in One's Madness".(Application)

Challenge Three:
Identify another idiom that is similar to "Method in One's Madness". (Analysis)

Challenge Four:
Recall **fictional** characters whom behaviors symbolized "A method in one's madness." Explain each character's behavior and reasoning in relation to the idiom.(Evaluation)

Suggested Start:
Using an American English Idiom dictionary, define the figurative meaning of "Method in One's Madness".

Potential Resources:
    1.) Idioms.thefreedictionary.com
    2.) Dictionary.reference.com/idioms

Challenge Five:
Create, draw or sketch three **individual** objects that represent the word "Puzzling". Based on your images, explain the connection(s) to the subject.(Synthesis)

Example 1:
Humbled

Example 2:
Driven

Challenge Six:

Create two or more images that express the feeling "I dislike broccoli!" But, use as few images and letters as possible. Then, repeat this process with the thought, "I love broccoli". Communicate the subtle or overt meaning of the objects inside your images.(Synthesis)

Example One: *I dislike brussel sprouts.*

Example Two: *I love brussel sprouts.*

Chapter 1
Section 2

Perspectives on:
Time

Common Core State Standards:
- CCSS.ELA-LITERACY.WHST.6-8.7
- CCSS.ELA-LITERACY.WHST.6-8.8
- CCSS.ELA-LITERACY.WHST.6-8.10
- CCSS.ELA-LITERACY.RST.6-8.1
- CCSS.ELA-LITERACY.RST.6-8.2

Learning Objectives:
- A. Gain perspective on vague writing
- B. Gain awareness of potential problems with "absolute" statements in writing
- C. Gain perspective on multiple answers

What time is it?

Instructions:
Place your answers to each challenge into a journal or folder

Challenge One:
Answer the question, "What time is it?" Explain. (Analysis)

Challenge Two:
Explain the concept(s) of time? Cite sources that defend your argument.(Evaluation)

Here are recommendations to keep in mind when answering the above questions:
1. What is time?
2. How is time measured?
3. Is there more than one type of time?
4. Cite sources that defend your argument.

Suggested Start:
   1. Pause before answering the question.
   2. Using a dictionary, define "Time".
   3. Using an encyclopedia, research "Time".

Potential Resources:
      1.) Merriam-Webster.com
      2.) Bartleby.com
      3.) Plato.Stanford.edu

Challenge Three:
Create a joke that you must answer in a figurative way and a literal way. Remember, keep it clean and respectful. NO PRACTICAL JOKES!(Analysis)

Example:
Joke(the setup): *They say "failure is a part of learning".*
Figurative answer (punchline): *Could someone please explain that to my parents.*
Literal answer: *This quote translates more often into "We learn from our mistakes". Whether a person is completing a quiz or learning to ride a bike, mistakes may occur, and they have the option to grow from their small failures.*

The secret to creating jokes is to ask questions about the world. In other words, analyze the world around you. If it doesn't make sense, question it. Then, research it.

To help, start with a statement like:
Why is it that...............
Ever notice that...........
Whose idea was it to make...
One day, there was a.................
Why does....
Where's the......
How is it that....
Don't forget to explore and explain the answer in a figurative and literal way. Creating jokes can be challenging. Worst case scenario, find and use a joke that you can answer in a figurative and literal way. Explain, why it is funny. Give credit to the comedian.

Challenge Four:

First, **define** the word, "Creativity". Second, create a two column chart with a "negative factors" side and a "positive factors" side. Third, contrast the positive factors and negative issues of the word, "Creativity". (Analysis)

Example:

According to _____'s dictionary, **failure** is....

Failure	
Negative Factors	**Positive Factors**
May spark negative emotions	Mistakes and failings are a part of the creation process
May affect interpersonal relationships	"When you quit that is true failure"
	Don't make failing a habit; however, if it happens, learn from your failure

Challenge Five:

Find an image. Then, create a chart that lists the directly observable features versus the not-visible, but inferable features of the image.(Analysis)

Example: Airplane	
Observable and Visible	**Not Visible, but Inferable**
is a vehicle	holds passengers
is on the ground	holds cargo
is jet propelled	has instruments

Chapter 1
Section 3

Exploring Quotations on: Travel

Common Core State Standards:
- CCSS.ELA-LITERACY.WHST.6-8.6
- CCSS.ELA-LITERACY.WHST.6-8.8
- CCSS.ELA-LITERACY.WHST.6-8.10
- CCSS.ELA-LITERACY.RH.6-8.1
- CCSS.ELA-LITERACY.RH.6-8.4
- CCSS.ELA-LITERACY.RH.6-8.7

Learning Objectives:
A. Gain knowledge on the topic of "travel"
B. Experience other perspectives on "travel"
C. Stimulate creative skills through research

Quotations on Travel

Instructions:
Place your answers to each challenge into a journal or folder

Challenge One:
Locate a quotation on the topic of "travel".(Knowledge)

Challenge Two:
Translate your selected quotation on "travel" into your own words.(Comprehension)

Challenge Three:
Compose a biographical statement using your chosen quotation on "travel".(Application)

Challenge Four:
Create your own quote on "travel".(Application)

Challenge Five:
Create or select a poem on "travel".(Application)

Suggested Start:
1. Reflect on traveling experiences, small or large.
2. Quotation resources are available at your library.

Potential Resources:
1.) Quoteland.com
2.) Brainyquote.com
3.) Quotationspage.com
4.) En.wikiquote.org

Challenge Six:

Using a quotation on "travel", discover a way to express the meaning through pictures and words. Then, create a comic strip that explains the quotation.(Synthesis)

Example:
"Hunger"
"Thou shouldst eat to live; not live to eat."
Socrates

Create a collection of images that relate to the quote. Then, add captions or messages that help express the quote. Lastly, connect images and create a comic strip.

Challenge Seven:
Complete the following sentence fragment with three or more separate statements. Figure out a way to incorporate a quotation, adage, or joke.(Application)

The school campus is...

Example:

The last movie that I saw...
1.) ...caused my mind to reflect on the possibilities of humans having superpowers. For instance, by combining advanced nanotechnology with our understanding of genetics, we could modify ourselves into more supercharged people.

2.) ...agitated me because it depicted the cruelties of mankind. However, I then reflected on an anonymous quote that "Unfortunately, the road to progress can have various levels of bumpiness".

3.) ...frightened me because it was a creepy horror film. Now, I want to sleep with the lights on, but my parents disagree. Even though, I don't pay the electric bill. I feel that I should be able to make this decision!

Chapter 1
Section 4

Exploration of Adages, Aphorisms, Proverbs, and Maxims:

Common Core State Standards:
- CCSS.ELA-LITERACY.WHST.6-8.6
- CCSS.ELA-LITERACY.WHST.6-8.8
- CCSS.ELA-LITERACY.WHST.6-8.10
- CCSS.ELA-LITERACY.RH.6-8.4
- CCSS.ELA-LITERACY.RH.6-8.7

Learning Objectives:
- A. Experience perceptive sayings from various cultures
- B. Examine beliefs and understandings of various individuals and groups
- C. Communicate information through visualization

Adages, Aphorisms, Proverbs, and Maxims

Instructions:
Place your answers to each challenge into a journal or folder

Challenge One:
Select an adage, aphorism, proverb, or maxim. Research the origin of the adage, aphorism, proverb, or maxim. Cite source(s).(Knowledge)

Challenge Two:
Translate your chosen adage, aphorism, proverb, or maxim into your own words.(Comprehension)

Challenge Three:
Compose a small paragraph or a short segment of dialogue that includes your chosen adage, aphorism, proverb, or maxim.(Application)

Challenge Four:
Do you agree or disagree with the message of your chosen adage, aphorism, proverb or maxim. Defend your response. Cite sources.(Analysis & Evaluation)

Suggested Start:
1. Reflect on your chosen adage, aphorism, proverb, or maxim.
2. Identify problems, if any.

Potential Resources:
1.) En.wikiquote.org
2.) Thinkexist.com

Challenge Five:
Select at least three pictures based on your selected adage, aphorism, proverb, or maxim. Next, build three posters by adding text to the chosen pictures. (Synthesis)

Suggested Start:
"Tomorrow Never Comes"
1. Make sure you understand the adage, aphorism, proverb, or maxim.
2. Reflect on the meaning(s) of your chosen adage, aphorism, proverb, or maxim.
3. Search for images that symbolize or reflect the adage, aphorism, proverb, or maxim.
4. Construct posters.

Tomorrow Never Comes

Carpe Diem - Sieze the Day!

Challenge Six:

Is it better to <u>succeed</u> or <u>fail</u>?

In this exercise, consider possible scenarios when it is better to do one or the other underlined options. Next, find scenarios that benefit from each underlined option. Then, try to find scenarios that do not benefit from each underlined option. Create a chart that represents your conclusions. Lastly, compose statements using historical examples or scientific data that validate each item inside your chart. (Evaluation)

Example: Is it better to <u>spark</u> or <u>spur</u>?

Neither	Spark	Spur	Both
malice	critical thoughts	truthfulness	healthy behavior
hatred	cooperation	obedience	innovations
ignorance	motivation	horse	inventions
	confidence		imagination
			students
			self-control

- A. <u>Hatred</u> can <u>spark</u> destructive behavior such as... (insert historical example).
- B. Although, at times effective, spurred obedience has a limited shelf life; eventually, the spurred will rebel or revolt such as a child or colony...
- C. According to _____ (author/researcher/expert), sparking confidence can boost students' comprehension.

Chapter 1
Section 5

Exploration of Business

Common Core State Standards:
- CCSS.ELA-LITERACY.WHST.6-8.6
- CCSS.ELA-LITERACY.WHST.6-8.7
- CCSS.ELA-LITERACY.WHST.6-8.8
- CCSS.ELA-LITERACY.WHST.6-8.9
- CCSS.ELA-LITERACY.WHST.6-8.10
- CCSS.ELA-LITERACY.RH.6-8.4
- CCSS.ELA-LITERACY.RH.6-8.7

Learning Objectives:
- A. Examine business costs and opportunities
- B. Communicate information through graphics and text such as diagrams and charts

Organization Path

Instructions:
Place your answers to each challenge into a journal or folder

Challenge One:
Name a business that you patronize frequently. Classify the type of business it is. Identify the main product or service.(Knowledge)

Challenge Two:
Identify three competitors of the business that you patronize frequently.(Comprehension)

Challenge Three:
Identify three products or services of your chosen company. Create a chart that displays the relationship among the main product and the additional products. Determine if these products are:
- Integrated and necessary for the main product to operate such as gasoline or motor oil for cars
- Complementary to the product and enhances product like air conditioning and power windows for cars
- Vital to the business such as their brand brake pads and spark plugs for cars(Application)

Main Product(Windows Operating System)			
	Integrated and Necessary	Enhances Main Product	Vital to Business
Microsoft Office	No	Yes	Yes
Internet Explorer	Yes	Yes	Yes
Xbox 360	No	No	No

Challenge Four:

Categorize the four chosen products by popularity among consumers, history of the products, revenue, profit, target audience(name their main customers), and strongest direct competitor, quasi-competitor and indirect competitor. Use a scale from 4 to 1, 4 being highest, to grade each category. Then, based on your chart, describe the growth potential (or lack of future potential) of each product. Which product is the strongest? Which product would you focus more resources on for the future of the company. Defend your decision. Cite sources.(Analysis)

Strengths and Weaknesses				
	Windows OS	Microsoft Office	Internet Explorer	Xbox 360
Popularity	3	4	2	1
Revenue	3	4	2	1
Profitabil- ity	3	4	2	1

Strengths and Weaknesses by Details				
	Windows OS	Microsoft Office	Internet Explorer	Xbox 360
Years Available	28 yrs.	23 yrs.	19 yrs.	8 yrs.
Direct Competitor	Mac OS X	LibreOf- fice	Chrome	Playsta- tion 3
Quasi- Competitor	Android OS	QuickOf- fice	Smart- TVs	Gameboy Advance
Indirect Competitor	Pen and Paper	Typewriter	Library Card	Mobile Device
Rankings among direct Com- petitors	#1	#1	#2	#1

Challenge Five:

Choose one of your chosen company's most popular or well-known products or services. Research this product or service and build a diagram that displays the fabrication process of the product or service. Cite sources.(Synthesis)

Your diagram or chart should display the work that goes into producing a product or service.

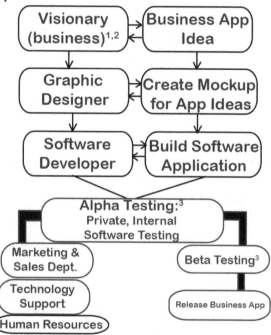

1 Does the app solve a problem?
2 Can it be profitable?
3 Testing may require restarts or revisions.

Challenge Six:

Create a chart that explains two of the product's major features. For example, an alarm clock normally has a minimum of two features, the time display and the alarm function. Use graphics, if possible. Cite sources.(Analysis)

Alarm Radio	
Radio	converts radio waves...
Alarm Buzzer	is a feature of the...

Challenge Seven:

Based on your gathered research and your product choice, create a visual flowchart or graphical diagram that demonstrates the interaction between human resources and non-human resources to produce the product or service. Start with the necessary (raw) materials required to produce the product or service. For example, an organic farmer needs supplies, materials, equipment, and workers. Then, your flowchart should display the interactions between the workforce and resources until the end-product reaches consumers. (Synthesis)

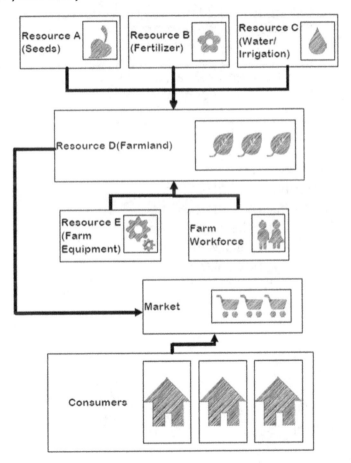

Challenge Eight:

Identify three individuals that had a major impact on your chosen company's industry. Create a multi-media chart to describe their impact. Based on your research of these three individuals, which individual had the biggest impact on their industry. Defend your argument. Cite sources.(Evaluation)

Industry: Telecommunications		
insert image	John Doe	was an inventor whose radical and unorthodox methods produced the first....
insert image	Jane Doe	was an amazing engineer who invented the first....
insert image	Dr. Cooper	was a well-known and well-respected physician that accidentally invented....

Potential Resources:
- www.bls.gov/ooh
- www.bls.gov/iag
- howstuffworks.com
- visual.merriam-webster.com
- finance.yahoo.com
- ehow.com
- sba.gov
- entrepreneur.com

Rubric for Chapter
See Appendix A

Reflective Questions for Chapter
See Appendix B

Chapter 2

Connections to
Common Core State Standards:

CCSS.ELA-LITERACY.WHST.6-8.6
Use technology, including the Internet, to produce and publish writing and present the relationships between information and ideas clearly and efficiently.(2010)

CCSS.ELA-LITERACY.WHST.6-8.7
Conduct short research projects to answer a question(including a self-generated question), drawing on several sources and generating additional related, focused questions that allow for multiple avenues of exploration.(2010)

CCSS.ELA-LITERACY.WHST.6-8.8
Gather relevant information from multiple print and digital sources, using search terms effectively; assess the credibility and accuracy of each source; and quote or paraphrase the data and conclusions of others while avoiding plagiarism and following a standard form of citation.(2010)

CCSS.ELA-LITERACY.WHST.6-8.9
Draw evidence from informational texts to support analysis, reflection, and research.(2010)

Connections to
Common Core State Standards:
(continued)

CCSS.ELA-LITERACY.WHST.6-8.10
Write routinely over extended time frames(time for revision and reflection) and shorter time frames(a single sitting or a day or two) for a range of discipline-specific tasks, purposes, and audiences.(2010)

CCSS.ELA-LITERACY.RH.6-8.1
Cite specific textual evidence to support analysis of primary and secondary sources.(2010)

CCSS.ELA-LITERACY.RH.6-8.4
Determine the meaning of words and phrases as they are used in a text, including vocabulary specific to domains related to history/social studies.(2010)

CCSS.ELA-LITERACY.RH.6-8.7
Integrate visual information(e.g., in charts, graphs, photographs, videos, or maps) with other information in print and digital text.(2010)

CCSS.ELA-LITERACY.RST.6-8.1
Cite specific textual evidence to support analysis of science and technical texts.(2010)

CCSS.ELA-LITERACY.RST.6-8.2
Determine the central ideas or conclusions of a text; provide an accurate summary of the text distinct from prior knowledge or opinions.(2010)

CCSS.ELA-LITERACY.RST.6-8.
Distinguish among facts, reasoned judgment based on research findings, and speculation in text.(2010)

Chapter 2
Section 1

Exploration of the Idiom: Catch Cold

Common Core State Standards:
- CCSS.ELA-LITERACY.WHST.6-8.8
- CCSS.ELA-LITERACY.WHST.6-8.10
- CCSS.ELA-LITERACY.RH.6-8.4
- CCSS.ELA-LITERACY.RH.6-8.7

Learning Objectives:
- A. Understand the figurative meaning of idioms
- B. Comprehend the problematic issues with literal translations of idioms

Catch Cold

Instructions:
Place your answers to each challenge into a journal or folder

Challenge One:
Translate "Catch Cold" or "Catch a Cold" **into your own words**.(Comprehension)

Challenge Two:
Create two separate sentences using the idiom "Catch Cold" or "Catch a Cold".(Application)

Challenge Three:
Identify another idiom that is similar to "Catch Cold". (Analysis)

Challenge Four:
List fictional characters that "Caught a Cold".(Evaluation)

Challenge Five:
Recall a fictional character that warns another fictional character about the potential of "Catching a Cold". Explain each character's behavior and action in relation to the idiom.(Evaluate)

Suggested Start:
Using an American English Idiom dictionary, define the figurative meaning of "Catch Cold".

Potential Resources:
    1.) Idioms.thefreedictionary.com
    2.) Dictionary.reference.com/idioms

Challenge Six:

Create, draw or sketch three **individual** objects that represent the word "Enrichment". Based on your images, explain the connection(s) to the subject.(Synthesis)

Example 1:
Humbled

Example 2:
Driven

Challenge Seven:

Create two or more images that express the statement "My hunger is no more!" But, use as few images and letters as possible. Then, repeat this process with the thought, "I'm full!".(Synthesis) Communicate the subtle or overt meaning of the objects inside your images.(Synthesis)

Example One: *I dislike bananas.*

Example Two: *I love bananas.*

Chapter 2
Section 2

Perspectives on:
Bacteria

Common Core State Standards:
- CCSS.ELA-LITERACY.WHST.6-8.7
- CCSS.ELA-LITERACY.WHST.6-8.8
- CCSS.ELA-LITERACY.WHST.6-8.10
- CCSS.ELA-LITERACY.RST.6-8.1
- CCSS.ELA-LITERACY.RST.6-8.2

Learning Objectives:
- A. Gain perspective on vague writing
- B. Gain awareness of potential problems with "absolute" statements in writing
- C. Gain perspective on multiple answers

All Bacteria are Harmful to Humans

Instructions:
Place your answers to each challenge into a journal or folder

Challenge One:
Respond to the statement, "All Bacteria are Harmful to Humans". Cite sources that defend your response. (Analysis)

Challenge Two:
Can bacteria be parasitic? Can bacteria be symbiotic? (Comprehension)

Challenge Three:
Is the common cold a
a.) A virus?
b.) A bacteria?
c.) A combination of a virus and bacteria?(knowledge)

Here are recommendations to keep in mind when answering the above questions:
1. Describe bacteria.
2. Compare bacteria versus other forms of life.

Suggested Start:
   1. Pause before answering the question.
   2. Using an encyclopedia, research "bacteria".

Potential Resources:
   1.) Merriam-Webster.com
   2.) Bartleby.com

Challenge Four:
Create a joke that you must answer in a figurative way and a literal way. Remember, keep it clean and respectful. NO PRACTICAL JOKES!(Analysis)

Example:
Joke(the setup): *They say "failure is a part of learning".*
Figurative answer (punchline): *Could someone please explain that to my parents.*
Literal answer: *This quote translates more often into "We learn from our mistakes". Whether a person is completing a quiz or learning to ride a bike, mistakes may occur, and they have the option to grow from their small failures.*

The secret to creating jokes is to ask questions about the world. In other words, analyze the world around you. If it doesn't make sense, question it. Then, research it.

To help, start with a statement like:
   Why is it that...............
   Ever notice that...........
   Whose idea was it to make...
   One day, there was a.................
   Why does....
   Where's the......
   How is it that....

Don't forget to explore and explain the answer in a figurative and literal way. Creating jokes can be challenging. Worst case scenario, find and use a joke that you can answer in a figurative and literal way. Explain, why it is funny. Give credit to the comedian.

Challenge Five:
First, **define** the word, "Mysterious". Second, create a two column chart with a "negative factors" side and a "positive factors" side. Third, contrast the positive factors and negative issues of the word, "Mysterious". (Analysis)
Example:
According to _____'s dictionary, **failure** is....

Failure	
Negative Factors	**Positive Factors**
May spark negative emotions	Mistakes and failings are a part of the creation process
May affect interpersonal relationships	"When you quit that is true failure"
	Don't make failing a habit; however, if it happens, learn from your failure

Challenge Six:
Find an image. Then, create a chart that lists the directly observable features versus the not-visible, but inferable features of the image.(Analysis)

Example: Military Airplane	
Observable and Visible	**Not Visible, but Inferable**
is a vehicle	holds pilots
is jet propelled	holds cargo
	has computer systems

Chapter 2
Section 3

Exploring Quotations on: Peace

Common Core State Standards:
- CCSS.ELA-LITERACY.WHST.6-8.6
- CCSS.ELA-LITERACY.WHST.6-8.8
- CCSS.ELA-LITERACY.WHST.6-8.10
- CCSS.ELA-LITERACY.RH.6-8.1
- CCSS.ELA-LITERACY.RH.6-8.4
- CCSS.ELA-LITERACY.RH.6-8.7

Learning Objectives:
- A. Gain knowledge on the topic of "peace"
- B. Experience other perspectives on "peace"

Quotations on Peace

Instructions:
Place your answers to each challenge into a journal or folder

Challenge One:
Locate a quotation on the topic of "peace".(Knowledge)

Challenge Two:
Translate your selected quotation on "peace" into your own words.(Comprehension)

Challenge Three:
Compose a biographical statement using your chosen quotation on "peace".(Application)

Challenge Four:
Create your own quote on "peace".(Synthesis)

Challenge Five:
Select or create a poem on "peace".(Syntheis)

Suggested Start:
1. Reflect on various views on the word "peace".
2. Quotation resources are available at your local library.

Potential Resources:
1.) Quoteland.com
2.) Brainyquote.com
3.) Quotationspage.com
4.) En.wikiquote.org

Challenge Six:

Using a quotation on "peace", discover a way to express the meaning through pictures and words. Then, create a comic strip that explains the quotation.(Synthesis)

Example:

"Hunger"

"Thou shouldst eat to live; not live to eat."

Socrates

Create a collection of images that relate to the quote. Then, add captions or messages that help express the quote. Lastly, connect images and create a comic strip.

Challenge Seven:

Complete the following sentence fragment with three or more separate statements. Figure out a way to incorporate a quotation, adage, or joke.(Application)

Our football team...

Example:

The last movie that I saw...

1.) ...caused my mind to reflect on the possibilities of humans having superpowers. For instance, by combining advanced nanotechnology with our understanding of genetics, we could modify ourselves into more supercharged people.

2.) ...agitated me because it depicted the cruelties of mankind. However, I then reflected on an anonymous quote that "Unfortunately, the road to progress can have various levels of bumpiness".

3.) ...frightened me because it was a creepy horror film. Now, I want to sleep with the lights on, but my parents disagree. Even though, I don't pay the electric bill. I feel that I should be able to make this decision!

Chapter 2
Section 4

Exploration of Adages, Aphorisms, Proverbs, and Maxims:

Common Core State Standards:
- CCSS.ELA-LITERACY.WHST.6-8.6
- CCSS.ELA-LITERACY.WHST.6-8.8
- CCSS.ELA-LITERACY.WHST.6-8.10
- CCSS.ELA-LITERACY.RH.6-8.4
- CCSS.ELA-LITERACY.RH.6-8.7

Learning Objectives:
- A. Experience perceptive sayings from various cultures
- B. Examine beliefs and understandings of various individuals and groups

Adages, Aphorisms, Proverbs, and Maxims

Instructions:
Place your answers to each challenge into a journal or folder

Challenge One:
Select an adage, aphorism, proverb, or maxim. Research the origin of the adage, aphorism, proverb, or maxim. Cite source(s).(Knowledge)

Challenge Two:
Translate your chosen adage, aphorism, proverb, or maxim into your own words.(Comprehension)

Challenge Three:
Compose a small paragraph or a short segment of dialogue that includes your chosen adage, aphorism, proverb, or maxim.(Application)

Challenge Four:
Do you agree or disagree with the message of your chosen adage, aphorism, proverb, or maxim. Defend your response. Cite sources.(Evaluation)

Suggested Start:
1. Reflect on your chosen adage, aphorism, proverb, or maxim.
2. Identify problems, if any.

Potential Resources:
1.) En.wikiquote.org
2.) Thinkexist.com

Challenge Five:

Select at least three pictures based on your selected adage, aphorism, proverb, or maxim. Next, build three posters by adding text to the chosen pictures. (Synthesis)

Suggested Start:
"Tomorrow Never Comes"

1. Make sure you understand the adage, aphorism, proverb, or maxim.
2. Reflect on the meaning(s) of your chosen adage, aphorism, proverb, or maxim.
3. Search for images that symbolize or reflect the adage, aphorism, proverb, or maxim.
4. Construct posters.

Tomorrow Never Comes

Carpe Diem - Sieze the Day!

Challenge Six:

Is it better to <u>invent</u> or <u>innovate</u>?

In this exercise, consider possible scenarios when it is better to do one or the other underlined options. Next, find scenarios that benefit from each underlined option. Then, try to find scenarios that do not benefit from each underlined option. Create a chart that represents your conclusions. Lastly, compose statements using historical examples or scientific data that validate each item inside your chart. (Evaluation)

Example: Is it better to <u>spark</u> or <u>spur</u>?

Neither	Spark	Spur	Both
malice	critical thoughts	truthfulness	healthy behavior
hatred	cooperation	obedience	innovations
ignorance	motivation	horse	inventions
	confidence		imagination
			students
			self-control

A. <u>Hatred</u> can <u>spark</u> destructive behavior such as... (insert historical example).
B. Although, at times effective, spurred obedience has a limited shelf life; eventually, the spurred will rebel or revolt such as a child or colony...
C. According to _____(author/researcher/expert), sparking confidence can boost students' comprehension.

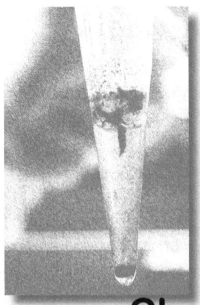

Chapter 2
Section 5

Exploration of Business

Common Core State Standards:
- CCSS.ELA-LITERACY.WHST.6-8.6
- CCSS.ELA-LITERACY.WHST.6-8.7
- CCSS.ELA-LITERACY.WHST.6-8.8
- CCSS.ELA-LITERACY.WHST.6-8.9
- CCSS.ELA-LITERACY.WHST.6-8.10
- CCSS.ELA-LITERACY.RH.6-8.4
- CCSS.ELA-LITERACY.RH.6-8.7

Learning Objectives:
- A. Examine products and services from the view of an organizational entity such as a business
- B. Communicate information through graphics and text such as diagrams and charts

Product and Service Path

Instructions:
Place your answers to each challenge into a journal or folder

Challenge One:
Identify an amazing product or service that you use frequently.(Knowledge)

Challenge Two:
Identify the type of companies that produce your chosen product or service. Classify their industry.(Comprehension)

Challenge Three:
Identify three direct competitors of your chosen product or service. Describe and chart the competition based on market share, business size (by employees), years available, marketing reach(local, regional, national, global), revenue and profits. Research and use industry averages if your chosen company or its competitors are not publicly traded.(Analysis)

Main Product (Web Browsers)				
	Market Share	**Business Size**	**Marketing Reach**	**Years Available**
Internet Explorer (product)	2	large enterprise	global	19
Chrome (competitor)	1	large enterprise	global	6
Firefox (competitor)	3	mid-size	global	12
Opera (competitor)	4	mid-size	global	18

Challenge four:

Create a diagram that displays the major parts or sequences of your chosen product or service. Next explain two of the product's major parts. For example, an Xbox 360 has multiple, specialized parts such as the central processing unit, the graphics processing unit and the hard drive. Use graphics. Cite sources. (Analysis)

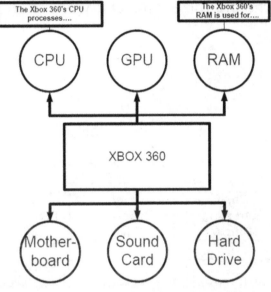

Challenge Five:

Based on your chosen product or service, identify three influential people that had a major impact on this industry through improvements, innovations, or inventions. Describe their effects on the industry. Cite sources.(Analysis)

Industry: Telecommunications		
insert image	John Doe	was an inventor whose radical and unorthodox methods produced the first....
insert image	Jane Doe	was an amazing engineer who invented the first....
insert image	Dr. Cooper	was a well-known and well-respected physician that accidentally invented....

Challenge Six:

Create an organizational chart (unofficial) of a company that offers your chosen product or service. Next, pinpoint the areas where your three previously chosen influential people would work. For example, if one of your selected influential people is a visionary executive leader, then they would fit somewhere at the top of the organizational chart(org chart).(Synthesis)

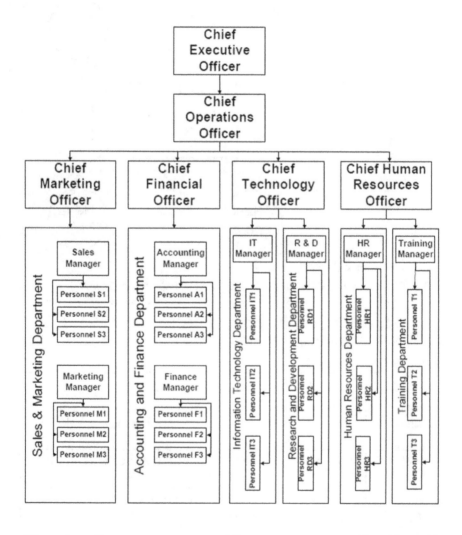

Challenge Seven:

Based on your gathered research and your product choice, create a visual flowchart or graphical diagram that demonstrates the interaction between human resources and non-human resources to produce the product or service. Start with the necessary (raw) materials required to produce the product or service. For example, an organic farmer needs supplies, materials, equipment, and workers. Then, your flowchart should display the interactions between the workforce and resources until the end-product reaches consumers. (Synthesis)

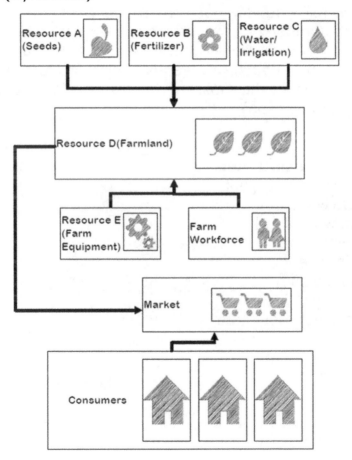

Challenge Eight:

Based on your product choice or service selection,
- Identify two supplemental/complementary products or services such as computer applications complement computer operating systems
- Identify two required/necessary products (computer operating system are necessary to operate computers)
- Identify two separate or indirectly connected products or services that the company produces(Xbox 360 or Zune)

Discover which product(s) is your strongest seller(s). Why? Would you eliminate any products or services from the company's product lineup? Explain. Which product or service deserves the most research and development? Elaborate. Lastly, which product or service deserves the most marketing. Explain. Cite sources.(Evaluation)

Potential Resources:
- www.bls.gov/ooh
- www.bls.gov/iag
- howstuffworks.com
- visual.merriam-webster.com
- finance.yahoo.com
- ehow.com
- sba.gov
- entrepreneur.com

Rubric for Chapter
See Appendix A

Reflective Questions for Chapter
See Appendix B

Chapter 3

Connections to Common Core State Standards:

CCSS.ELA-LITERACY.WHST.6-8.6
Use technology, including the Internet, to produce and publish writing and present the relationships between information and ideas clearly and efficiently.(2010)

CCSS.ELA-LITERACY.WHST.6-8.7
Conduct short research projects to answer a question(including a self-generated question), drawing on several sources and generating additional related, focused questions that allow for multiple avenues of exploration.(2010)

CCSS.ELA-LITERACY.WHST.6-8.8
Gather relevant information from multiple print and digital sources, using search terms effectively; assess the credibility and accuracy of each source; and quote or paraphrase the data and conclusions of others while avoiding plagiarism and following a standard form of citation.(2010)

CCSS.ELA-LITERACY.WHST.6-8.9
Draw evidence from informational texts to support analysis, reflection, and research.(2010)

Connections to
Common Core State Standards:
(continued)

CCSS.ELA-LITERACY.WHST.6-8.10
Write routinely over extended time frames(time for revision and reflection) and shorter time frames(a single sitting or a day or two) for a range of discipline-specific tasks, purposes, and audiences.(2010)

CCSS.ELA-LITERACY.RH.6-8.1
Cite specific textual evidence to support analysis of primary and secondary sources.(2010)

CCSS.ELA-LITERACY.RH.6-8.4
Determine the meaning of words and phrases as they are used in a text, including vocabulary specific to domains related to history/social studies.(2010)

CCSS.ELA-LITERACY.RH.6-8.7
Integrate visual information(e.g., in charts, graphs, photographs, videos, or maps) with other information in print and digital text.(2010)

CCSS.ELA-LITERACY.RST.6-8.1
Cite specific textual evidence to support analysis of science and technical texts.(2010)

CCSS.ELA-LITERACY.RST.6-8.2
Determine the central ideas or conclusions of a text; provide an accurate summary of the text distinct from prior knowledge or opinions.(2010)

CCSS.ELA-LITERACY.RST.6-8.
Distinguish among facts, reasoned judgment based on research findings, and speculation in text.(2010)

Chapter 3
Section 1

Exploration of the Idiom:
Get the Picture

Common Core State Standards:
- CCSS.ELA-LITERACY.WHST.6-8.8
- CCSS.ELA-LITERACY.WHST.6-8.10
- CCSS.ELA-LITERACY.RH.6-8.4
- CCSS.ELA-LITERACY.RH.6-8.7

Learning Objectives:
A. Understand the figurative meaning of idioms
B. Comprehend the problematic issues with literal translations of idioms

Get the Picture

Instructions:
Place your answers to each challenge into a journal or folder

Challenge One:
Translate "Get the Picture" **into your own words.**
(Comprehension)

Challenge Two:
Create two separate sentences using the idiom "Get the Picture".(Application)

Challenge Three:
Identify another idiom that is similar to "Get the Picture".(Analysis)

Challenge Four:
List **fictional** characters who "Got the Picture" at an important time in their fictional works. Evaluate and explain each character's behavior and action in relation to the idiom.(Evaluation)

Suggested Start:
Using an American English Idiom dictionary, define the figurative meaning of "Get the Picture".

Potential Resources:
1.) Idioms.thefreedictionary.com
2.) Dictionary.reference.com/idioms

Challenge Five:

Create, draw or sketch three **individual** objects that represent the word "caustic". Based on your images, explain the connection(s) to the subject.(Synthesis)

Example 1:
Humbled

Example 2:
Driven

Challenge Six:

Create two or more images that express the statement "Eureka!" But, use as few images and letters as possible. Then, repeat this process with the thought, "Oops!" Communicate the subtle or overt meaning of the objects inside your images.(Synthesis)

Example One: *I dislike cantaloupe.*

Example Two: *I love cantaloupe.*

Chapter 3
Section 2

Perspectives on:
Height

Common Core State Standards:
- CCSS.ELA-LITERACY.WHST.6-8.7
- CCSS.ELA-LITERACY.WHST.6-8.8
- CCSS.ELA-LITERACY.WHST.6-8.10
- CCSS.ELA-LITERACY.RST.6-8.1
- CCSS.ELA-LITERACY.RST.6-8.2

Learning Objectives:
- A. Gain perspective on vague writing
- B. Gain awareness of potential problems with "absolute" statements in writing
- C. Gain perspective on multiple answers

What is Your Height?

Instructions:
Place your answers to each challenge into a journal or folder

Challenge One:
Answer the question, "What is your height?"(Analysis)

Challenge Two:
Explain height? Cite sources that defend your explanation.(Evaluation)

Here are recommendations to keep in mind when answering the above questions.
1. What exactly is height?
2. Is there more than one way to answer this question?
3. Cite sources that defend your argument.

Suggested Start:
    4. Pause before answering the question.
    5. Using a dictionary, define "Height".

Potential Resources:
    1.) Merriam-Webster.com
    2.) Bartleby.com

Challenge Three:
Create a joke that you must answer in a figurative way and a literal way. Remember, keep it clean and respectful. NO PRACTICAL JOKES!(Analysis)

Example:
Joke(the setup): *They say "failure is a part of learning".*
Figurative answer (punchline): *Could someone please explain that to my parents.*
Literal answer: *This quote translates more often into "We learn from our mistakes". Whether a person is completing a quiz or learning to ride a bike, mistakes may occur, and they have the option to grow from their small failures.*

The secret to creating jokes is to ask questions about the world. In other words, analyze the world around you. If it doesn't make sense, question it. Then, research it.

To help, start with a statement like:
Why is it that...............
Ever notice that...........
Whose idea was it to make...
One day, there was a.................
Why does....
Where's the......
How is it that....

Don't forget to explore and explain the answer in a figurative and literal way. Creating jokes can be challenging. Worst case scenario, find and use a joke that you can answer in a figurative and literal way. Explain, why it is funny. Give credit to the comedian.

Challenge Four:

First, **define** the word, "Venerable". Second, create a two column chart with a "negative factors" side and a "positive factors" side. Third, contrast the positive factors and negative issues of the word, "Venerable". (Analysis)

Example:

According to _____'s dictionary, **failure** is....

Failure	
Negative Factors	**Positive Factors**
May spark negative emotions	Mistakes and failings are a part of the creation process
May affect interpersonal relationships	"When you quit that is true failure"
	Don't make failing a habit; however, if it happens, learn from your failure

Challenge Five:

Find an image. Then, create a chart that lists the directly observable features versus the not-visible, but inferable features of the image.(Analysis)

Example: Military Helicopter	
Observable and Visible	**Not Visible, but Inferable**
is a vehicle	holds pilots
has two propellors	holds passengers
is in the air	has computer systems

Chapter 3
Section 3

Exploring Quotations on: War

Common Core State Standards:
- CCSS.ELA-LITERACY.WHST.6-8.6
- CCSS.ELA-LITERACY.WHST.6-8.8
- CCSS.ELA-LITERACY.WHST.6-8.10
- CCSS.ELA-LITERACY.RH.6-8.1
- CCSS.ELA-LITERACY.RH.6-8.4
- CCSS.ELA-LITERACY.RH.6-8.7

Learning Objectives:
- A. Gain knowledge on the topic of "war"
- B. Experience other perspectives on "war"

Quotations on War

Instructions:
Place your answers to each challenge into a journal or folder

Challenge One:
Locate a quotation on the topic of "war".(Knowledge)

Challenge Two:
Translate your selected quotation on "war" into your own words.(Comprehension)

Challenge Three:
Provide historical context on your selected quotation. Draw connections between the quote, the author, and the time period.(Analysis)

Challenge Four:
Locate a historical document or famous statement that relates to your selected quotation on "war".(Application)

Suggested Start:
1. Reflect on the time period of quotation.
2. Quotation resources are available at your local library.

Potential Resources:
1.) Quoteland.com
2.) Brainyquote.com
3.) Quotationspage.com
4.) En.wikiquote.org

Challenge Five:

Using a quotation on "war", discover a way to communicate the meaning through pictures and words. Then, create a comic strip that explains the quotation. (Synthesis)

Example:
"Hunger"
"Thou shouldst eat to live; not live to eat."
Socrates

Create a collection of images that relate to the quote. Then, add captions or messages that help express the quote. Lastly, connect images and create a comic strip.

Challenge Six:
Complete the following sentence fragment with three or more separate statements. Figure out a way to incorporate a quotation, adage, or joke.(Application)

The Grand Canyon...

Example:

The last movie that I saw...
1.) ...caused my mind to reflect on the possibilities of humans having superpowers. For instance, by combining advanced nanotechnology with our understanding of genetics, we could modify ourselves into more supercharged people.

2.) ...agitated me because it depicted the cruelties of mankind. However, I then reflected on an anonymous quote that "Unfortunately, the road to progress can have various levels of bumpiness".

3.) ...frightened me because it was a creepy horror film. Now, I want to sleep with the lights on, but my parents disagree. Even though, I don't pay the electric bill. I feel that I should be able to make this decision!

Chapter 3
Section 4

Exploration of Adages,
Aphorisms, Proverbs, and Maxims:

Common Core State Standards:
- CCSS.ELA-LITERACY.WHST.6-8.6
- CCSS.ELA-LITERACY.WHST.6-8.8
- CCSS.ELA-LITERACY.WHST.6-8.10
- CCSS.ELA-LITERACY.RH.6-8.4
- CCSS.ELA-LITERACY.RH.6-8.7

Learning Objectives:
A. Experience perceptive sayings from various cultures
B. Examine beliefs and understandings of various individuals and groups

Adages, Aphorisms, Proverbs, and Maxims

Instructions:
Place your answers to each challenge into a journal or folder

Challenge One:
Select an adage, aphorism, proverb, or maxim. Research the origin of the adage, aphorism, proverb, or maxim. Cite source(s).(Knowledge)

Challenge Two:
Translate your chosen adage, aphorism, proverb, or maxim into your own words.(Comprehension)

Challenge Three:
Compose a small paragraph or a short segment of dialogue that includes your chosen adage, aphorism, proverb, or maxim.(Application)

Challenge Four:
Do you agree or disagree with the message of your chosen adage, aphorism, proverb, or maxim. Defend your response. Cite sources.(Evaluation)

Suggested Start:
1. Reflect on your chosen adage, aphorism, proverb, or maxim.
2. Identify problems, if any.

Potential Resources:
1.) En.wikiquote.org
2.) Thinkexist.com

Challenge Five:

Select at least three pictures based on your selected adage, aphorism, proverb, or maxim. Next, build three posters by adding text to the chosen pictures. (Synthesis)

Suggested Start:
"Tomorrow Never Comes"

1. Make sure you understand the adage, aphorism, proverb, or maxim.
2. Reflect on the meaning(s) of your chosen adage, aphorism, proverb, or maxim.
3. Search for images that symbolize or reflect the adage, aphorism, proverb, or maxim.
4. Construct posters.

Tomorrow Never Comes

Carpe Diem - Sieze the Day!

Challenge Six:

Is it better to <u>duplicate</u> or <u>replicate</u>?

In this exercise, consider possible scenarios when it is better to do one or the other underlined options. Next, find scenarios that benefit from each underlined option. Then, try to find scenarios that do not benefit from each underlined option. Create a chart that represents your conclusions. Lastly, compose statements using historical examples or scientific data that validate each item inside your chart.(Evaluation)

Example: Is it better to <u>spark</u> or <u>spur</u>?

Neither	Spark	Spur	Both
malice	critical thoughts	truthfulness	healthy behavior
hatred	cooperation	obedience	innovations
ignorance	motivation	horse	inventions
	confidence		imagination
			students
			self-control

A. <u>Hatred</u> can <u>spark</u> destructive behavior such as... (insert historical example).
B. Although, at times effective, spurred obedience has a limited shelf life; eventually, the spurred will rebel or revolt such as a child or colony...
C. According to _____(author/researcher/expert), sparking confidence can boost students' comprehension.

Chapter 3
Section 5

Exploration of Business

Common Core State Standards:
- CCSS.ELA-LITERACY.WHST.6-8.6
- CCSS.ELA-LITERACY.WHST.6-8.7
- CCSS.ELA-LITERACY.WHST.6-8.8
- CCSS.ELA-LITERACY.WHST.6-8.9
- CCSS.ELA-LITERACY.WHST.6-8.10
- CCSS.ELA-LITERACY.RH.6-8.4
- CCSS.ELA-LITERACY.RH.6-8.7

Learning Objectives:
- A. Examine business costs and opportunities
- B. Communicate information through graphics and text such as diagrams and charts

Organization Path

Instructions:
Place your answers to each challenge into a journal or folder

Challenge One:
Name a business that you would like to own. Classify the type of business it is. Identify your main product. (Knowledge)

Challenge Two:
Identify three competitors of the business that you would like to own.(Comprehension)

Challenge Three:
Identify three products or services that your company offers. In a chart, illustrate the function(s) of each product or service. Next, in relationship to your chosen product or service, identify if these products are:
- Integrated and necessary for the main product to operate such as gasoline or motor oil for cars
- Complementary to the product and enhances product like air conditioning and power windows for cars
- Vital to the business such as their brand brake pads and spark plugs for cars (Application)

Main Product(Windows Operating System)			
	Integrated and Necessary	Enhances Main Product	Vital to Business
Microsoft Office	No	Yes	Yes
Internet Explorer	Yes	Yes	Yes
Xbox 360	No	No	No

Challenge Four:

Categorize the four chosen products by popularity among consumers, history of the products, revenue, profit, target audience(name their main customers), and strongest direct competitor, quasi-competitor and indirect competitor. Use a scale from 4 to 1, 4 being highest, to grade each category. Then, based on your chart, describe the growth potential (or lack of future potential) of each product. Which product is the strongest? Which product would you focus more resources on for the future of the company. Defend your decision. Cite sources.(Analysis)

Strengths and Weaknesses				
	Windows OS	Microsoft Office	Internet Explorer	Xbox 360
Popularity	3	4	2	1
Revenue	3	4	2	1
Profitabil-ity	3	4	2	1

Strengths and Weaknesses by Details				
	Windows OS	Microsoft Office	Internet Explorer	Xbox 360
Years Available	28 yrs.	23 yrs.	19 yrs.	8 yrs.
Direct Competitor	Mac OS X	LibreOffice	Chrome	Playstation 3
Quasi-Competitor	Android OS	QuickOffice	Smart-TVs	Gameboy Advance
Indirect Competitor	Pen and Paper	Typewriter	Library Card	Mobile Device
Rankings among direct Competitors	#1	#1	#2	#1

Challenge Five:

Choose one of your company's most popular or well-known products or services based on industry average data. Research this product or service and build a diagram that displays the fabrication process of the product or service. Cite sources.(Synthesis)

Your diagram or chart should display the work that goes into producing a product or service.

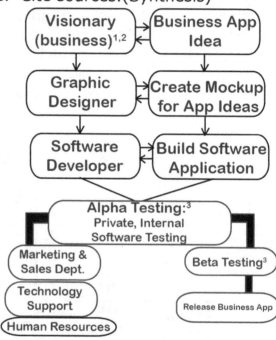

1 Does the app solve a problem?
2 Can it be profitable?
3 Testing may require restarts or revisions.

Challenge Six:

Create a chart that explains two of the product's major features. For example, an alarm clock normally has a minimum of two features, the time display and the alarm function. Use graphics, if possible. Cite sources.(Analysis)

Alarm Radio	
Radio	converts radio waves...
Alarm Buzzer	is a feature of the...

Challenge Seven:

Based on your gathered research and your product choice, create a visual flowchart or graphical diagram that demonstrates the interaction between human resources and non-human resources to produce the product or service. Start with the necessary (raw) materials required to produce the product or service. For example, an organic farmer needs supplies, materials, equipment, and workers. Then, your flowchart should display the interactions between the workforce and resources until the end-product reaches consumers. (Synthesis)

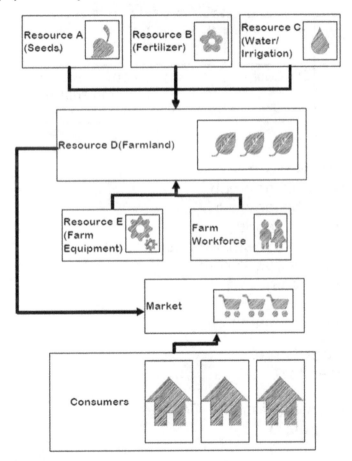

Challenge Eight:

Identify three individuals that had a major impact on your company's industry. Create a multimedia chart to describe their impact. Based on your research of these three individuals, which individual had the biggest impact on their industry. Defend your argument. Cite sources.(Evaluation)

Industry: Telecommunications		
insert image	John Doe	was an inventor whose radical and unorthodox methods produced the first....
insert image	Jane Doe	was an amazing engineer who invented the first....
insert image	Dr. Cooper	was a well-known and well-respected physician that accidentally invented....

Potential Resources:
- www.bls.gov/ooh
- www.bls.gov/iag
- howstuffworks.com
- visual.merriam-webster.com
- finance.yahoo.com
- ehow.com
- sba.gov
- entrepreneur.com

Rubric for Chapter
See Appendix A

Reflective Questions for Chapter
See Appendix B

Chapter 4

Connections to
Common Core State Standards:

CCSS.ELA-LITERACY.WHST.6-8.6
Use technology, including the Internet, to produce and publish writing and present the relationships between information and ideas clearly and efficiently.(2010)

CCSS.ELA-LITERACY.WHST.6-8.7
Conduct short research projects to answer a question(including a self-generated question), drawing on several sources and generating additional related, focused questions that allow for multiple avenues of exploration.(2010)

CCSS.ELA-LITERACY.WHST.6-8.8
Gather relevant information from multiple print and digital sources, using search terms effectively; assess the credibility and accuracy of each source; and quote or paraphrase the data and conclusions of others while avoiding plagiarism and following a standard form of citation.(2010)

CCSS.ELA-LITERACY.WHST.6-8.9
Draw evidence from informational texts to support analysis, reflection, and research.(2010)

Connections to
Common Core State Standards:
(continued)

CCSS.ELA-LITERACY.WHST.6-8.10
Write routinely over extended time frames(time for revision and reflection) and shorter time frames(a single sitting or a day or two) for a range of discipline-specific tasks, purposes, and audiences.(2010)

CCSS.ELA-LITERACY.RH.6-8.1
Cite specific textual evidence to support analysis of primary and secondary sources.(2010)

CCSS.ELA-LITERACY.RH.6-8.4
Determine the meaning of words and phrases as they are used in a text, including vocabulary specific to domains related to history/social studies.(2010)

CCSS.ELA-LITERACY.RH.6-8.7
Integrate visual information(e.g., in charts, graphs, photographs, videos, or maps) with other information in print and digital text.(2010)

CCSS.ELA-LITERACY.RST.6-8.1
Cite specific textual evidence to support analysis of science and technical texts.(2010)

CCSS.ELA-LITERACY.RST.6-8.2
Determine the central ideas or conclusions of a text; provide an accurate summary of the text distinct from prior knowledge or opinions.(2010)

CCSS.ELA-LITERACY.RST.6-8.
Distinguish among facts, reasoned judgment based on research findings, and speculation in text.(2010)

Chapter 4
Section 1

Exploration of the Idiom: Fair-Weather Friend

Common Core State Standards:
- CCSS.ELA-LITERACY.WHST.6-8.8
- CCSS.ELA-LITERACY.WHST.6-8.10
- CCSS.ELA-LITERACY.RH.6-8.4
- CCSS.ELA-LITERACY.RH.6-8.7

Learning Objectives:
A. Understand the figurative meaning of idioms
B. Comprehend the problematic issues with literal translations of idioms

Fair-Weather Friend

Instructions:
Place your answers to each challenge into a journal or folder

Challenge One:
Translate "Fair-Weather Friend" **into your own word**s.(Comprehension)

Challenge Two:
Create two separate sentences using the idiom "Fair-Weather Friend".(Application)

Challenge Three:
Identify another idiom that is similar to "Fair-Weather Friend".(Analysis)

Challenge Four:
List **fictional** characters that were "Fair-Weather Friends". Describe each character's behavior and action in relation to the idiom.(Evaluation)

Suggested Start:
Using an American English Idiom dictionary, define the figurative meaning of "Fair-Weather Friend".

Potential Resources:
    1.) Idioms.thefreedictionary.com
    2.) Dictionary.reference.com/idioms

Challenge Five:

Create, draw or sketch three **individual** objects that represent the word "Feudal". Based on your images, explain the connection(s) to the subject.(Synthesis)

Example 1:
Humbled

Example 2:
Driven

Challenge Six:

Create two or more images that express the statement "I'm contentious!" But, use as few images and letters as possible. Then, repeat this process with the thought, "I am a pacifist". Communicate the subtle or overt meaning of the objects inside your images. (Synthesis)

Example One: *I dislike carrots.*

Example Two: *I love carrots.*

Chapter 4
Section 2

Perspectives on:
Colors

Common Core State Standards:
- CCSS.ELA-LITERACY.WHST.6-8.7
- CCSS.ELA-LITERACY.WHST.6-8.8
- CCSS.ELA-LITERACY.WHST.6-8.10
- CCSS.ELA-LITERACY.RST.6-8.1
- CCSS.ELA-LITERACY.RST.6-8.2

Learning Objectives:
- A. Gain perspective on vague writing
- B. Gain awareness of potential problems with "absolute" statements in writing
- C. Gain perspective on multiple answers

What Color is the sky?

Instructions:
Place your answers to each challenge into a journal or folder

Challenge One:
Respond to the following question. "What color is the sky?"(Analysis)

Challenge Two:
Explain the concept of color? Cite sources that defend your explanation.(Evaluation)

Here are recommendations to keep in mind when answering the above questions:
1. What is color?
2. What are colors?
3. Do colors actually exist?
4. Cite sources that defend your argument.

Suggested Start:
1. Pause before answering the question.
2. Using a dictionary, define "Color".
3. Using an encyclopedia, research "Color".

Potential Resources:
1.) Merriam-Webster.com
2.) Bartleby.com
3.) Plato.Stanford.edu

Challenge Three:
Create a joke that you must answer in a figurative way and a literal way. Remember, keep it clean and respectful. NO PRACTICAL JOKES!(Analysis)

Example:
Joke(the setup): *They say "failure is a part of learning".*
Figurative answer (punchline): *Could someone please explain that to my parents.*
Literal answer: *This quote translates more often into "We learn from our mistakes". Whether a person is completing a quiz or learning to ride a bike, mistakes may occur, and they have the option to grow from their small failures.*

The secret to creating jokes is to ask questions about the world. In other words, analyze the world around you. If it doesn't make sense, question it. Then, research it.

To help, start with a statement like:
Why is it that...............
Ever notice that...........
Whose idea was it to make...
One day, there was a.................
Why does....
Where's the......
How is it that....

Don't forget to explore and explain the answer in a figurative and literal way. Creating jokes can be challenging. Worst case scenario, find and use a joke that you can answer in a figurative and literal way. Explain, why it is funny. Give credit to the comedian.

Challenge Four:

First, **define** the word, "Curiosity". Second, create a two column chart with a "negative factors" side and a "positive factors" side. Third, contrast the positive factors and negative issues of the word, "Curiosity". (Analysis)

Example:

According to _____'s dictionary, **failure** is....

Failure	
Negative Factors	**Positive Factors**
May spark negative emotions	Mistakes and failings are a part of the creation process
May affect interpersonal relationships	"When you quit that is true failure"
	Don't make failing a habit; however, if it happens, learn from your failure

Challenge Five:

Find an image. Then, create a chart that lists the directly observable features versus the not-visible, but inferable features of the image.(Analysis)

Example: Jet Fighter	
Observable and Visible	**Not Visible, but Inferable**
is a vehicle	holds pilots
is in the air	has weapons
is jet propelled	has computer systems

Chapter 4
Section 3

Exploring Quotations on: Health and Exercise

Common Core State Standards:
- CCSS.ELA-LITERACY.WHST.6-8.6
- CCSS.ELA-LITERACY.WHST.6-8.8
- CCSS.ELA-LITERACY.WHST.6-8.10
- CCSS.ELA-LITERACY.RH.6-8.1
- CCSS.ELA-LITERACY.RH.6-8.4
- CCSS.ELA-LITERACY.RH.6-8.7

Learning Objectives:
- A. Gain knowledge on the topic of "Health and Exercise"
- B. Experience other perspectives on "Health and Exercise"

Quotations on Health and Exercise

Instructions:
Place your answers to each challenge into a journal or folder

Challenge One:
Locate a quotation on the topic of "Health and Exercise".(Knowledge)

Challenge Two:
Translate your selected quotation on "Health and Exercise" into your own words.(Comprehension)

Challenge Three:
Compose a biographical statement using your chosen quotation on "Health and Exercise".(Application)

Challenge Four:
Create your own quote on "Health and Exercise".(Synthesis)

Challenge Five:
Select or create a poem on "Health and Exercise". (Synthesis)

Suggested Start:
1. Reflect on "Health and Exercise" experiences.
2. Quotation resources are available at your local library.

Potential Resources:
1.) Quoteland.com
2.) En.wikiquote.org

Challenge Six:

Using a quotation on "Health and Exercise", discover a way to express the meaning through pictures and words. Then, create a comic strip that explains the quotation.(Synthesis)

Example:
"Hunger"
"Thou shouldst eat to live; not live to eat."
Socrates

Create a collection of images that relate to the quote. Then, add captions or messages that help express the quote. Lastly, connect images and create a comic strip.

Challenge Seven:
Complete the following sentence fragment with three or more separate statements. Figure out a way to incorporate a quotation, adage, or joke.(Application)

Mount Everest...

Example:

The last movie that I saw...
1.) ...caused my mind to reflect on the possibilities of humans having superpowers. For instance, by combining advanced nanotechnology with our understanding of genetics, we could modify ourselves into more supercharged people.

2.) ...agitated me because it depicted the cruelties of mankind. However, I then reflected on an anonymous quote that "Unfortunately, the road to progress can have various levels of bumpiness".

3.) ...frightened me because it was a creepy horror film. Now, I want to sleep with the lights on, but my parents disagree. Even though, I don't pay the electric bill. I feel that I should be able to make this decision!

Chapter 4
Section 4

Exploration of Adages, Aphorisms, Proverbs, and Maxims:

Common Core State Standards:
- CCSS.ELA-LITERACY.WHST.6-8.6
- CCSS.ELA-LITERACY.WHST.6-8.8
- CCSS.ELA-LITERACY.WHST.6-8.10
- CCSS.ELA-LITERACY.RH.6-8.4
- CCSS.ELA-LITERACY.RH.6-8.7

Learning Objectives:
- A. Experience perceptive sayings from various cultures
- B. Examine beliefs and understandings of various individuals and groups

Adages, Aphorisms, Proverbs, and Maxims

Instructions:
Place your answers to each challenge into a journal or folder

Challenge One:
Select an adage, aphorism, proverb, or maxim. Research the origin of the adage, aphorism, proverb, or maxim. Cite source(s).(Knowledge)

Challenge Two:
Translate your chosen adage, aphorism, proverb, or maxim into your own words.(Comprehension)

Challenge Three:
Compose a small paragraph or a short segment of dialogue that includes your chosen adage, aphorism, proverb, or maxim.(Application)

Challenge Four:
Do you agree or disagree with the message of your chosen adage, aphorism, proverb, or maxim. Defend your response. Cite sources.(Evaluation)

Suggested Start:
1. Reflect on your chosen adage, aphorism, proverb, or maxim.
2. Identify problems, if any.

Potential Resources:
1.) En.wikiquote.org
2.) Thinkexist.com

Challenge Five:
Select at least three pictures based on your selected adage, aphorism, proverb, or maxim. Next, build three posters by adding text to the chosen pictures. (Synthesis)

Suggested Start:
"Tomorrow Never Comes"
1. Make sure you understand the adage, aphorism, proverb, or maxim.
2. Reflect on the meaning(s) of your chosen adage, aphorism, proverb, or maxim.
3. Search for images that symbolize or reflect the adage, aphorism, proverb, or maxim.
4. Construct posters.

Tomorrow Never Comes

Carpe Diem - Sieze the Day!

Challenge Six:

Is it better to **think** or **act**?

In this exercise, consider possible scenarios when it is better to do one or the other underlined options. Next, find scenarios that benefit from each underlined option. Then, try to find scenarios that do not benefit from each underlined option. Create a chart that represents your conclusions. Lastly, compose statements using historical examples or scientific data that validate each item inside your chart. (Evaluation)

Example: Is it better to **spark** or **spur**?

Neither	Spark	Spur	Both
malice	critical thoughts	truthfulness	healthy behavior
hatred	cooperation	obedience	innovations
ignorance	motivation	horse	inventions
	confidence		imagination
			students
			self-control

A. Hatred can spark destructive behavior such as... (insert historical example).
B. Although, at times effective, spurred obedience has a limited shelf life; eventually, the spurred will rebel or revolt such as a child or colony...
C. According to _____(author/researcher/expert), sparking confidence can boost students' comprehension.

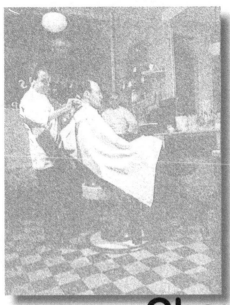

Chapter 4
Section 5

Exploration of Business

Common Core State Standards:
- CCSS.ELA-LITERACY.WHST.6-8.6
- CCSS.ELA-LITERACY.WHST.6-8.7
- CCSS.ELA-LITERACY.WHST.6-8.8
- CCSS.ELA-LITERACY.WHST.6-8.9
- CCSS.ELA-LITERACY.WHST.6-8.10
- CCSS.ELA-LITERACY.RH.6-8.4
- CCSS.ELA-LITERACY.RH.6-8.7

Learning Objectives:
- A. Examine products and services from the view of an organizational entity such as a business
- B. Communicate information through graphics and text such as diagrams and charts

Product and Service Path

Instructions:
Place your answers to each challenge into a journal or folder

Challenge One:
Identify a highly-anticipated, upcoming, unreleased product or service.(Knowledge)

Challenge Two:
Identify the type of companies that will most likely produce your chosen product or service. Classify their industry.(Comprehension)

Challenge Three:
Identify three future direct competitors of your chosen product or service. Describe and chart the competition based on possible business size (by employees), financial strength(early investments), potential revenue. Research and use industry estimates and averages.(Analysis)

Main Product (Web Browsers)				
	Market Share	Business Size	Marketing Reach	Years Available
Internet Explorer (product)	2	large enterprise	global	19
Chrome (competitor)	1	large enterprise	global	6
Firefox (competitor)	3	mid-size	global	12
Opera (competitor)	4	mid-size	global	18

Challenge four:

Create a diagram that displays the upcoming major parts or sequences of your chosen product or service. Next explain two of the product's major parts. For example, an Xbox 360 has multiple, specialized parts such as the central processing unit and the graphics processing unit. Use graphics. Cite sources.(Analysis)

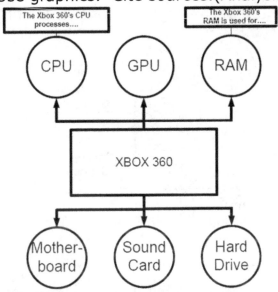

Challenge Five:

Based on your chosen product or service, identify three influential people that had a major impact on this industry through improvements, innovations, or inventions. Describe their effects on the industry. Cite sources.(Analysis)

Industry: Telecommunications		
insert image	John Doe	was an inventor whose radical and unorthodox methods produced the first....
insert image	Jane Doe	was an amazing engineer who invented the first....
insert image	Dr. Cooper	was a well-known and well-respected physician that accidentally invented....

Challenge Six:

Create an organizational chart (unofficial) of a company that offers your upcoming product or service. Next, pinpoint the areas where your three previously chosen influential people would work. For example, if one of your selected influential people is a visionary executive leader, then they would fit somewhere at the top of the organizational chart(org chart).(Synthesis)

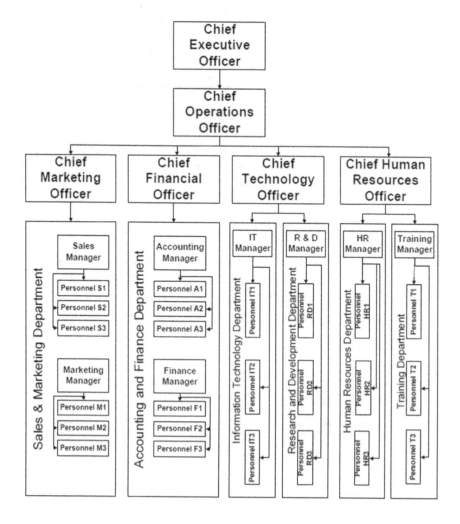

Challenge Seven:

Based on your gathered research and your upcoming product choice, create a visual flowchart or graphical diagram that demonstrates the interaction between human resources and non-human resources to produce the product or service. Start with the necessary (raw) materials required to produce the product or service. For example, an organic farmer needs supplies, materials, equipment, and workers. Then, your flowchart should display the interactions between the workforce and resources until the end-product reaches consumers. (Synthesis)

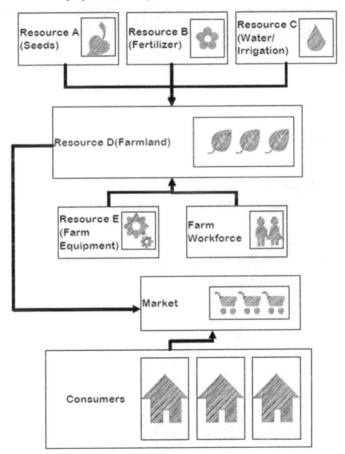

Challenge Eight:

Based on your upcoming chosen product or service selection,

- Identify two supplemental/complementary products or services such as computer applications complement computer operating systems
- Identify two required/necessary products (computer operating system are necessary to operate computers)
- Identify two separate or indirectly connected products or services that the company produces(Xbox 360 or Zune)

Discover which product(s) is your strongest seller(s). Why? Would you eliminate any products or services from the company's product lineup? Explain. Which product or service deserves the most research and development? Elaborate. Lastly, which product or service deserves the most marketing. Explain. Cite sources.(Evaluation)

Potential Resources:

- www.bls.gov/ooh
- www.bls.gov/iag
- howstuffworks.com
- visual.merriam-webster.com
- finance.yahoo.com
- ehow.com
- sba.gov
- entrepreneur.com

Rubric for Chapter
See Appendix A

Reflective Questions for Chapter
See Appendix B

Chapter 5

Connections to
Common Core State Standards:

CCSS.ELA-LITERACY.WHST.6-8.6
Use technology, including the Internet, to produce and publish writing and present the relationships between information and ideas clearly and efficiently.(2010)

CCSS.ELA-LITERACY.WHST.6-8.7
Conduct short research projects to answer a question(including a self-generated question), drawing on several sources and generating additional related, focused questions that allow for multiple avenues of exploration.(2010)

CCSS.ELA-LITERACY.WHST.6-8.8
Gather relevant information from multiple print and digital sources, using search terms effectively; assess the credibility and accuracy of each source; and quote or paraphrase the data and conclusions of others while avoiding plagiarism and following a standard form of citation.(2010)

CCSS.ELA-LITERACY.WHST.6-8.9
Draw evidence from informational texts to support analysis, reflection, and research.(2010)

Connections to
Common Core State Standards:
(continued)

CCSS.ELA-LITERACY.WHST.6-8.10
Write routinely over extended time frames(time for revision and reflection) and shorter time frames(a single sitting or a day or two) for a range of discipline-specific tasks, purposes, and audiences.(2010)

CCSS.ELA-LITERACY.RH.6-8.1
Cite specific textual evidence to support analysis of primary and secondary sources.(2010)

CCSS.ELA-LITERACY.RH.6-8.4
Determine the meaning of words and phrases as they are used in a text, including vocabulary specific to domains related to history/social studies.(2010)

CCSS.ELA-LITERACY.RH.6-8.7
Integrate visual information(e.g., in charts, graphs, photographs, videos, or maps) with other information in print and digital text.(2010)

CCSS.ELA-LITERACY.RST.6-8.1
Cite specific textual evidence to support analysis of science and technical texts.(2010)

CCSS.ELA-LITERACY.RST.6-8.2
Determine the central ideas or conclusions of a text; provide an accurate summary of the text distinct from prior knowledge or opinions.(2010)

CCSS.ELA-LITERACY.RST.6-8.
Distinguish among facts, reasoned judgment based on research findings, and speculation in text.(2010)

Chapter 5
Section 1

Exploration of the Idiom:
Fall Through the Cracks

Common Core State Standards:
- CCSS.ELA-LITERACY.WHST.6-8.8
- CCSS.ELA-LITERACY.WHST.6-8.10
- CCSS.ELA-LITERACY.RH.6-8.4
- CCSS.ELA-LITERACY.RH.6-8.7

Learning Objectives:
- A. Understand the figurative meaning of idioms
- B. Comprehend the problematic issues with literal translations of idioms

Fall Through the Cracks

Instructions:
Place your answers to each challenge into a journal or folder

Challenge One:
Translate "Fall Through the Cracks" **into your own words**.(Comprehension)

Challenge Two:
Create two separate sentences using the idiom "Fall Through the Cracks".(Application)

Challenge Three:
Identify another idiom that is similar to "Fall Through the Cracks".(Analysis)

Challenge Four:
Recall environments, fictional or non-fictional, where people can "fall through the cracks". Explain.(Evaluation)

Suggested Start:
Using an American English Idiom dictionary, define the figurative meaning of "Fall Through the Cracks".

Potential Resources:
　　1.) Idioms.thefreedictionary.com
　　2.) Dictionary.reference.com/idioms

Challenge Five:

Create, draw or sketch three **individual** objects that represent the word "Parity". Based on your images, explain the connection(s) to the subject.(Synthesis)

Example 1:
Humbled

Example 2:
Driven

Challenge Six:

Create two or more images that express the command "Don't lie!" But, use as few images and letters as possible. Then, repeat this process with the thought, "What is the truth?" Communicate the subtle or overt meaning of the objects inside your images.(Synthesis)

Example One: *I dislike grapes.*

Example Two: *I love grapes.*

Chapter 5
Section 2

Perspectives on:
Day

Common Core State Standards:
- CCSS.ELA-LITERACY.WHST.6-8.7
- CCSS.ELA-LITERACY.WHST.6-8.8
- CCSS.ELA-LITERACY.WHST.6-8.10
- CCSS.ELA-LITERACY.RST.6-8.1
- CCSS.ELA-LITERACY.RST.6-8.2

Learning Objectives:
- A. Gain perspective on vague writing
- B. Gain awareness of potential problems with "absolute" statements in writing
- C. Gain perspective on multiple answers

A day is equal to 24 hours

Instructions:
Place your answers to each challenge into a journal or folder

Challenge One:
Respond to the following statement. "A day is equal to 24 hours." Cite sources that defend your argument.(Analysis)

Challenge Two:
Respond to the previous statement in more than three ways.(Analysis)

Here are recommendations to keep in mind when answering the above questions:
1. What is a day?
2. How is a day measured?
3. If a day is greater than 24 hours, is it still a day?
4. Cite sources that defend your argument.

Suggested Start:
   1. Pause before answering the question.
   2. Using a dictionary, define "day".
   3. Using an encyclopedia, research "day".

Potential Resources:
   1.) Merriam-Webster.com
   2.) Bartleby.com

Challenge Three:
Create a joke that you must answer in a figurative way and a literal way. Remember, keep it clean and respectful. NO PRACTICAL JOKES!(Analysis)

Example:
Joke(the setup):   *They say "failure is a part of learning".*
Figurative answer (punchline): *Could someone please explain that to my parents.*
Literal answer: *This quote translates more often into "We learn from our mistakes". Whether a person is completing a quiz or learning to ride a bike, mistakes may occur, and they have the option to grow from their small failures.*

The secret to creating jokes is to ask questions about the world. In other words, analyze the world around you. If it doesn't make sense, question it. Then, research it.

To help, start with a statement like:
    Why is it that...............
    Ever notice that...........
    Whose idea was it to make...
    One day, there was a..................
    Why does....
    Where's the......
    How is it that....

Don't forget to explore and explain the answer in a figurative and literal way. Creating jokes can be challenging. Worst case scenario, find and use a joke that you can answer in a figurative and literal way. Explain, why it is funny. Give credit to the comedian.

Challenge Four:
First, **define** the word, "Innovative". Second, create a two column chart with a "negative factors" side and a "positive factors" side. Third, contrast the positive factors and negative issues of the word, "Innovative". (Analysis)
Example:
According to _____'s dictionary, **failure** is....

Failure	
Negative Factors	**Positive Factors**
May spark negative emotions	Mistakes and failings are a part of the creation process
May affect interpersonal relationships	"When you quit that is true failure"
	Don't make failing a habit; however, if it happens, learn from your failure

Challenge Five:
Find an image. Then, create a chart that lists the directly observable features versus the not-visible, but inferable features of the image.(Analysis)

Example: Blimp	
Observable and Visible	**Not Visible, but Inferable**
is a vehicle	holds pilots
uses hydrogen or helium	has controls
	has instruments

Chapter 5
Section 3

Exploring Quotations on: Thinking

Common Core State Standards:
- CCSS.ELA-LITERACY.WHST.6-8.6
- CCSS.ELA-LITERACY.WHST.6-8.8
- CCSS.ELA-LITERACY.WHST.6-8.10
- CCSS.ELA-LITERACY.RH.6-8.1
- CCSS.ELA-LITERACY.RH.6-8.4
- CCSS.ELA-LITERACY.RH.6-8.7

Learning Objectives:
- A. Gain knowledge on the topic of "thinking"
- B. Experience other perspectives on "thinking"

Quotations on Thinking

Instructions:
Place your answers to each challenge into a journal or folder

Challenge One:
Locate a quotation on the topic of "Thinking".(Knowledge)

Challenge Two:
Translate your selected quotation on "Thinking" into your own words.(Comprehension)

Challenge Three:
Compose a biographical statement using your chosen quotation on "Thinking".(Application)

Challenge Four:
Create your own quote on "Thinking".(Synthesis)

Challenge Five:
Select or create a poem on "Thinking".(Synthesis)

Suggested Start:
1. Reflect on an academic epiphany.
2. Reflect on a difficult or confusing experience.

Potential Resources:
1.) Quoteland.com
2.) Brainyquote.com
3.) Quotationspage.com
4.) En.wikiquote.org

Challenge Six:

Using a quotation on "thinking", discover a way to express the meaning through pictures and words. Then, create a comic strip that explains the quotation.(Synthesis)

Example:
"Hunger"
"Thou shouldst eat to live; not live to eat."
Socrates

Create a collection of images that relate to the quote. Then, add captions or messages that help express the quote. Lastly, connect images and create a comic strip.

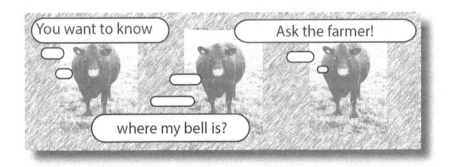

Challenge Seven:
Complete the following sentence fragment with three or more separate statements. Figure out a way to incorporate a quotation, adage, or joke.(Application)

A lunar calendar

Example:

The last movie that I saw...
1.) ...caused my mind to reflect on the possibilities of humans having superpowers. For instance, by combining advanced nanotechnology with our understanding of genetics, we could modify ourselves into more supercharged people.

2.) ...agitated me because it depicted the cruelties of mankind. However, I then reflected on an anonymous quote that "Unfortunately, the road to progress can have various levels of bumpiness".

3.) ...frightened me because it was a creepy horror film. Now, I want to sleep with the lights on, but my parents disagree. Even though, I don't pay the electric bill. I feel that I should be able to make this decision!

Chapter 5
Section 4

Exploration of Adages, Aphorisms, Proverbs, and Maxims:

Common Core State Standards:
- CCSS.ELA-LITERACY.WHST.6-8.6
- CCSS.ELA-LITERACY.WHST.6-8.8
- CCSS.ELA-LITERACY.WHST.6-8.10
- CCSS.ELA-LITERACY.RH.6-8.4
- CCSS.ELA-LITERACY.RH.6-8.7

Learning Objectives:
- A. Experience perceptive sayings from various cultures
- B. Examine beliefs and understandings of various individuals and groups

Adages, Aphorisms, Proverbs, and Maxims

Instructions:
Place your answers to each challenge into a journal or folder

Challenge One:
Select an adage, aphorism, proverb, or maxim. Research the origin of the adage, aphorism, proverb, or maxim. Cite source(s).(Knowledge)

Challenge Two:
Translate your chosen adage, aphorism, proverb, or maxim into your own words.(Comprehension)

Challenge Three:
Compose a small paragraph or a short segment of dialogue that includes your chosen adage, aphorism, proverb, or maxim.(Application)

Challenge Four:
Do you agree or disagree with the message of your chosen adage, aphorism, proverb, or maxim. Defend your response. Cite sources.(Evaluation)

Suggested Start:
1. Reflect on your chosen adage, aphorism, proverb, or maxim.
2. Identify problems, if any.

Potential Resources:
1.) En.wikiquote.org
2.) Thinkexist.com

Challenge Five:
Select at least three pictures based on your selected adage, aphorism, proverb, or maxim. Next, build three posters by adding text to the chosen pictures. (Synthesis)

Suggested Start:
"Tomorrow Never Comes"
1. Make sure you understand the adage, aphorism, proverb, or maxim.
2. Reflect on the meaning(s) of your chosen adage, aphorism, proverb, or maxim.
3. Search for images that symbolize or reflect the adage, aphorism, proverb, or maxim.
4. Construct posters.

Tomorrow Never Comes

Carpe Diem - Sieze the Day!

Challenge Six:

Is it better to <u>give</u> or <u>receive</u>?

In this exercise, consider possible scenarios when it is better to do one or the other underlined options. Next, find scenarios that benefit from each underlined option. Then, try to find scenarios that do not benefit from each underlined option. Create a chart that represents your conclusions. Lastly, compose statements using historical examples or scientific data that validate each item inside your chart. (Evaluation)

Example: Is it better to <u>spark</u> or <u>spur</u>?

Neither	Spark	Spur	Both
malice	critical thoughts	truthfulness	healthy behavior
hatred	cooperation	obedience	innovations
ignorance	motivation	horse	inventions
	confidence		imagination
			students
			self-control

A. <u>Hatred</u> can <u>spark</u> destructive behavior such as... (insert historical example).
B. Although, at times effective, spurred obedience has a limited shelf life; eventually, the spurred will rebel or revolt such as a child or colony...
C. According to _____(author/researcher/expert), sparking confidence can boost students' comprehension.

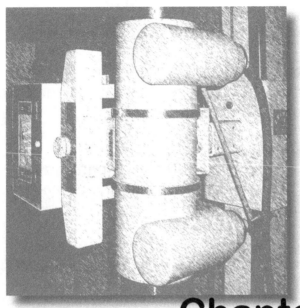

Chapter 5
Section 5

Exploration of Business

Common Core State Standards:
- CCSS.ELA-LITERACY.WHST.6-8.6
- CCSS.ELA-LITERACY.WHST.6-8.7
- CCSS.ELA-LITERACY.WHST.6-8.8
- CCSS.ELA-LITERACY.WHST.6-8.9
- CCSS.ELA-LITERACY.WHST.6-8.10
- CCSS.ELA-LITERACY.RH.6-8.4
- CCSS.ELA-LITERACY.RH.6-8.7

Learning Objectives:
- A. Examine business costs and opportunities
- B. Communicate information through graphics and text such as diagrams and charts

Organization Path

Instructions:
Place your answers to each challenge into a journal or folder

Challenge One:
Name the last business that you patronized. Classify the type of business it is. Identify its main product. (Knowledge)

Challenge Two:
Identify three competitors of this business.(Comprehension)

Challenge Three:
Identify three products or services of your chosen company. Create a chart that displays the relationship among the main product and the additional products. Determine if these products are:
- Integrated and necessary for the main product to operate such as gasoline or motor oil for cars
- Complementary to the product and enhances product like air conditioning and power windows for cars
- Vital to the business such as their brand brake pads and spark plugs for cars(Application)

Main Product(Windows Operating System)			
	Integrated and Necessary	Enhances Main Product	Vital to Business
Microsoft Office	No	Yes	Yes
Internet Explorer	Yes	Yes	Yes
Xbox 360	No	No	No

Challenge Four:

Categorize the four chosen products by popularity among consumers, history of the products, revenue, profit, target audience(name their main customers), and strongest direct competitor, quasi-competitor and indirect competitor. Use a scale from 4 to 1, 4 being highest, to grade each category. Then, based on your chart, describe the growth potential (or lack of future potential) of each product. Which product is the strongest? Which product would you focus more resources on for the future of the company. Defend your decision. Cite sources.(Analysis)

Strengths and Weaknesses				
	Windows OS	Microsoft Office	Internet Explorer	Xbox 360
Popularity	3	4	2	1
Revenue	3	4	2	1
Profitabil-ity	3	4	2	1

Strengths and Weaknesses by Details				
	Windows OS	Microsoft Office	Internet Explorer	Xbox 360
Years Available	28 yrs.	23 yrs.	19 yrs.	8 yrs.
Direct Competitor	Mac OS X	LibreOffice	Chrome	Playstation 3
Quasi-Competitor	Android OS	QuickOffice	Smart-TVs	Gameboy Advance
Indirect Competitor	Pen and Paper	Typewriter	Library Card	Mobile Device
Rankings among direct Competitors	#1	#1	#2	#1

Challenge Five:

Choose one of your chosen company's most popular or well-known products or services. Research this product or service and build a diagram that displays the fabrication process of the product or service. Cite sources.(Synthesis)

Your diagram or chart should display the work that goes into producing a product or service.

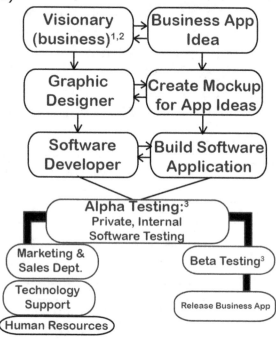

1 Does the app solve a problem?
2 Can it be profitable?
3 Testing may require restarts or revisions.

Challenge Six:

Create a chart that explains two of the product's major features. For example, an alarm clock normally has a minimum of two features, the time display and the alarm function. Use graphics, if possible. Cite sources.(Analysis)

Alarm Radio	
Radio	converts radio waves...
Alarm Buzzer	is a feature of the...

Challenge Seven:

Based on your gathered research and your product choice, create a visual flowchart or graphical diagram that demonstrates the interaction between human resources and non-human resources to produce the product or service. Start with the necessary (raw) materials required to produce the product or service. For example, an organic farmer needs supplies, materials, equipment, and workers. Then, your flowchart should display the interactions between the workforce and resources until the end-product reaches consumers. (Synthesis)

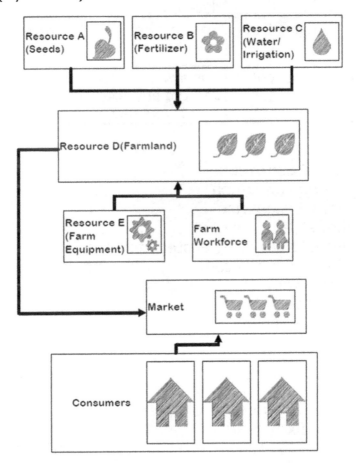

Challenge Eight:

Identify three individuals that had a major impact on your chosen company's industry. Create a multimedia chart to describe their impact. Based on your research of these three individuals, which individual had the biggest impact on their industry. Defend your argument. Cite sources.(Evaluation)

Industry: Telecommunications		
insert image	John Doe	was an inventor whose radical and unorthodox methods produced the first....
insert image	Jane Doe	was an amazing engineer who invented the first....
insert image	Dr. Cooper	was a well-known and well-respected physician that accidentally invented....

Potential Resources:
- www.bls.gov/ooh
- www.bls.gov/iag
- howstuffworks.com
- visual.merriam-webster.com
- finance.yahoo.com
- ehow.com
- sba.gov
- entrepreneur.com

Rubric for Chapter
See Appendix A

Reflective Questions for Chapter
See Appendix B

Chapter 6

Connections to Common Core State Standards:

CCSS.ELA-LITERACY.WHST.6-8.6
Use technology, including the Internet, to produce and publish writing and present the relationships between information and ideas clearly and efficiently.(2010)

CCSS.ELA-LITERACY.WHST.6-8.7
Conduct short research projects to answer a question(including a self-generated question), drawing on several sources and generating additional related, focused questions that allow for multiple avenues of exploration.(2010)

CCSS.ELA-LITERACY.WHST.6-8.8
Gather relevant information from multiple print and digital sources, using search terms effectively; assess the credibility and accuracy of each source; and quote or paraphrase the data and conclusions of others while avoiding plagiarism and following a standard form of citation.(2010)

CCSS.ELA-LITERACY.WHST.6-8.9
Draw evidence from informational texts to support analysis, reflection, and research.(2010)

Connections to
Common Core State Standards:
<u>(continued)</u>

CCSS.ELA-LITERACY.WHST.6-8.10
Write routinely over extended time frames(time for revision and reflection) and shorter time frames(a single sitting or a day or two) for a range of discipline-specific tasks, purposes, and audiences.(2010)

CCSS.ELA-LITERACY.RH.6-8.1
Cite specific textual evidence to support analysis of primary and secondary sources.(2010)

CCSS.ELA-LITERACY.RH.6-8.4
Determine the meaning of words and phrases as they are used in a text, including vocabulary specific to domains related to history/social studies.(2010)

CCSS.ELA-LITERACY.RH.6-8.7
Integrate visual information(e.g., in charts, graphs, photographs, videos, or maps) with other information in print and digital text.(2010)

CCSS.ELA-LITERACY.RST.6-8.1
Cite specific textual evidence to support analysis of science and technical texts.(2010)

CCSS.ELA-LITERACY.RST.6-8.2
Determine the central ideas or conclusions of a text; provide an accurate summary of the text distinct from prior knowledge or opinions.(2010)

CCSS.ELA-LITERACY.RST.6-8.
Distinguish among facts, reasoned judgment based on research findings, and speculation in text.(2010)

Chapter 6
Section 1

Exploration of the Idiom:
In the Same Boat

Common Core State Standards:
- CCSS.ELA-LITERACY.WHST.6-8.8
- CCSS.ELA-LITERACY.WHST.6-8.10
- CCSS.ELA-LITERACY.RH.6-8.4
- CCSS.ELA-LITERACY.RH.6-8.7

Learning Objectives:
- A. Understand the figurative meaning of idioms
- B. Comprehend the problematic issues with literal translations of idioms

In the Same Boat

Instructions:
Place your answers to each challenge into a journal or folder

Challenge One:
Translate "In the Same Boat" **into your own words**. (Comprehension)

Challenge Two:
Create two separate sentences using the idiom "In the Same Boat".(Application)

Challenge Three:
Identify another idiom that is similar to "In the Same Boat".(Analysis)

Challenge Four:
Recall a situation where **fictional** characters were symbolically "In the Same Boat". Based on your memory, were the situations often more negative or more positive.(Analysis)

Challenge Five:
Research additional sources. Is the idiom, "In the Same Boat", a more negative or more positive statement. Defend your analysis.(Evaluation)

Suggested Start:
Using an American English Idiom dictionary, define the figurative meaning of "In the Same Boat".

Potential Resources:
      1.) Idioms.thefreedictionary.com
      2.) Dictionary.reference.com/idioms

Challenge Six:

Create, draw or sketch three **individual** objects that represent the word "Homogenous". Based on your images, explain the connection(s) to the subject.(Synthesis)

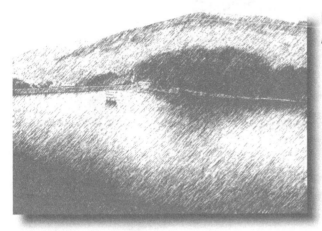

Example 1:
Humbled

Example 2:
Driven

Challenge Seven:

Create two or more images that express the statement "I'm a junk food aficionado!" But, use as few images and letters as possible. Then, repeat this process with the thought, "I dislike rollercoasters!". Communicate the subtle or overt meaning of the objects inside your images.(Synthesis)

Example One: *I dislike corn.*

Example Two: *I love corn.*

Chapter 6
Section 2

Perspectives on:
Time Zones

Common Core State Standards:
- CCSS.ELA-LITERACY.WHST.6-8.7
- CCSS.ELA-LITERACY.WHST.6-8.8
- CCSS.ELA-LITERACY.WHST.6-8.10
- CCSS.ELA-LITERACY.RST.6-8.1
- CCSS.ELA-LITERACY.RST.6-8.2

Learning Objectives:
- A. Gain perspective on vague writing
- B. Gain awareness of potential problems with "absolute" statements in writing
- C. Gain perspective on multiple answers

There are Only 24 Time Zones

Instructions:
Place your answers to each challenge into a journal or folder

Challenge One:
"There are only 24 time zones."   Respond to this statement.(Analysis)

Challenge Two:
Explain time zones in your own words. Cite sources that defend your explanation.(Evaluation)

Here are recommendations to keep in mind when answering the above questions:
1. What is a time zone?
2. How do time zones work?
3. Operationalize the term "Time Zone".
4. Cite sources that defend your argument.

Suggested Start:
   1. Pause before answering the question.
   2. Using a dictionary, define "Time Zone".
   3. Using an encyclopedia, research "Time Zone".

Potential Resources:
   1.) Merriam-Webster.com
   2.) Bartleby.com

Challenge Three:
Create a joke that you must answer in a figurative way and a literal way. Remember, keep it clean and respectful. NO PRACTICAL JOKES!(Analysis)

Example:
Joke(the setup): *They say "failure is a part of learning".*
Figurative answer (punchline): *Could someone please explain that to my parents.*
Literal answer: *This quote translates more often into "We learn from our mistakes". Whether a person is completing a quiz or learning to ride a bike, mistakes may occur, and they have the option to grow from their small failures.*

The secret to creating jokes is to ask questions about the world. In other words, analyze the world around you. If it doesn't make sense, question it. Then, research it.

To help, start with a statement like:
    Why is it that...............
    Ever notice that...........
    Whose idea was it to make...
    One day, there was a.................
    Why does....
    Where's the......
    How is it that....

Don't forget to explore and explain the answer in a figurative and literal way. Creating jokes can be challenging. Worst case scenario, find and use a joke that you can answer in a figurative and literal way. Explain, why it is funny. Give credit to the comedian.

Challenge Four:

First, **define** the word, "Cautious". Second, create a two column chart with a "negative factors" side and a "positive factors" side. Third, contrast the positive factors and negative issues of the word, "Cautious". (Analysis)

Example:

According to _____'s dictionary, **failure** is....

Failure	
Negative Factors	**Positive Factors**
May spark negative emotions	Mistakes and failings are a part of the creation process
May affect interpersonal relationships	"When you quit that is true failure"
	Don't make failing a habit; however, if it happens, learn from your failure

Challenge Five:

Find an image. Then, create a chart that lists the directly observable features versus the not-visible, but inferable features of the image.(Analysis)

Example: Space Shuttle	
Observable and Visible	**Not Visible, but Inferable**
is a vehicle	holds crew
is in the air	holds cargo
	has computer systems

Chapter 6
Section 3

Exploring Quotations on: Inspiration

Common Core State Standards:
- CCSS.ELA-LITERACY.WHST.6-8.6
- CCSS.ELA-LITERACY.WHST.6-8.8
- CCSS.ELA-LITERACY.WHST.6-8.10
- CCSS.ELA-LITERACY.RH.6-8.1
- CCSS.ELA-LITERACY.RH.6-8.4
- CCSS.ELA-LITERACY.RH.6-8.7

Learning Objectives:
A. Gain knowledge on the topic of "inspiration"
B. Experience other perspectives on "inspiration"

Quotations on Inspiration

Instructions:
Place your answers to each challenge into a journal or folder

Challenge One:
Locate a quotation on the topic of "inspiration". (Knowledge)

Challenge Two:
Translate your selected quotation on "inspiration" into your own words.(Comprehension)

Challenge Three:
Compose a biographical statement using your chosen quotation on "inspiration".(Application)

Challenge Four:
Create your own quote on "inspiration".(Synthesis)

Challenge Five:
Select or create an inspirational poem.(Synthesis)

Suggested Start:
1. Reflect on inspiring experiences.
2. Quotation resources are available at your local library.

Potential Resources:
1.) Quoteland.com
2.) Brainyquote.com
3.) Quotationspage.com
4.) En.wikiquote.org

Challenge Six:
Using a quotation on "inspiration", discover a way to express the meaning through pictures and words. Then, create a comic strip that explains the quotation. (Synthesis)

Example:
"Hunger"
"Thou shouldst eat to live; not live to eat."
Socrates

Create a collection of images that relate to the quote. Then, add captions or messages that help express the quote. Lastly, connect images and create a comic strip.

Challenge Seven:
Complete the following sentence fragment with three or more separate statements. Figure out a way to incorporate a quotation, adage, or joke.(Application)

The planet Mars...

Example:

The last movie that I saw...
1.) ...caused my mind to reflect on the possibilities of humans having superpowers. For instance, by combining advanced nanotechnology with our understanding of genetics, we could modify ourselves into more supercharged people.

2.) ...agitated me because it depicted the cruelties of mankind. However, I then reflected on an anonymous quote that "Unfortunately, the road to progress can have various levels of bumpiness".

3.) ...frightened me because it was a creepy horror film. Now, I want to sleep with the lights on, but my parents disagree. Even though, I don't pay the electric bill. I feel that I should be able to make this decision!

Chapter 6
Section 4

Exploration of Adages, Aphorisms, Proverbs, and Maxims:

Common Core State Standards:
- CCSS.ELA-LITERACY.WHST.6-8.6
- CCSS.ELA-LITERACY.WHST.6-8.8
- CCSS.ELA-LITERACY.WHST.6-8.10
- CCSS.ELA-LITERACY.RH.6-8.4
- CCSS.ELA-LITERACY.RH.6-8.7

Learning Objectives:
- A. Experience perceptive sayings from various cultures
- B. Examine beliefs and understandings of various individuals and groups

Adages, Aphorisms, Proverbs, and Maxims

Instructions:
Place your answers to each challenge into a journal or folder

Challenge One:
Select an adage, aphorism, proverb, or maxim. Research the origin of the adage, aphorism, proverb, or maxim. Cite source(s).(Knowledge)

Challenge Two:
Translate your chosen adage, aphorism, proverb, or maxim into your own words.(Comprehension)

Challenge Three:
Compose a small paragraph or a short segment of dialogue that includes your chosen adage, aphorism, proverb, or maxim.(Application)

Challenge Four:
Do you agree or disagree with the message of your chosen adage, aphorism, proverb, or maxim. Defend your response. Cite sources.(Evaluation)

Suggested Start:
1. Reflect on your chosen adage, aphorism, proverb, or maxim.
2. Identify problems, if any.

Potential Resources:
1.) En.wikiquote.org
2.) Thinkexist.com

Challenge Five:

Select at least three pictures based on your selected adage, aphorism, proverb, or maxim. Next, build three posters by adding text to the chosen pictures. (Synthesis)

Suggested Start:
"Knowledge is Power"

1. Make sure you understand the adage, aphorism, proverb, or maxim.
2. Reflect on the meaning(s) of your chosen adage, aphorism, proverb, or maxim.
3. Search for images that symbolize or reflect the adage, aphorism, proverb, or maxim.
4. Construct posters.

Challenge Six:

Is it better to <u>argue</u> or <u>concede</u>?

In this exercise, consider possible scenarios when it is better to do one or the other underlined options. Next, find scenarios that benefit from each underlined option. Then, try to find scenarios that do not benefit from each underlined option. Create a chart that represents your conclusions. Lastly, compose statements using historical examples or scientific data that validate each item inside your chart. (Evaluation)

Example: Is it better to <u>spark</u> or <u>spur</u>?

Neither	Spark	Spur	Both
malice	critical thoughts	truthfulness	healthy behavior
hatred	cooperation	obedience	innovations
ignorance	motivation	horse	inventions
	confidence		imagination
			students
			self-control

A. <u>Hatred</u> can <u>spark</u> destructive behavior such as... (insert historical example).
B. Although, at times effective, spurred obedience has a limited shelf life; eventually, the spurred will rebel or revolt such as a child or colony...
C. According to _____(author/researcher/expert), sparking confidence can boost students' comprehension.

Chapter 6
Section 5

Exploration of Business

Common Core State Standards:
- CCSS.ELA-LITERACY.WHST.6-8.6
- CCSS.ELA-LITERACY.WHST.6-8.7
- CCSS.ELA-LITERACY.WHST.6-8.8
- CCSS.ELA-LITERACY.WHST.6-8.9
- CCSS.ELA-LITERACY.WHST.6-8.10
- CCSS.ELA-LITERACY.RH.6-8.4
- CCSS.ELA-LITERACY.RH.6-8.7

Learning Objectives:
- A. Examine products and services from the view of an organizational entity such as a business
- B. Communicate information through graphics and text such as diagrams and charts

Product and Service Path

Instructions:
Place your answers to each challenge into a journal or folder

Challenge One:
Identify a product or service that you use daily. (Knowledge)

Challenge Two:
Identify the type of companies that produce your chosen product or service. Classify their industry.(Comprehension)

Challenge Three:
Identify three direct competitors of your chosen product or service. Describe and chart the competition based on market share, business size (by employees), years available, marketing reach(local, regional, national, global), revenue and profits. Research and use industry averages if your chosen company or its competitors are not publicly traded.(Analysis)

Main Product (Web Browsers)				
	Market Share	Business Size	Marketing Reach	Years Available
Internet Explorer (product)	2	large enterprise	global	19
Chrome (competitor)	1	large enterprise	global	6
Firefox (competitor)	3	mid-size	global	12
Opera (competitor)	4	mid-size	global	18

Challenge four:

Create a diagram that displays the major parts or sequences of your chosen product or service. Next explain two of the product's major parts. For example, an Xbox 360 has multiple, specialized parts such as the central processing unit, the graphics processing unit and the hard drive. Use graphics. Cite sources. (Analysis)

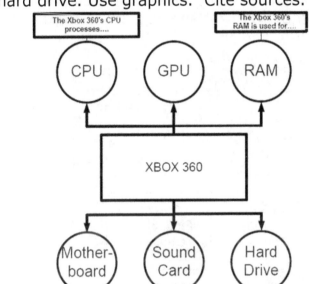

Challenge Five:

Based on your chosen product or service, identify three influential people that had a major impact on this industry through improvements, innovations, or inventions. Describe their effects on the industry. Cite sources.(Analysis)

Industry: Telecommunications		
insert image	John Doe	was an inventor whose radical and unorthodox methods produced the first....
insert image	Jane Doe	was an amazing engineer who invented the first....
insert image	Dr. Cooper	was a well-known and well-respected physician that accidentally invented....

Challenge Six:

Create an organizational chart (unofficial) of a company that offers your chosen product or service. Next, pinpoint the areas where your three previously chosen influential people would work. For example, if one of your selected influential people is a visionary executive leader, then they would fit somewhere at the top of the organizational chart(org chart).(Synthesis)

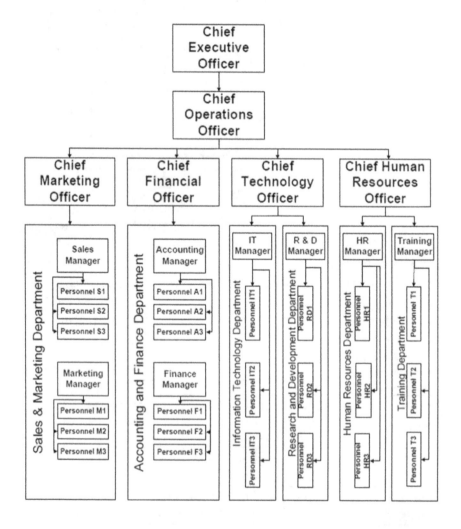

Challenge Seven:

Based on your gathered research and your product choice, create a visual flowchart or graphical diagram that demonstrates the interaction between human resources and non-human resources to produce the product or service. Start with the necessary (raw) materials required to produce the product or service. For example, an organic farmer needs supplies, materials, equipment, and workers. Then, your flowchart should display the interactions between the workforce and resources until the end-product reaches consumers. (Synthesis)

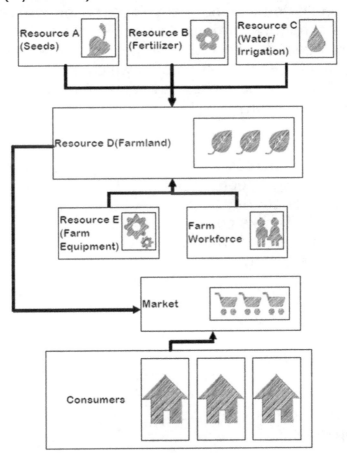

Challenge Eight:

Based on your product choice or service selection,

- Identify two supplemental/complementary products or services such as computer applications complement computer operating systems
- Identify two required/necessary products (computer operating system are necessary to operate computers)
- Identify two separate or indirectly connected products or services that the company produces(Xbox 360 or Zune)

Discover which product(s) is your strongest seller(s). Why? Would you eliminate any products or services from the company's product lineup? Explain. Which product or service deserves the most research and development? Elaborate. Lastly, which product or service deserves the most marketing. Explain. Cite sources.(Evaluation)

Potential Resources:

- www.bls.gov/ooh
- www.bls.gov/iag
- howstuffworks.com
- visual.merriam-webster.com
- finance.yahoo.com
- ehow.com
- sba.gov
- entrepreneur.com

Rubric for Chapter
See Appendix A

Reflective Questions for Chapter
See Appendix B

Chapter 7

Connections to
Common Core State Standards:

CCSS.ELA-LITERACY.WHST.6-8.6
Use technology, including the Internet, to produce and publish writing and present the relationships between information and ideas clearly and efficiently.(2010)

CCSS.ELA-LITERACY.WHST.6-8.7
Conduct short research projects to answer a question(including a self-generated question), drawing on several sources and generating additional related, focused questions that allow for multiple avenues of exploration.(2010)

CCSS.ELA-LITERACY.WHST.6-8.8
Gather relevant information from multiple print and digital sources, using search terms effectively; assess the credibility and accuracy of each source; and quote or paraphrase the data and conclusions of others while avoiding plagiarism and following a standard form of citation.(2010)

CCSS.ELA-LITERACY.WHST.6-8.9
Draw evidence from informational texts to support analysis, reflection, and research.(2010)

Connections to
Common Core State Standards:
<u>(continued)</u>

CCSS.ELA-LITERACY.WHST.6-8.10
Write routinely over extended time frames(time for revision and reflection) and shorter time frames(a single sitting or a day or two) for a range of discipline-specific tasks, purposes, and audiences.(2010)

CCSS.ELA-LITERACY.RH.6-8.1
Cite specific textual evidence to support analysis of primary and secondary sources.(2010)

CCSS.ELA-LITERACY.RH.6-8.4
Determine the meaning of words and phrases as they are used in a text, including vocabulary specific to domains related to history/social studies.(2010)

CCSS.ELA-LITERACY.RH.6-8.7
Integrate visual information(e.g., in charts, graphs, photographs, videos, or maps) with other information in print and digital text.(2010)

CCSS.ELA-LITERACY.RST.6-8.1
Cite specific textual evidence to support analysis of science and technical texts.(2010)

CCSS.ELA-LITERACY.RST.6-8.2
Determine the central ideas or conclusions of a text; provide an accurate summary of the text distinct from prior knowledge or opinions.(2010)

CCSS.ELA-LITERACY.RST.6-8.
Distinguish among facts, reasoned judgment based on research findings, and speculation in text.(2010)

Chapter 7
Section 1

Exploration of the Idiom: Elephant in the Room

Common Core State Standards:
- CCSS.ELA-LITERACY.WHST.6-8.8
- CCSS.ELA-LITERACY.WHST.6-8.10
- CCSS.ELA-LITERACY.RH.6-8.4
- CCSS.ELA-LITERACY.RH.6-8.7

Learning Objectives:
- A. Understand the figurative meaning of idioms
- B. Comprehend the problematic issues with literal translations of idioms

Elephant in the Room

Instructions:
Place your answers to each challenge into a journal or folder

Challenge One:
Translate "Elephant in the Room" **into your own words**.(Comprehension)

Challenge Two:
Create two separate sentences using the idiom "Elephant in the Room".(Application)

Challenge Three:
Identify another idiom that is similar to "Elephant in the Room".(Analysis)

Challenge Four:
Create or recall a situation where there was, in a figurative sense, an "Elephant in the Room".(Analysis)

Challenge Five:
Is this idiom a positive statement, negative statement, or a neutral statement. If possible, create positive scenarios and negative situations using the idiom, "Elephant in the Room".(Evaluation)

Suggested Start:
Using an American English Idiom dictionary, define the figurative meaning of "Elephant in the Room".

Potential Resources:
    1.) Idioms.thefreedictionary.com
    2.) Dictionary.reference.com/idioms

Challenge Six:

Create, draw or sketch three **individual** objects that represent the word "Expansive". Based on your images, explain the connection(s) to the subject.(Synthesis)

Example 1:
Humbled

Example 2:
Driven

Challenge Seven:

Create two or more images that express the command "Cancel the order!" But, use as few images and letters as possible. Then, repeat this process with the thought, "Take a break!". Communicate the subtle or overt meaning of the objects inside your images. (Synthesis)

Example One: *I dislike garlic.*

Example Two: *I love garlic.*

Chapter 7
Section 2

Perspectives on: Computers

Common Core State Standards:
- CCSS.ELA-LITERACY.WHST.6-8.7
- CCSS.ELA-LITERACY.WHST.6-8.8
- CCSS.ELA-LITERACY.WHST.6-8.10
- CCSS.ELA-LITERACY.RST.6-8.1
- CCSS.ELA-LITERACY.RST.6-8.2

Learning Objectives:
- A. Gain perspective on vague writing
- B. Gain awareness of potential problems with "absolute" statements in writing
- C. Gain perspective on multiple answers

Can a Computer Run While the Power is Off?

Instructions:
Place your answers to each challenge into a journal or folder

Challenge One:
Answer the question, "Can a computer run while the power is off?" Cite sources that defend your argument.(Analysis)

Challenge Two:
Answer the question, "What is computing?" (Analysis)

Here are recommendations to keep in mind when answering the above questions:
1. What is a computer?
2. What is power?
3. List various types of computers. List types of power.
4. Reflect on the history of computers.
5. Cite sources that defend your argument.

Suggested Start:
1. Pause before answering the question.
2. Define "run".
3. Define "power".
4. Define "off".

Potential Resources:
1.) Merriam-Webster.com
2.) Bartleby.com

Challenge Three:
Create a joke that you must answer in a figurative way and a literal way. Remember, keep it clean and respectful. NO PRACTICAL JOKES!(Analysis)

Example:
Joke(the setup): *They say "failure is a part of learning".*
Figurative answer (punchline): *Could someone please explain that to my parents.*
Literal answer: *This quote translates more often into "We learn from our mistakes". Whether a person is completing a quiz or learning to ride a bike, mistakes may occur, and they have the option to grow from their small failures.*

The secret to creating jokes is to ask questions about the world. In other words, analyze the world around you. If it doesn't make sense, question it. Then, research it.

To help, start with a statement like:
    Why is it that...............
    Ever notice that...........
    Whose idea was it to make...
    One day, there was a.................
    Why does....
    Where's the......
    How is it that....

Don't forget to explore and explain the answer in a figurative and literal way. Creating jokes can be challenging. Worst case scenario, find and use a joke that you can answer in a figurative and literal way. Explain, why it is funny. Give credit to the comedian.

Challenge Four:

First, **define** the word, "Apathy". Second, create a two column chart with a "negative factors" side and a "positive factors" side. Third, contrast the positive factors and negative issues of the word, "Apathy". (Analysis)

Example:

According to _____'s dictionary, **failure** is....

Failure	
Negative Factors	**Positive Factors**
May spark negative emotions	Mistakes and failings are a part of the creation process
May affect interpersonal relationships	"When you quit that is true failure"
	Don't make failing a habit; however, if it happens, learn from your failure

Challenge Five:

Find an image. Then, create a chart that lists the directly observable features versus the not-visible, but inferable features of the image.(Analysis)

Example: Helicopter	
Observable and Visible	**Not Visible, but Inferable**
is a vehicle	holds pilots
is in the air	holds passengers

Chapter 7
Section 3

Exploring Quotations on:
Literacy

Common Core State Standards:
- CCSS.ELA-LITERACY.WHST.6-8.6
- CCSS.ELA-LITERACY.WHST.6-8.8
- CCSS.ELA-LITERACY.WHST.6-8.10
- CCSS.ELA-LITERACY.RH.6-8.1
- CCSS.ELA-LITERACY.RH.6-8.4
- CCSS.ELA-LITERACY.RH.6-8.7

Learning Objectives:
- A. Gain knowledge on the topic of "literacy"
- B. Experience other perspectives on "literacy"

Quotations on Literacy

Instructions:
Place your answers to each challenge into a journal or folder

Challenge One:
Locate a quotation on the topic of "literacy".(Knowledge)

Challenge Two:
Translate your selected quotation on "literacy" into your own words.(Comprehension)

Challenge Three:
Compose a biographical statement using your chosen quotation on "literacy".(Application)

Challenge Four:
Create your own quote on "literacy".(Synthesis)

Challenge Five:
Select or create a poem on "literacy".(Synthesis)

Suggested Start:
1. Reflect on your views on "literacy".
2. Quotation resources are available at your local library.

Potential Resources:
1.) Quoteland.com
2.) Brainyquote.com
3.) Quotationspage.com
4.) En.wikiquote.org

Challenge Six:
Using a quotation on "literacy", discover a way to express the meaning through pictures and words. Then, create a comic strip that explains the quotation.(Synthesis)

Example:
"Hunger"
"Thou shouldst eat to live; not live to eat."
Socrates

Create a collection of images that relate to the quote. Then, add captions or messages that help express the quote. Lastly, connect images and create a comic strip.

Challenge Seven:
Complete the following sentence fragment with three or more separate statements. Figure out a way to incorporate a quotation, adage, or joke.(Application)

The tome was...

Example:

The last movie that I saw...
1.) ...caused my mind to reflect on the possibilities of humans having superpowers. For instance, by combining advanced nanotechnology with our understanding of genetics, we could modify ourselves into more supercharged people.

2.) ...agitated me because it depicted the cruelties of mankind. However, I then reflected on an anonymous quote that "Unfortunately, the road to progress can have various levels of bumpiness".

3.) ...frightened me because it was a creepy horror film. Now, I want to sleep with the lights on, but my parents disagree. Even though, I don't pay the electric bill. I feel that I should be able to make this decision!

Chapter 7
Section 4

Exploration of Adages, Aphorisms, Proverbs, and Maxims:

Common Core State Standards:
- CCSS.ELA-LITERACY.WHST.6-8.6
- CCSS.ELA-LITERACY.WHST.6-8.8
- CCSS.ELA-LITERACY.WHST.6-8.10
- CCSS.ELA-LITERACY.RH.6-8.4
- CCSS.ELA-LITERACY.RH.6-8.7

Learning Objectives:
- A. Experience perceptive sayings from various cultures
- B. Examine beliefs and understandings of various individuals and groups

Adages, Aphorisms, Proverbs, and Maxims

Instructions:
Place your answers to each challenge into a journal or folder

Challenge One:
Select an adage, aphorism, proverb, or maxim. Research the origin of the adage, aphorism, proverb, or maxim. Cite source(s).(Knowledge)

Challenge Two:
Translate your chosen adage, aphorism, proverb, or maxim into your own words.(Comprehension)

Challenge Three:
Compose a small paragraph or a short segment of dialogue that includes your chosen adage, aphorism, proverb, or maxim.(Application)

Challenge Four:
Do you agree or disagree with the message of your chosen adage, aphorism, proverb, or maxim. Defend your response. Cite sources.(Evaluation)

Suggested Start:
1. Reflect on your chosen adage, aphorism, proverb, or maxim.
2. Identify problems, if any.

Potential Resources:
    1.) En.wikiquote.org
    2.) Thinkexist.com

Challenge Five:

Select at least three pictures based on your selected adage, aphorism, proverb, or maxim. Next, build three posters by adding text to the chosen pictures. (Synthesis)

Suggested Start:
"Knowledge is Power"

1. Make sure you understand the adage, aphorism, proverb, or maxim.
2. Reflect on the meaning(s) of your chosen adage, aphorism, proverb, or maxim.
3. Search for images that symbolize or reflect the adage, aphorism, proverb, or maxim.
4. Construct posters.

Challenge Six:

Is it better to <u>consume</u> or <u>produce</u>?

In this exercise, consider possible scenarios when it is better to do one or the other underlined options. Next, find scenarios that benefit from each underlined option. Then, try to find scenarios that do not benefit from each underlined option. Create a chart that represents your conclusions. Lastly, compose statements using historical examples or scientific data that validate each item inside your chart. (Evaluation)

Example: Is it better to <u>spark</u> or <u>spur</u>?

Neither	Spark	Spur	Both
malice	critical thoughts	truthfulness	healthy behavior
hatred	cooperation	obedience	innovations
ignorance	motivation	horse	inventions
	confidence		imagination
			students
			self-control

    A. <u>Hatred</u> can <u>spark</u> destructive behavior such as... (insert historical example).
    B. Although, at times effective, spurred obedience has a limited shelf life; eventually, the spurred will rebel or revolt such as a child or colony...
    C. According to _____(author/researcher/expert), sparking confidence can boost students' comprehension.

Chapter 7
Section 5

Exploration of Business

Common Core State Standards:
- CCSS.ELA-LITERACY.WHST.6-8.6
- CCSS.ELA-LITERACY.WHST.6-8.7
- CCSS.ELA-LITERACY.WHST.6-8.8
- CCSS.ELA-LITERACY.WHST.6-8.9
- CCSS.ELA-LITERACY.WHST.6-8.10
- CCSS.ELA-LITERACY.RH.6-8.4
- CCSS.ELA-LITERACY.RH.6-8.7

Learning Objectives:
- A. Examine business costs and opportunities
- B. Communicate information through graphics and text such as diagrams and charts

Organization Path

Instructions:
Place your answers to each challenge into a journal or folder

Challenge One:
Name a business or organization that you patronize on a daily basis. Classify the type of business it is. Identify its main product or service.(Knowledge)

Challenge Two:
Identify three competitors of this business.(Comprehension)

Challenge Three:
Identify three products or services of your chosen company. Create a chart that displays the relationship among the main product and the additional products. Determine if these products are:
- Integrated and necessary for the main product to operate such as gasoline or motor oil for cars
- Complementary to the product and enhances product like air conditioning and power windows for cars
- Vital to the business such as their brand brake pads and spark plugs for cars(Application)

Main Product(Windows Operating System)			
	Integrated and Necessary	Enhances Main Product	Vital to Business
Microsoft Office	No	Yes	Yes
Internet Explorer	Yes	Yes	Yes
Xbox 360	No	No	No

Challenge Four:

Categorize the four chosen products by popularity among consumers, history of the products, revenue, profit, target audience(name their main customers), and strongest direct competitor, quasi-competitor and indirect competitor. Use a scale from 4 to 1, 4 being highest, to grade each category. Then, based on your chart, describe the growth potential (or lack of future potential) of each product. Which product is the strongest? Which product would you focus more resources on for the future of the company. Defend your decision. Cite sources.(Analysis)

Strengths and Weaknesses				
	Windows OS	Microsoft Office	Internet Explorer	Xbox 360
Popularity	3	4	2	1
Revenue	3	4	2	1
Profitabil-ity	3	4	2	1

Strengths and Weaknesses by Details				
	Windows OS	Microsoft Office	Internet Explorer	Xbox 360
Years Available	28 yrs.	23 yrs.	19 yrs.	8 yrs.
Direct Competitor	Mac OS X	LibreOffice	Chrome	Playstation 3
Quasi-Competitor	Android OS	QuickOffice	Smart-TVs	Gameboy Advance
Indirect Competitor	Pen and Paper	Typewriter	Library Card	Mobile Device
Rankings among direct Competitors	#1	#1	#2	#1

Challenge Five:

Choose one of your chosen company's most popular or well-known products or services. Research this product or service and build a diagram that displays the fabrication process of the product or service. Cite sources.(Synthesis)

Your diagram or chart should display the work that goes into producing a product or service.

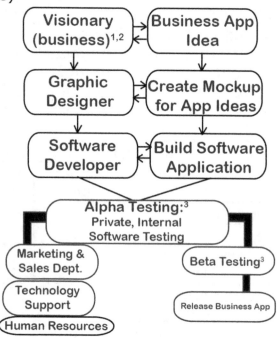

1 Does the app solve a problem?
2 Can it be profitable?
3 Testing may require restarts or revisions.

Challenge Six:

Create a chart that explains two of the product's major features. For example, an alarm clock normally has a minimum of two features, the time display and the alarm function. Use graphics, if possible. Cite sources.(Analysis)

Alarm Radio	
Radio	converts radio waves...
Alarm Buzzer	is a feature of the...

Challenge Seven:

Based on your gathered research and your product choice, create a visual flowchart or graphical diagram that demonstrates the interaction between human resources and non-human resources to produce the product or service. Start with the necessary (raw) materials required to produce the product or service. For example, an organic farmer needs supplies, materials, equipment, and workers. Then, your flowchart should display the interactions between the workforce and resources until the end-product reaches consumers. (Synthesis)

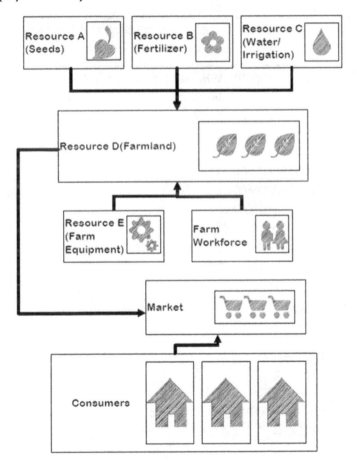

Challenge Eight:

Identify three individuals that had a major impact on your chosen company's industry. Create a multimedia chart to describe their impact. Based on your research of these three individuals, which individual had the biggest impact on their industry. Defend your argument. Cite sources.(Evaluation)

Industry: Telecommunications		
insert image	John Doe	was an inventor whose radical and unorthodox methods produced the first....
insert image	Jane Doe	was an amazing engineer who invented the first....
insert image	Dr. Cooper	was a well-known and well-respected physician that accidentally invented....

Potential Resources:
- www.bls.gov/ooh
- www.bls.gov/iag
- howstuffworks.com
- visual.merriam-webster.com
- finance.yahoo.com
- ehow.com
- sba.gov
- entrepreneur.com

Rubric for Chapter
See Appendix A

Reflective Questions for Chapter
See Appendix B

Chapter 8

Connections to
Common Core State Standards:

CCSS.ELA-LITERACY.WHST.6-8.6
Use technology, including the Internet, to produce and publish writing and present the relationships between information and ideas clearly and efficiently.(2010)

CCSS.ELA-LITERACY.WHST.6-8.7
Conduct short research projects to answer a question(including a self-generated question), drawing on several sources and generating additional related, focused questions that allow for multiple avenues of exploration.(2010)

CCSS.ELA-LITERACY.WHST.6-8.8
Gather relevant information from multiple print and digital sources, using search terms effectively; assess the credibility and accuracy of each source; and quote or paraphrase the data and conclusions of others while avoiding plagiarism and following a standard form of citation.(2010)

CCSS.ELA-LITERACY.WHST.6-8.9
Draw evidence from informational texts to support analysis, reflection, and research.(2010)

Connections to
Common Core State Standards:
<u>(continued)</u>

CCSS.ELA-LITERACY.WHST.6-8.10
Write routinely over extended time frames(time for revision and reflection) and shorter time frames(a single sitting or a day or two) for a range of discipline-specific tasks, purposes, and audiences.(2010)

CCSS.ELA-LITERACY.RH.6-8.1
Cite specific textual evidence to support analysis of primary and secondary sources.(2010)

CCSS.ELA-LITERACY.RH.6-8.4
Determine the meaning of words and phrases as they are used in a text, including vocabulary specific to domains related to history/social studies.(2010)

CCSS.ELA-LITERACY.RH.6-8.7
Integrate visual information(e.g., in charts, graphs, photographs, videos, or maps) with other information in print and digital text.(2010)

CCSS.ELA-LITERACY.RST.6-8.1
Cite specific textual evidence to support analysis of science and technical texts.(2010)

CCSS.ELA-LITERACY.RST.6-8.2
Determine the central ideas or conclusions of a text; provide an accurate summary of the text distinct from prior knowledge or opinions.(2010)

CCSS.ELA-LITERACY.RST.6-8.
Distinguish among facts, reasoned judgment based on research findings, and speculation in text.(2010)

Chapter 8
Section 1

Exploration of the Idiom: Get It?

Common Core State Standards:
- CCSS.ELA-LITERACY.WHST.6-8.8
- CCSS.ELA-LITERACY.WHST.6-8.10
- CCSS.ELA-LITERACY.RH.6-8.4
- CCSS.ELA-LITERACY.RH.6-8.7

Learning Objectives:
A. Understand the figurative meaning of idioms
B. Comprehend the problematic issues with literal translations of idioms

Get It?

Instructions:
Place your answers to each challenge into a journal or folder

Challenge One:
Translate "Get It?" **into your own words.**(Comprehension)

Challenge Two:
Create two separate sentences using the idiom "Get It?"(Comprehension)

Challenge Three:
Identify another idiom that is similar to "Get It?" (Analysis)

Challenge Four:
List an experience where you "Got It." Or, list an experience where you could not "Get It?"(Knowledge)

Challenge Five:
List **fictional** characters that "Get it?" at the right time. List **fictional** characters that "Get It?" at a bad or inopportune time.(Analysis)

Suggested Start:
Using an American English Idiom dictionary, define the figurative meaning of "Get It".

Potential Resources:
    1.) Idioms.thefreedictionary.com
    2.) Dictionary.reference.com/idioms

Challenge Six:

Create, draw or sketch three **individual** objects that represent the word "Condensed". Based on your images, explain the connection(s) to the subject.(Synthesis)

Example 1:
Humbled

Example 2:
Driven

Challenge Seven:

Create two or more images that express the command "Use your imagination!" But, use as few images and letters as possible. Then, repeat this process with the thought, "Sounds logical to me!" Communicate the subtle or overt meaning of the objects inside your images.(Synthesis)

Example One: *I dislike onions.*

Example Two: *I love onions.*

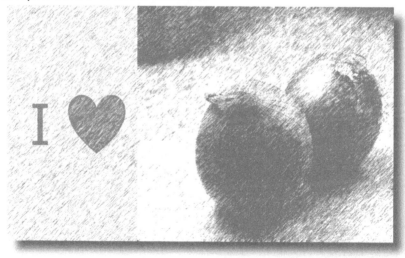

Chapter 8
Section 2

Perspectives on:
No one

Common Core State Standards:
- CCSS.ELA-LITERACY.WHST.6-8.7
- CCSS.ELA-LITERACY.WHST.6-8.8
- CCSS.ELA-LITERACY.WHST.6-8.10
- CCSS.ELA-LITERACY.RST.6-8.1
- CCSS.ELA-LITERACY.RST.6-8.2

Learning Objectives:
- A. Gain perspective on vague writing
- B. Gain awareness of potential problems with "absolute" statements in writing
- C. Gain perspective on multiple answers

No one can hold their breath for 90 seconds

Instructions:
Place your answers to each challenge into a journal or folder

Challenge One:
Respond to the statement, "No one can hold their breath for 90 seconds". (Analysis)

Challenge Two:
List activities that require holding your breath for long periods of time.(Knowledge)

Challenge Three:
List groups or communities that are known for holding their breath for long periods of time. Cite sources. (Knowledge)

Here are recommendations to keep in mind when answering the above questions:
1. Reflect on the words, "No one" and "Groups".
2. Cite sources that defend your argument.

Suggested Start:
1. Pause before answering the question.
2. Using a dictionary, define "No one".

Potential Resources:
1.) Merriam-Webster.com
2.) Bartleby.com

Challenge Four:
Create a joke that you must answer in a figurative way and a literal way. Remember, keep it clean and respectful. NO PRACTICAL JOKES!(Analysis)

Example:
Joke(the setup): *They say "failure is a part of learning".*
Figurative answer (punchline): *Could someone please explain that to my parents.*
Literal answer: *This quote translates more often into "We learn from our mistakes". Whether a person is completing a quiz or learning to ride a bike, mistakes may occur, and they have the option to grow from their small failures.*

The secret to creating jokes is to ask questions about the world. In other words, analyze the world around you. If it doesn't make sense, question it. Then, research it.

To help, start with a statement like:
    Why is it that...............
    Ever notice that...........
    Whose idea was it to make...
    One day, there was a.................
    Why does....
    Where's the......
    How is it that....

Don't forget to explore and explain the answer in a figurative and literal way. Creating jokes can be challenging. Worst case scenario, find and use a joke that you can answer in a figurative and literal way. Explain, why it is funny. Give credit to the comedian.

Challenge Five:

First, **define** the word, "Fearless". Second, create a two column chart with a "negative factors" side and a "positive factors" side. Third, contrast the positive factors and negative issues of the word, "Fearless". (Analysis)

Example:

According to _____'s dictionary, **failure** is....

Failure	
Negative Factors	**Positive Factors**
May spark negative emotions	Mistakes and failings are a part of the creation process
May affect interpersonal relationships	"When you quit that is true failure"
	Don't make failing a habit; however, if it happens, learn from your failure

Challenge Six:

Find an image. Then, create a chart that lists the directly observable features versus the not-visible, but inferable features of the image.(Analysis)

Example: Aircraft Carrier	
Observable and Visible	**Not Visible, but Inferable**
is a vehicle	holds crew
is in the ocean	has computer systems
holds aircraft	

Chapter 8
Section 3

Exploring Quotations on:
Friendship

Common Core State Standards:
- CCSS.ELA-LITERACY.WHST.6-8.6
- CCSS.ELA-LITERACY.WHST.6-8.8
- CCSS.ELA-LITERACY.WHST.6-8.10
- CCSS.ELA-LITERACY.RH.6-8.1
- CCSS.ELA-LITERACY.RH.6-8.4
- CCSS.ELA-LITERACY.RH.6-8.7

Learning Objectives:
- A. Gain knowledge on the topic of "friendship"
- B. Experience other perspectives on "friendship"

Quotations on Friendship

Instructions:
Place your answers to each challenge into a journal or folder

Challenge One:
Locate a quotation on the topic of "friendship".(Knowledge)

Challenge Two:
Translate your selected quotation on "friendship" into your own words.(Comprehension)

Challenge Three:
Compose a biographical statement using your chosen quotation on "friendship".(Application)

Challenge Four:
Create your own quote on "friendship".(Synthesis)

Challenge Five:
Select or create a poem on "friendship".(Synthesis)

Suggested Start:
1. Reflect on "friendship".
2. Quotation resources are available at your local library.

Potential Resources:
1.) Quoteland.com
2.) Brainyquote.com
3.) En.wikiquote.org

Challenge Six:

Using a quotation on "friendship", discover a way to express the meaning through pictures and words. Then, create a comic strip that explains the quotation. (Synthesis)

Example:

"Hunger"
"Thou shouldst eat to live; not live to eat."
Socrates

Create a collection of images that relate to the quote. Then, add captions or messages that help express the quote. Lastly, connect images and create a comic strip.

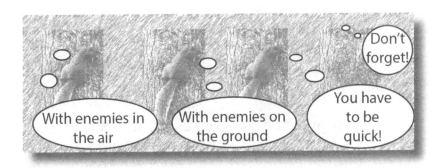

Challenge Seven:
Complete the following sentence fragment with three or more separate statements. Figure out a way to incorporate a quotation, adage, or joke.(Application)

The computer network...

Example:

The last movie that I saw...
1.) ...caused my mind to reflect on the possibilities of humans having superpowers. For instance, by combining advanced nanotechnology with our understanding of genetics, we could modify ourselves into more supercharged people.

2.) ...agitated me because it depicted the cruelties of mankind. However, I then reflected on an anonymous quote that "Unfortunately, the road to progress can have various levels of bumpiness".

3.) ...frightened me because it was a creepy horror film. Now, I want to sleep with the lights on, but my parents disagree. Even though, I don't pay the electric bill. I feel that I should be able to make this decision!

Chapter 8
Section 4

Exploration of Adages, Aphorisms, Proverbs, and Maxims:

Common Core State Standards:
- CCSS.ELA-LITERACY.WHST.6-8.6
- CCSS.ELA-LITERACY.WHST.6-8.8
- CCSS.ELA-LITERACY.WHST.6-8.10
- CCSS.ELA-LITERACY.RH.6-8.4
- CCSS.ELA-LITERACY.RH.6-8.7

Learning Objectives:
- A. Experience perceptive sayings from various cultures
- B. Examine beliefs and understandings of various individuals and groups

Adages, Aphorisms, Proverbs, and Maxims

Instructions:
Place your answers to each challenge into a journal or folder

Challenge One:
Select an adage, aphorism, proverb, or maxim. Research the origin of the adage, aphorism, proverb, or maxim. Cite source(s).(Knowledge)

Challenge Two:
Translate your chosen adage, aphorism, proverb, or maxim into your own words.(Comprehension)

Challenge Three:
Compose a small paragraph or a short segment of dialogue that includes your chosen adage, aphorism, proverb, or maxim.(Application)

Challenge Four:
Do you agree or disagree with the message of your chosen adage, aphorism, proverb, or maxim. Defend your response. Cite sources.(Evaluation)

Suggested Start:
1. Reflect on your chosen adage, aphorism, proverb, or maxim.
2. Identify problems, if any.

Potential Resources:
1.) En.wikiquote.org
2.) Thinkexist.com

Challenge Five:
Select at least three pictures based on your selected adage, aphorism, proverb, or maxim. Next, build three posters by adding text to the chosen pictures. (Synthesis)

Suggested Start:
"Knowledge is Power"
1. Make sure you understand the adage, aphorism, proverb, or maxim.
2. Reflect on the meaning(s) of your chosen adage, aphorism, proverb, or maxim.
3. Search for images that symbolize or reflect the adage, aphorism, proverb, or maxim.
4. Construct posters.

Challenge Six:

Is it better to <u>understand</u> or <u>digest</u>?

In this exercise, consider possible scenarios when it is better to do one or the other underlined options. Next, find scenarios that benefit from each underlined option. Then, try to find scenarios that do not benefit from each underlined option. Create a chart that represents your conclusions. Lastly, compose statements using historical examples or scientific data that validate each item inside your chart. (Evaluation)

Example: Is it better to <u>spark</u> or <u>spur</u>?

Neither	Spark	Spur	Both
malice	critical thoughts	truthfulness	healthy behavior
hatred	cooperation	obedience	innovations
ignorance	motivation	horse	inventions
	confidence		imagination
			students
			self-control

A. <u>Hatred</u> can <u>spark</u> destructive behavior such as... (insert historical example).
B. Although, at times effective, spurred obedience has a limited shelf life; eventually, the spurred will rebel or revolt such as a child or colony...
C. According to _____(author/researcher/expert), sparking confidence can boost students' comprehension.

Chapter 8
Section 5

Exploration of Business

Common Core State Standards:
- CCSS.ELA-LITERACY.WHST.6-8.6
- CCSS.ELA-LITERACY.WHST.6-8.7
- CCSS.ELA-LITERACY.WHST.6-8.8
- CCSS.ELA-LITERACY.WHST.6-8.9
- CCSS.ELA-LITERACY.WHST.6-8.10
- CCSS.ELA-LITERACY.RH.6-8.4
- CCSS.ELA-LITERACY.RH.6-8.7

Learning Objectives:
- A. Examine products and services from the view of an organizational entity such as a business
- B. Communicate information through graphics and text such as diagrams and charts

Product and Service Path

Instructions:
Place your answers to each challenge into a journal or folder

Challenge One:
Identify your favorite product or service. Then, identify its historical predecessor.(Knowledge)

Challenge Two:
Identify the type of companies that produced the historical predecessor of your favorite product or service. Classify their industry.(Comprehension)

Challenge Three:
Identify three direct competitors of the histororical predecessor. Describe and chart the competition based on market share, business size (by employees), years available, marketing reach(local, regional, national, global), revenue and profits. Research and use industry averages if the predecessor or its competitors are not publicly traded.(Analysis)

Main Product (Web Browsers)				
	Market Share	Business Size	Marketing Reach	Years Available
Internet Explorer (product)	2	large enterprise	global	19
Chrome (competitor)	1	large enterprise	global	6
Firefox (competitor)	3	mid-size	global	12
Opera (competitor)	4	mid-size	global	18

Challenge four:

Create a diagram that displays the major parts or sequences of the historical predecessor. Next explain two of the product's major parts. For example, an Xbox 360 has multiple, specialized parts such as the central processing unit, the graphics processing unit and the hard drive. Use graphics. Cite sources. (Analysis)

The Xbox 360's CPU processes....

The Xbox 360's RAM is used for....

CPU   GPU   RAM

XBOX 360

Mother-board   Sound Card   Hard Drive

Challenge Five:

Based on the predecessor of your chosen product or service, identify three influential people that had a major impact on its industry through improvements, innovations, or inventions. Describe their effects on the industry. Cite sources.(Analysis)

Industry: Telecommunications		
insert image	John Doe	was an inventor whose radical and unorthodox methods produced the first....
insert image	Jane Doe	was an amazing engineer who invented the first....
insert image	Dr. Cooper	was a well-known and well-respected physician that accidentally invented....

Challenge Six:

Create an organizational chart (unofficial) of a company that offers the predecessor. Next, pinpoint the areas where your three previously chosen influential people would work. For example, if one of your selected influential people is a visionary executive leader, then they would fit somewhere at the top of the organizational chart(org chart).(Synthesis)

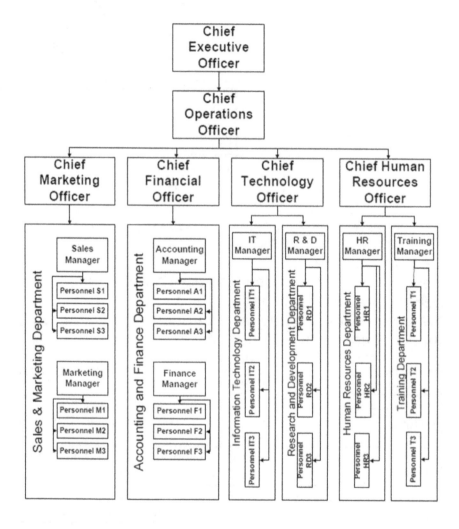

Challenge Seven:

Based on your gathered research and the predecessor of your product/service choice, create a visual flowchart or graphical diagram that demonstrates the interaction between human resources and non-human resources to produce the product or service. Start with the necessary (raw) materials required to produce the product or service. For example, an organic farmer needs supplies, materials, equipment, and workers. Then, your flowchart should display the interactions between the workforce and resources until the end-product reaches consumers. (Synthesis)

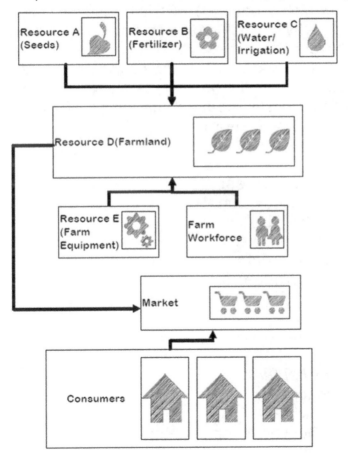

Challenge Eight:

Based on the predecessor of your product choice or service selection,

- Identify two supplemental/complementary products or services such as computer applications complement computer operating systems
- Identify two required/necessary products (computer operating system are necessary to operate computers)
- Identify two separate or indirectly connected products or services that the company produces(Xbox 360 or Zune)

Discover which product(s) was/is the strongest seller(s). Why? Would you eliminate any products or services from the company's product lineup? Explain. Which product or service deserves the most research and development? Elaborate. Lastly, which product or service deserves the most marketing. Explain. Cite sources.(Evaluation)

Potential Resources:

- www.bls.gov/ooh
- www.bls.gov/iag
- howstuffworks.com
- visual.merriam-webster.com
- finance.yahoo.com
- ehow.com
- sba.gov
- entrepreneur.com

Rubric for Chapter
See Appendix A

Reflective Questions for Chapter
See Appendix B

Chapter 9

Connections to
Common Core State Standards:

CCSS.ELA-LITERACY.WHST.6-8.6
Use technology, including the Internet, to produce and publish writing and present the relationships between information and ideas clearly and efficiently.(2010)

CCSS.ELA-LITERACY.WHST.6-8.7
Conduct short research projects to answer a question(including a self-generated question), drawing on several sources and generating additional related, focused questions that allow for multiple avenues of exploration.(2010)

CCSS.ELA-LITERACY.WHST.6-8.8
Gather relevant information from multiple print and digital sources, using search terms effectively; assess the credibility and accuracy of each source; and quote or paraphrase the data and conclusions of others while avoiding plagiarism and following a standard form of citation.(2010)

CCSS.ELA-LITERACY.WHST.6-8.9
Draw evidence from informational texts to support analysis, reflection, and research.(2010)

Connections to
Common Core State Standards:
(continued)

CCSS.ELA-LITERACY.WHST.6-8.10
Write routinely over extended time frames(time for revision and reflection) and shorter time frames(a single sitting or a day or two) for a range of discipline-specific tasks, purposes, and audiences.(2010)

CCSS.ELA-LITERACY.RH.6-8.1
Cite specific textual evidence to support analysis of primary and secondary sources.(2010)

CCSS.ELA-LITERACY.RH.6-8.4
Determine the meaning of words and phrases as they are used in a text, including vocabulary specific to domains related to history/social studies.(2010)

CCSS.ELA-LITERACY.RH.6-8.7
Integrate visual information(e.g., in charts, graphs, photographs, videos, or maps) with other information in print and digital text.(2010)

CCSS.ELA-LITERACY.RST.6-8.1
Cite specific textual evidence to support analysis of science and technical texts.(2010)

CCSS.ELA-LITERACY.RST.6-8.2
Determine the central ideas or conclusions of a text; provide an accurate summary of the text distinct from prior knowledge or opinions.(2010)

CCSS.ELA-LITERACY.RST.6-8.
Distinguish among facts, reasoned judgment based on research findings, and speculation in text.(2010)

Chapter 9
Section 1

Exploration of the Idiom:
Down Memory Lane

Common Core State Standards:
- CCSS.ELA-LITERACY.WHST.6-8.8
- CCSS.ELA-LITERACY.WHST.6-8.10
- CCSS.ELA-LITERACY.RH.6-8.4
- CCSS.ELA-LITERACY.RH.6-8.7

Learning Objectives:
- A. Understand the figurative meaning of idioms
- B. Comprehend the problematic issues with literal translations of idioms

Down Memory Lane

Instructions:
Place your answers to each challenge into a journal or folder

Challenge One:
Translate "Down Memory Lane" **into your own words**.(Comprehension)

Challenge Two:
Create two separate sentences using the idiom "Down Memory Lane".(Application)

Challenge Three:
Identify another idiom that is similar to "Down Memory Lane".(Analysis)

Challenge Four:
Is memory lane a place?   Defend your answer.(Analysis)

Challenge Five:
Recall **fictional** characters that use similar idiomatic expressions.(Evaluation)

Suggested Start:
Using an American English Idiom dictionary, define the figurative meaning of "Down Memory Lane".
1. Define "place"?

Potential Resources:
      1.) Idioms.thefreedictionary.com
      2.) Dictionary.reference.com/idioms

Challenge Six:

Create, draw or sketch three **individual** objects that represent the word "Simplicity". Based on your images, explain the connection(s) to the subject.(Synthesis)

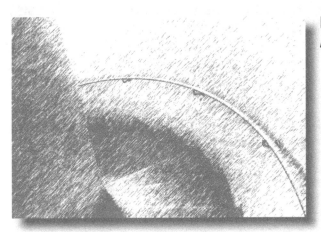

Example 1:
Humbled

Example 2:
Driven

Challenge Seven:

Create two or more images that express the statement "This links us to our past!" But, use as few images and letters as possible. Then, repeat this process with the command, "Give me three more laps around the track!". Communicate the subtle or overt meaning of the objects inside your images.(Synthesis)
Example One: *I dislike peppers.*

Example Two: *I love peppers.*

Chapter 9
Section 2

Perspectives on:
Anyone

Common Core State Standards:
- CCSS.ELA-LITERACY.WHST.6-8.7
- CCSS.ELA-LITERACY.WHST.6-8.8
- CCSS.ELA-LITERACY.WHST.6-8.10
- CCSS.ELA-LITERACY.RST.6-8.1
- CCSS.ELA-LITERACY.RST.6-8.2

Learning Objectives:
- A. Gain perspective on vague writing
- B. Gain awareness of potential problems with "absolute" statements in writing
- C. Gain perspective on multiple answers

Anyone can learn how to swim.

Instructions:
Place your answers to each challenge into a journal or folder

Challenge One:
Respond to the statement, "Anyone can learn how to swim". Cite sources that defend your argument.(Analysis)

Challenge Two:
Respond to the statement, "Swimming is an extremely easy form of exercise to master. Anyone can swim."(Evaluation)

Here are recommendations to keep in mind when answering the above questions:
1. Reflect on the word, "anyone".
2. Cite sources that defend your argument.

Suggested Start:
   1. Pause before answering the question.
   2. Operationalize the word, "swim".

Potential Resources:
   1.) Merriam-Webster.com
   2.) Bartleby.com

Challenge Three:
Create a joke that you must answer in a figurative way and a literal way. Remember, keep it clean and respectful. NO PRACTICAL JOKES!(Analysis)

Example:
Joke(the setup): *They say "failure is a part of learning".*
Figurative answer (punchline): *Could someone please explain that to my parents.*
Literal answer: *This quote translates more often into "We learn from our mistakes". Whether a person is completing a quiz or learning to ride a bike, mistakes may occur, and they have the option to grow from their small failures.*

The secret to creating jokes is to ask questions about the world. In other words, analyze the world around you. If it doesn't make sense, question it. Then, research it.

To help, start with a statement like:
Why is it that...............
Ever notice that...........
Whose idea was it to make...
One day, there was a.................
Why does....
Where's the......
How is it that....

Don't forget to explore and explain the answer in a figurative and literal way. Creating jokes can be challenging. Worst case scenario, find and use a joke that you can answer in a figurative and literal way. Explain, why it is funny. Give credit to the comedian.

Challenge Four:

First, **define** the word, "Transcendent". Second, create a two column chart with a "negative factors" side and a "positive factors" side. Third, contrast the positive factors and negative issues of the word, "Transcendent".(Analysis)

Example:

According to _____'s dictionary, **failure** is....

Failure	
Negative Factors	**Positive Factors**
May spark negative emotions	Mistakes and failings are a part of the creation process
May affect interpersonal relationships	"When you quit that is true failure"
	Don't make failing a habit; however, if it happens, learn from your failure

Challenge Five:

Find an image. Then, create a chart that lists the directly observable features versus the not-visible, but inferable features of the image.(Analysis)

Example: Barge	
Observable and Visible	**Not Visible, but Inferable**
is a vehicle	runs on fuel
is in a river	
has cargo	

Chapter 9
Section 3

Exploring Quotations on:
Success

Common Core State Standards:
- CCSS.ELA-LITERACY.WHST.6-8.6
- CCSS.ELA-LITERACY.WHST.6-8.8
- CCSS.ELA-LITERACY.WHST.6-8.10
- CCSS.ELA-LITERACY.RH.6-8.1
- CCSS.ELA-LITERACY.RH.6-8.4
- CCSS.ELA-LITERACY.RH.6-8.7

Learning Objectives:
- A. Gain knowledge on the topic of "success"
- B. Experience other perspectives on "success"

Quotations on Success

Instructions:
Place your answers to each challenge into a journal or folder

Challenge One:
Locate a quotation on the topic of "success".(Knowledge)

Challenge Two:
Translate your selected quotation on "success" into your own words.(Comprehension)

Challenge Three:
Compose a biographical statement using your chosen quotation on "success".(Application)

Challenge Four:
Create your own quote on "success".(Synthesis)

Challenge Five:
Select or create a poem on "success".(Synthesis)

Suggested Start:
1. Reflect on successful experiences.
2. Quotation resources are available at your local library.

Potential Resources:
1.) Quoteland.com
2.) Brainyquote.com
3.) En.wikiquote.org

Challenge Six:

Using a quotation on "success", discover a way to express the meaning through pictures and words. Then, create a comic strip that explains the quotation.(Synthesis)

Example:
"Hunger"
"Thou shouldst eat to live; not live to eat."
Socrates

Create a collection of images that relate to the quote. Then, add captions or messages that help express the quote. Lastly, connect images and create a comic strip.

Challenge Seven:

Complete the following sentence fragment with three or more separate statements. Figure out a way to incorporate a quotation, adage, or joke.(Application)

The Technology Initiative was...

Example:

The last movie that I saw...

1.) ...caused my mind to reflect on the possibilities of humans having superpowers. For instance, by combining advanced nanotechnology with our understanding of genetics, we could modify ourselves into more supercharged people.

2.) ...agitated me because it depicted the cruelties of mankind. However, I then reflected on an anonymous quote that "Unfortunately, the road to progress can have various levels of bumpiness".

3.) ...frightened me because it was a creepy horror film. Now, I want to sleep with the lights on, but my parents disagree. Even though, I don't pay the electric bill. I feel that I should be able to make this decision!

Chapter 9
Section 4

Exploration of Adages, Aphorisms, Proverbs, and Maxims:

Common Core State Standards:
- CCSS.ELA-LITERACY.WHST.6-8.6
- CCSS.ELA-LITERACY.WHST.6-8.8
- CCSS.ELA-LITERACY.WHST.6-8.10
- CCSS.ELA-LITERACY.RH.6-8.4
- CCSS.ELA-LITERACY.RH.6-8.7

Learning Objectives:
- A. Experience perceptive sayings from various cultures
- B. Examine beliefs and understandings of various individuals and groups

Adages, Aphorisms, Proverbs, and Maxims

Instructions:
Place your answers to each challenge into a journal or folder

Challenge One:
Select an adage, aphorism, proverb, or maxim. Research the origin of the adage, aphorism, proverb, or maxim. Cite source(s).(Knowledge)

Challenge Two:
Translate your chosen adage, aphorism, proverb, or maxim into your own words.(Comprehension)

Challenge Three:
Compose a small paragraph or a short segment of dialogue that includes your chosen adage, aphorism, proverb, or maxim.(Application)

Challenge Four:
Do you agree or disagree with the message of your chosen adage, aphorism, proverb, or maxim. Defend your response. Cite sources.(Evaluation)

Suggested Start:
1. Reflect on your chosen adage, aphorism, proverb, or maxim.
2. Identify problems, if any.

Potential Resources:
1.) En.wikiquote.org
2.) Thinkexist.com

Challenge Five:
Select at least three pictures based on your selected adage, aphorism, proverb, or maxim. Next, build three posters by adding text to the chosen pictures. (Synthesis)

Suggested Start:
"Knowledge is Power"
1. Make sure you understand the adage, aphorism, proverb, or maxim.
2. Reflect on the meaning(s) of your chosen adage, aphorism, proverb, or maxim.
3. Search for images that symbolize or reflect the adage, aphorism, proverb, or maxim.
4. Construct posters.

Challenge Six:

Is it better to <u>blend</u> or <u>separate</u>?

In this exercise, consider possible scenarios when it is better to do one or the other underlined options. Next, find scenarios that benefit from each underlined option. Then, try to find scenarios that do not benefit from each underlined option. Create a chart that represents your conclusions. Lastly, compose statements using historical examples or scientific data that validate each item inside your chart. (Evaluation)

Example: Is it better to <u>spark</u> or <u>spur</u>?

Neither	Spark	Spur	Both
malice	critical thoughts	truthfulness	healthy behavior
hatred	cooperation	obedience	innovations
ignorance	motivation	horse	inventions
	confidence		imagination
			students
			self-control

A. <u>Hatred</u> can <u>spark</u> destructive behavior such as... (insert historical example).
B. Although, at times effective, spurred obedience has a limited shelf life; eventually, the spurred will rebel or revolt such as a child or colony...
C. According to _____(author/researcher/expert), sparking confidence can boost students' comprehension.

Chapter 9
Section 5

Exploration of Business

Common Core State Standards:
- CCSS.ELA-LITERACY.WHST.6-8.6
- CCSS.ELA-LITERACY.WHST.6-8.7
- CCSS.ELA-LITERACY.WHST.6-8.8
- CCSS.ELA-LITERACY.WHST.6-8.9
- CCSS.ELA-LITERACY.WHST.6-8.10
- CCSS.ELA-LITERACY.RH.6-8.4
- CCSS.ELA-LITERACY.RH.6-8.7

Learning Objectives:
- A. Examine business costs and opportunities
- B. Communicate information through graphics and text such as diagrams and charts

Organization Path

Instructions:
Place your answers to each challenge into a journal or folder

Challenge One:
Name a business or organization that you patronize on a weekly basis. Classify the type of business it is. Identify its main product.(Knowledge)

Challenge Two:
Identify three competitors of this business.(Comprehension)

Challenge Three:
Identify three products or services of your chosen company. Create a chart that displays the relationship among the main product and the additional products. Determine if these products are:
- Integrated and necessary for the main product to operate such as gasoline or motor oil for cars
- Complementary to the product and enhances product like air conditioning and power windows for cars
- Vital to the business such as their brand brake pads and spark plugs for cars

Main Product(Windows Operating System)			
	Integrated and Necessary	Enhances Main Product	Vital to Business
Microsoft Office	No	Yes	Yes
Internet Explorer	Yes	Yes	Yes
Xbox 360	No	No	No

Challenge Four:

Categorize the four chosen products by popularity among consumers, history of the products, revenue, profit, target audience(name their main customers), and strongest direct competitor, quasi-competitor and indirect competitor. Use a scale from 4 to 1, 4 being highest, to grade each category. Then, based on your chart, describe the growth potential (or lack of future potential) of each product. Which product is the strongest? Which product would you focus more resources on for the future of the company. Defend your decision. Cite sources.(Analysis)

Strengths and Weaknesses				
	Windows OS	Microsoft Office	Internet Explorer	Xbox 360
Popularity	3	4	2	1
Revenue	3	4	2	1
Profitabil-ity	3	4	2	1

Strengths and Weaknesses by Details				
	Windows OS	Microsoft Office	Internet Explorer	Xbox 360
Years Available	28 yrs.	23 yrs.	19 yrs.	8 yrs.
Direct Competitor	Mac OS X	LibreOffice	Chrome	Playstation 3
Quasi-Competitor	Android OS	QuickOffice	Smart-TVs	Gameboy Advance
Indirect Competitor	Pen and Paper	Typewriter	Library Card	Mobile Device
Rankings among direct Competitors	#1	#1	#2	#1

Challenge Five:

Choose one of your chosen company's most popular or well-known products or services. Research this product or service and build a diagram that displays the fabrication process of the product or service. Cite sources.(Synthesis)

Your diagram or chart should display the work that goes into producing a product or service.

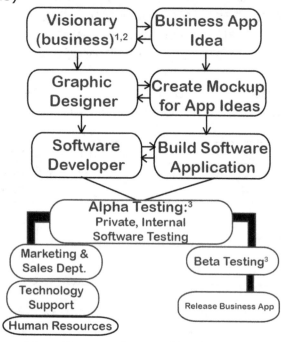

1 Does the app solve a problem?
2 Can it be profitable?
3 Testing may require restarts or revisions.

Challenge Six:

Create a chart that explains two of the product's major features. For example, an alarm clock normally has a minimum of two features, the time display and the alarm function. Use graphics, if possible. Cite sources.(Analysis)

Alarm Radio	
Radio	converts radio waves...
Alarm Buzzer	is a feature of the...

Challenge Seven:

Based on your gathered research and your product choice, create a visual flowchart or graphical diagram that demonstrates the interaction between human resources and non-human resources to produce the product or service. Start with the necessary (raw) materials required to produce the product or service. For example, an organic farmer needs supplies, materials, equipment, and workers. Then, your flowchart should display the interactions between the workforce and resources until the end-product reaches consumers. (Synthesis)

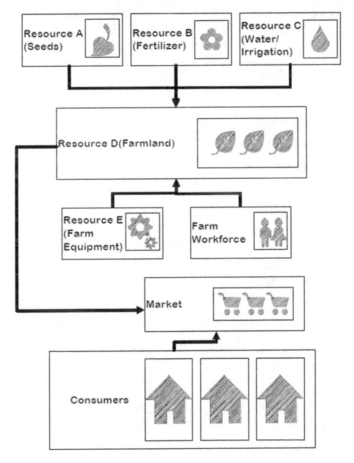

Challenge Eight:

Identify three individuals that had a major impact on your chosen company's industry. Create a multimedia chart to describe their impact. Based on your research of these three individuals, which individual had the biggest impact on their industry. Defend your argument. Cite sources.(Evaluation)

Industry: Telecommunications		
insert image	John Doe	was an inventor whose radical and unorthodox methods produced the first....
insert image	Jane Doe	was an amazing engineer who invented the first....
insert image	Dr. Cooper	was a well-known and well-respected physician that accidentally invented....

Potential Resources:
- www.bls.gov/ooh
- www.bls.gov/iag
- howstuffworks.com
- visual.merriam-webster.com
- finance.yahoo.com
- ehow.com
- sba.gov
- entrepreneur.com

Rubric for Chapter
See Appendix A

Reflective Questions for Chapter
See Appendix B

Chapter 10

Connections to
Common Core State Standards:

CCSS.ELA-LITERACY.WHST.6-8.6
Use technology, including the Internet, to produce and publish writing and present the relationships between information and ideas clearly and efficiently.(2010)

CCSS.ELA-LITERACY.WHST.6-8.7
Conduct short research projects to answer a question(including a self-generated question), drawing on several sources and generating additional related, focused questions that allow for multiple avenues of exploration.(2010)

CCSS.ELA-LITERACY.WHST.6-8.8
Gather relevant information from multiple print and digital sources, using search terms effectively; assess the credibility and accuracy of each source; and quote or paraphrase the data and conclusions of others while avoiding plagiarism and following a standard form of citation.(2010)

CCSS.ELA-LITERACY.WHST.6-8.9
Draw evidence from informational texts to support analysis, reflection, and research.(2010)

Connections to
Common Core State Standards:
(continued)

CCSS.ELA-LITERACY.WHST.6-8.10
Write routinely over extended time frames(time for revision and reflection) and shorter time frames(a single sitting or a day or two) for a range of discipline-specific tasks, purposes, and audiences.(2010)

CCSS.ELA-LITERACY.RH.6-8.1
Cite specific textual evidence to support analysis of primary and secondary sources.(2010)

CCSS.ELA-LITERACY.RH.6-8.4
Determine the meaning of words and phrases as they are used in a text, including vocabulary specific to domains related to history/social studies.(2010)

CCSS.ELA-LITERACY.RH.6-8.7
Integrate visual information(e.g., in charts, graphs, photographs, videos, or maps) with other information in print and digital text.(2010)

CCSS.ELA-LITERACY.RST.6-8.1
Cite specific textual evidence to support analysis of science and technical texts.(2010)

CCSS.ELA-LITERACY.RST.6-8.2
Determine the central ideas or conclusions of a text; provide an accurate summary of the text distinct from prior knowledge or opinions.(2010)

CCSS.ELA-LITERACY.RST.6-8.
Distinguish among facts, reasoned judgment based on research findings, and speculation in text.(2010)

Chapter 10
Section 1

Exploration of the Idiom:
Get a Life

Common Core State Standards:
- CCSS.ELA-LITERACY.WHST.6-8.8
- CCSS.ELA-LITERACY.WHST.6-8.10
- CCSS.ELA-LITERACY.RH.6-8.4
- CCSS.ELA-LITERACY.RH.6-8.7

Learning Objectives:
- A. Understand the figurative meaning of idioms
- B. Comprehend the problematic issues with literal translations of idioms

Get a Life

Instructions:
Place your answers to each challenge into a journal or folder

Challenge One:
Translate "Get a Life" **into your own words.**(Comprehension)

Challenge Two:
Create two separate sentences using the idiom "Get a Life".(Application)

Challenge Three:
Identify another idiom that is similar to "Get a Life". (Analysis)

Challenge Four:
Recall **fictional** characters that use similar idiomatic expressions.(Analysis)

Suggested Start:
Using an American English Idiom dictionary, define the figurative meaning of "Get a Life".

Potential Resources:
      1.) Idioms.thefreedictionary.com
      2.) Dictionary.reference.com/idioms

Challenge Five:

Create, draw or sketch three **individual** objects that represent the word "divergent". Based on your images, explain the connection(s) to the subject.(Synthesis)

Example 1:
Humbled

Example 2:
Driven

Challenge Six:

Create two or more images that express the statement "You broke my toy!" But, use as few images and letters as possible. Then, repeat this process with the thought, "You're very brave!". Communicate the subtle or overt meaning of the objects inside your images.(Synthesis)

Example One: *I dislike potatoes.*

Example Two: *I love potatoes.*

Chapter 10
Section 2

Perspectives on:
Panacea

Common Core State Standards:
- CCSS.ELA-LITERACY.WHST.6-8.7
- CCSS.ELA-LITERACY.WHST.6-8.8
- CCSS.ELA-LITERACY.WHST.6-8.10
- CCSS.ELA-LITERACY.RST.6-8.1
- CCSS.ELA-LITERACY.RST.6-8.2

Learning Objectives:
- A. Gain perspective on vague writing
- B. Gain awareness of potential problems with "absolute" statements in writing
- C. Gain perspective on multiple answers

Peanut Butter is a Panacea

Instructions:
Place your answers to each challenge into a journal or folder

Challenge One:
Respond to the statement, "Peanut Butter is a Panacea".(Analysis)

Challenge Two:
Respond to the statement, "The peanut is a panacea". (Analysis)

Challenge Three:
Is there such a thing as a panacea? Defend your argument. (Evaluation)

Here are recommendations to keep in mind when answering the above questions:
1. Recall examples of panaceas from previous readings.
2. Recall a non-fiction understatement.
3. Recall an overstatement in print or digital media.
4. Cite sources that defend your argument.

Suggested Start:
1. Pause before answering the question.
2. Using a dictionary, define "panacea".

Potential Resources:
1.) Merriam-Webster.com
2.) Bartleby.com

Challenge Four:
Create a joke that you must answer in a figurative way and a literal way. Remember, keep it clean and respectful. NO PRACTICAL JOKES!(Analysis)

Example:
Joke(the setup): *They say "failure is a part of learning".*
Figurative answer (punchline): *Could someone please explain that to my parents.*
Literal answer: *This quote translates more often into "We learn from our mistakes". Whether a person is completing a quiz or learning to ride a bike, mistakes may occur, and they have the option to grow from their small failures.*

The secret to creating jokes is to ask questions about the world. In other words, analyze the world around you. If it doesn't make sense, question it. Then, research it.

To help, start with a statement like:
    Why is it that...............
    Ever notice that...........
    Whose idea was it to make...
    One day, there was a.................
    Why does....
    Where's the......
    How is it that....

Don't forget to explore and explain the answer in a figurative and literal way. Creating jokes can be challenging. Worst case scenario, find and use a joke that you can answer in a figurative and literal way. Explain, why it is funny. Give credit to the comedian.

Challenge Five:

First, **define** the word, "Empathy". Second, create a two column chart with a "negative factors" side and a "positive factors" side. Third, contrast the positive factors and negative issues of the word, "Empathy". (Analysis)

Example:

According to _____'s dictionary, **failure** is....

Failure	
Negative Factors	**Positive Factors**
May spark negative emotions	Mistakes and failings are a part of the creation process
May affect interpersonal relationships	"When you quit that is true failure"
	Don't make failing a habit; however, if it happens, learn from your failure

Challenge Six:

Find an image. Then, create a chart that lists the directly observable features versus the not-visible, but inferable features of the image.(Analysis)

Example: Battleship	
Observable and Visible	**Not Visible, but Inferable**
is a vehicle	holds crew
is in the ocean	holds cargo
	has computer systems

Chapter 10
Section 3

Exploring Quotations on:
Dreams

Common Core State Standards:
- CCSS.ELA-LITERACY.WHST.6-8.6
- CCSS.ELA-LITERACY.WHST.6-8.8
- CCSS.ELA-LITERACY.WHST.6-8.10
- CCSS.ELA-LITERACY.RH.6-8.1
- CCSS.ELA-LITERACY.RH.6-8.4
- CCSS.ELA-LITERACY.RH.6-8.7

Learning Objectives:
- A. Gain knowledge on the topic of "dreams"
- B. Experience other perspectives on "dreams"

Quotations on Dreams

Instructions:
Place your answers to each challenge into a journal or folder

Challenge One:
Locate a quotation on the topic of "dreams".

Challenge Two:
Translate your selected quotation on "dreams" into your own words.(Comprehension)

Challenge Three:
Compose a biographical statement using your chosen quotation on "dreams".(Application)

Challenge Four:
Create your own quote on "dreams".(Synthesis)

Challenge Five:
Select or create a poem on "dreams".(Synthesis)

Suggested Start:
1. Reflect on dreaming.
2. Quotation resources are available at your local library.

Potential Resources:
1.) Quoteland.com
2.) Brainyquote.com
3.) Quotationspage.com
4.) En.wikiquote.org

Challenge Six:

Using a quotation on "dreams", discover a way to express the meaning through pictures and words. Then, create a comic strip that explains the quotation.(Synthesis)

Example:
"Hunger"

"Thou shouldst eat to live; not live to eat."

Socrates

Create a collection of images that relate to the quote. Then, add captions or messages that help express the quote. Lastly, connect images and create a comic strip.

Challenge Seven:
Complete the following sentence fragment with three or more separate statements. Figure out a way to incorporate a quotation, adage, or joke.(Application)

My dreams about the future...

Example:

The last movie that I saw...
1.) ...caused my mind to reflect on the possibilities of humans having superpowers. For instance, by combining advanced nanotechnology with our understanding of genetics, we could modify ourselves into more supercharged people.

2.) ...agitated me because it depicted the cruelties of mankind. However, I then reflected on an anonymous quote that "Unfortunately, the road to progress can have various levels of bumpiness".

3.) ...frightened me because it was a creepy horror film. Now, I want to sleep with the lights on, but my parents disagree. Even though, I don't pay the electric bill. I feel that I should be able to make this decision!

Chapter 10
Section 4

Exploration of Adages, Aphorisms, Proverbs, and Maxims:

Common Core State Standards:
- CCSS.ELA-LITERACY.WHST.6-8.6
- CCSS.ELA-LITERACY.WHST.6-8.8
- CCSS.ELA-LITERACY.WHST.6-8.10
- CCSS.ELA-LITERACY.RH.6-8.4
- CCSS.ELA-LITERACY.RH.6-8.7

Learning Objectives:
- A. Experience perceptive sayings from various cultures
- B. Examine beliefs and understandings of various individuals and groups

Adages, Aphorisms, Proverbs, and Maxims

Instructions:
Place your answers to each challenge into a journal or folder

Challenge One:
Select an adage, aphorism, proverb, or maxim. Research the origin of the adage, aphorism, proverb, or maxim. Cite source(s).(Knowledge)

Challenge Two:
Translate your chosen adage, aphorism, proverb, or maxim into your own words.(Comprehension)

Challenge Three:
Compose a small paragraph or a short segment of dialogue that includes your chosen adage, aphorism, proverb, or maxim.(Application)

Challenge Four:
Do you agree or disagree with the message of your chosen adage, aphorism, proverb, or maxim. Defend your response. Cite sources.(Evaluation)

Suggested Start:
1. Reflect on your chosen adage, aphorism, proverb, or maxim.
2. Identify problems, if any.

Potential Resources:
1.) En.wikiquote.org
2.) Thinkexist.com

Challenge Five:

Select at least three pictures based on your selected adage, aphorism, proverb, or maxim. Next, build three posters by adding text to the chosen pictures. (Synthesis)

Suggested Start:
"Knowledge is Power"

1. Make sure you understand the adage, aphorism, proverb, or maxim.
2. Reflect on the meaning(s) of your chosen adage, aphorism, proverb, or maxim.
3. Search for images that symbolize or reflect the adage, aphorism, proverb, or maxim.
4. Construct posters.

Challenge Six:

Is it better to <u>demonstrate</u> or <u>explain</u>?

In this exercise, consider possible scenarios when it is better to do one or the other underlined options. Next, find scenarios that benefit from each underlined option. Then, try to find scenarios that do not benefit from each underlined option. Create a chart that represents your conclusions. Lastly, compose statements using historical examples or scientific data that validate each item inside your chart. (Evaluation)

Example: Is it better to <u>spark</u> or <u>spur</u>?

Neither	Spark	Spur	Both
malice	critical thoughts	truthfulness	healthy behavior
hatred	cooperation	obedience	innovations
ignorance	motivation	horse	inventions
	confidence		imagination
			students
			self-control

A. <u>Hatred</u> can <u>spark</u> destructive behavior such as... (insert historical example).
B. Although, at times effective, spurred obedience has a limited shelf life; eventually, the spurred will rebel or revolt such as a child or colony...
C. According to _____(author/researcher/expert), sparking confidence can boost students' comprehension.

Chapter 10
Section 5

Exploration of Business

Common Core State Standards:
- CCSS.ELA-LITERACY.WHST.6-8.6
- CCSS.ELA-LITERACY.WHST.6-8.7
- CCSS.ELA-LITERACY.WHST.6-8.8
- CCSS.ELA-LITERACY.WHST.6-8.9
- CCSS.ELA-LITERACY.WHST.6-8.10
- CCSS.ELA-LITERACY.RH.6-8.4
- CCSS.ELA-LITERACY.RH.6-8.7

Learning Objectives:
- A. Examine products and services from the view of an organizational entity such as a business
- B. Communicate information through graphics and text such as diagrams and charts

Product and Service Path

Instructions:
Place your answers to each challenge into a journal or folder

Challenge One:
Identify a complex product or service that is not necessary for your survival.(Knowledge)

Challenge Two:
Identify the type of organizations that produce your chosen product or service. Classify their industry. (Comprehension)

Challenge Three:
Identify three direct competitors of your chosen product or service. Describe and chart the competition based on market share, business size (by employees), years available, marketing reach(local, regional, national, global), revenue and profits. Research and use industry averages if your chosen company or its competitors are not publicly traded.(Analysis)

Main Product (Web Browsers)				
	Market Share	Business Size	Marketing Reach	Years Available
Internet Explorer (product)	2	large enterprise	global	19
Chrome (competitor)	1	large enterprise	global	6
Firefox (competitor)	3	mid-size	global	12
Opera (competitor)	4	mid-size	global	18

Challenge four:

Create a diagram that displays the major parts or sequences of your chosen product or service. Next explain two of the product's major parts. For example, an Xbox 360 has multiple, specialized parts such as the central processing unit, the graphics processing unit and the hard drive. Use graphics. Cite sources. (Analysis)

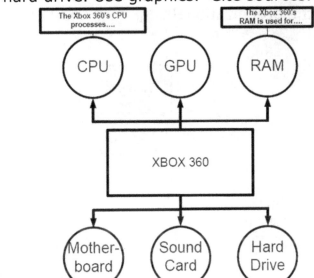

Challenge Five:

Based on your chosen product or service, identify three influential people that had a major impact on this industry through improvements, innovations, or inventions. Describe their effects on the industry. Cite sources.(Analysis)

Industry: Telecommunications		
insert image	John Doe	was an inventor whose radical and unorthodox methods produced the first....
insert image	Jane Doe	was an amazing engineer who invented the first....
insert image	Dr. Cooper	was a well-known and well-respected physician that accidentally invented....

Challenge Six:

Create an organizational chart (unofficial) of a company that offers your chosen product or service. Next, pinpoint the areas where your three previously chosen influential people would work. For example, if one of your selected influential people is a visionary executive leader, then they would fit somewhere at the top of the organizational chart(org chart).(Synthesis)

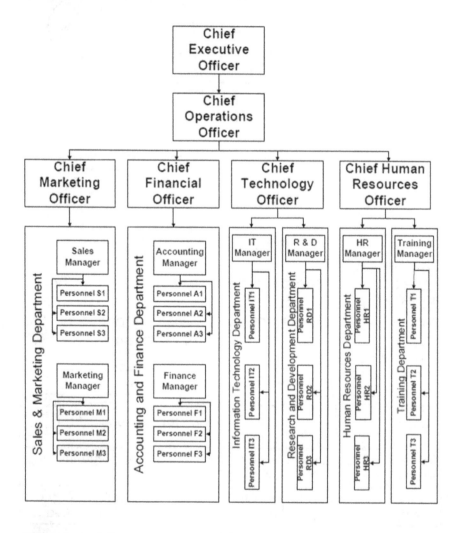

Challenge Seven:

Based on your gathered research and your product choice, create a visual flowchart or graphical diagram that demonstrates the interaction between human resources and non-human resources to produce the product or service. Start with the necessary (raw) materials required to produce the product or service. For example, an organic farmer needs supplies, materials, equipment, and workers. Then, your flowchart should display the interactions between the workforce and resources until the end-product reaches consumers. (Synthesis)

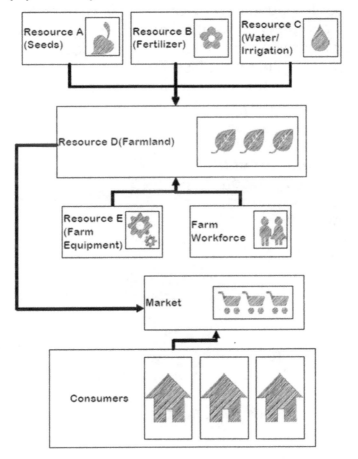

Challenge Eight:

Based on your product choice or service selection,

- Identify two supplemental/complementary products or services such as computer applications complement computer operating systems
- Identify two required/necessary products (computer operating system are necessary to operate computers)
- Identify two separate or indirectly connected products or services that the company produces(Xbox 360 or Zune)

Discover which product(s) is your strongest seller(s). Why? Would you eliminate any products or services from the company's product lineup? Explain. Which product or service deserves the most research and development? Elaborate. Lastly, which product or service deserves the most marketing. Explain. Cite sources.(Evaluation)

Potential Resources:

- www.bls.gov/ooh
- www.bls.gov/iag
- howstuffworks.com
- visual.merriam-webster.com
- finance.yahoo.com
- ehow.com
- sba.gov
- entrepreneur.com

Rubric for Chapter
See Appendix A

Reflective Questions for Chapter
See Appendix B

Chapter 11

Connections to
Common Core State Standards:

CCSS.ELA-LITERACY.WHST.6-8.6
Use technology, including the Internet, to produce and publish writing and present the relationships between information and ideas clearly and efficiently.(2010)

CCSS.ELA-LITERACY.WHST.6-8.7
Conduct short research projects to answer a question(including a self-generated question), drawing on several sources and generating additional related, focused questions that allow for multiple avenues of exploration.(2010)

CCSS.ELA-LITERACY.WHST.6-8.8
Gather relevant information from multiple print and digital sources, using search terms effectively; assess the credibility and accuracy of each source; and quote or paraphrase the data and conclusions of others while avoiding plagiarism and following a standard form of citation.(2010)

CCSS.ELA-LITERACY.WHST.6-8.9
Draw evidence from informational texts to support analysis, reflection, and research.(2010)

Connections to
Common Core State Standards:
<u>(continued)</u>

CCSS.ELA-LITERACY.WHST.6-8.10
Write routinely over extended time frames(time for revision and reflection) and shorter time frames(a single sitting or a day or two) for a range of discipline-specific tasks, purposes, and audiences.(2010)

CCSS.ELA-LITERACY.RH.6-8.1
Cite specific textual evidence to support analysis of primary and secondary sources.(2010)

CCSS.ELA-LITERACY.RH.6-8.4
Determine the meaning of words and phrases as they are used in a text, including vocabulary specific to domains related to history/social studies.(2010)

CCSS.ELA-LITERACY.RH.6-8.7
Integrate visual information(e.g., in charts, graphs, photographs, videos, or maps) with other information in print and digital text.(2010)

CCSS.ELA-LITERACY.RST.6-8.1
Cite specific textual evidence to support analysis of science and technical texts.(2010)

CCSS.ELA-LITERACY.RST.6-8.2
Determine the central ideas or conclusions of a text; provide an accurate summary of the text distinct from prior knowledge or opinions.(2010)

CCSS.ELA-LITERACY.RST.6-8.
Distinguish among facts, reasoned judgment based on research findings, and speculation in text.(2010)

Chapter 11
Section 1

Exploration of the Idiom:
Let the Cat out of the Bag

Common Core State Standards:
- CCSS.ELA-LITERACY.WHST.6-8.8
- CCSS.ELA-LITERACY.WHST.6-8.10
- CCSS.ELA-LITERACY.RH.6-8.4
- CCSS.ELA-LITERACY.RH.6-8.7

Learning Objectives:
- A. Understand the figurative meaning of idioms
- B. Comprehend the problematic issues with literal translations of idioms

Let the Cat out of the Bag

Instructions:
Place your answers to each challenge into a journal or folder

Challenge One:
Translate "Let the cat out of the bag" **into your own words**.(Comprehension)

Challenge Two:
Create two separate sentences using the idiom "Let the cat out of the bag".(Application)

Challenge Three:
Identify another idiom that is similar to "Let the cat out of the bag".(Analysis)

Challenge Four:
List **fictional** characters that unintentionally "Let the cat out of the bag".(Analysis)

Challenge Five:
List **fictional** characters that intentionally "Let the cat out of the bag".(Analysis)

Suggested Start:
Using an American English Idiom dictionary, define the figurative meaning of "Let the cat out of the bag".

Potential Resources:
1.) Idioms.thefreedictionary.com
2.) Dictionary.reference.com/idioms

Challenge Six:

Create, draw or sketch three **individual** objects that represent the word "Gregarious". Based on your images, explain the connection(s) to the subject.(Synthesis)

Example 1:
Humbled

Example 2:
Driven

Challenge Seven:

Create two or more images that express the feeling "I need to exercise!" But, use as few images and letters as possible. Then, repeat this process with the thought, "I enjoy exercising!". Communicate the subtle or overt meaning of the objects inside your images.(Synthesis)

Example One: *I dislike strawberries.*

Example Two: *I love strawberries.*

Chapter 11
Section 2

Perspectives on:
Every

Common Core State Standards:
- CCSS.ELA-LITERACY.WHST.6-8.7
- CCSS.ELA-LITERACY.WHST.6-8.8
- CCSS.ELA-LITERACY.WHST.6-8.10
- CCSS.ELA-LITERACY.RST.6-8.1
- CCSS.ELA-LITERACY.RST.6-8.2

Learning Objectives:
- A. Gain perspective on vague writing
- B. Gain awareness of potential problems with "absolute" statements in writing
- C. Gain perspective on multiple answers

Aloe Vera Cures Every Type of Disease and Illness

Instructions:
Place your answers to each challenge into a journal or folder

Challenge One:
Respond to the following statement. "Aloe Vera Cures Every Type of Disease and Illness". (Analysis)

Challenge Two:
Recall a panacea from a fictional work.(Analysis)

Challenge Three:
Respond to the following statement, "New diseases and illnesses will emerge".

Here are recommendations to keep in mind when answering the above questions:
1. Is there a difference between a disease and an illness.
2. Cite sources that defend your argument.

Suggested Start:
1. Pause and study the statement.
2. Using a dictionary, define "illness".
3. Using an encyclopedia, research "disease".

Potential Resources:
1.) Merriam-Webster.com
2.) Bartleby.com

Challenge Four:
Create a joke that you must answer in a figurative way and a literal way. Remember, keep it clean and respectful. NO PRACTICAL JOKES!(Analysis)

Example:
Joke(the setup): *They say "failure is a part of learning".*
Figurative answer (punchline): *Could someone please explain that to my parents.*
Literal answer: *This quote translates more often into "We learn from our mistakes". Whether a person is completing a quiz or learning to ride a bike, mistakes may occur, and they have the option to grow from their small failures.*

The secret to creating jokes is to ask questions about the world. In other words, analyze the world around you. If it doesn't make sense, question it. Then, research it.

To help, start with a statement like:
Why is it that...............
Ever notice that...........
Whose idea was it to make...
One day, there was a.................
Why does....
Where's the......
How is it that....

Don't forget to explore and explain the answer in a figurative and literal way. Creating jokes can be challenging. Worst case scenario, find and use a joke that you can answer in a figurative and literal way. Explain, why it is funny. Give credit to the comedian.

Challenge Five:

First, **define** the word, "Pragmatic". Second, create a two column chart with a "negative factors" side and a "positive factors" side. Third, contrast the positive factors and negative issues of the word, "Pragmatic". (Analysis)

Example:

According to _____'s dictionary, **failure** is....

Failure	
Negative Factors	**Positive Factors**
May spark negative emotions	Mistakes and failings are a part of the creation process
May affect interpersonal relationships	"When you quit that is true failure"
	Don't make failing a habit; however, if it happens, learn from your failure

Challenge Six:

Find an image. Then, create a chart that lists the directly observable features versus the not-visible, but inferable features of the image.(Analysis)

Example: Hovercraft	
Observable and Visible	**Not Visible, but Inferable**
is a vehicle	holds passengers
hovers off the ground	holds cargo

Chapter 11
Section 3

Exploring Quotations on:
Art

Common Core State Standards:
- CCSS.ELA-LITERACY.WHST.6-8.6
- CCSS.ELA-LITERACY.WHST.6-8.8
- CCSS.ELA-LITERACY.WHST.6-8.10
- CCSS.ELA-LITERACY.RH.6-8.1
- CCSS.ELA-LITERACY.RH.6-8.4
- CCSS.ELA-LITERACY.RH.6-8.7

Learning Objectives:
- A. Gain knowledge on the topic of "art"
- B. Experience other perspectives on "art"

Quotations on Art

Instructions:
Place your answers to each challenge into a journal or folder

Challenge One:
Locate a quotation on the topic of "Art".(Knowledge)

Challenge Two:
Translate your selected quotation on "Art" into your own words.(Comprehension)

Challenge Three:
Compose a biographical statement using your chosen quotation on "Art".(Application)

Challenge Four:
Create your own quote on "Art".(Synthesis)

Challenge Five:
Select or create a poem on "Art".(Synthesis)

Suggested Start:
1. Reflect on past experiences with "Art".
2. Quotation resources are available at your local library.

Potential Resources:
1.) Quoteland.com
2.) Brainyquote.com
3.) Quotationspage.com
4.) En.wikiquote.org

Challenge Six:

Using a quotation on "art", discover a way to express the meaning through pictures and words. Then, create a comic strip that explains the quotation.(Synthesis)

Example:
"Hunger"
"Thou shouldst eat to live; not live to eat."
Socrates

Create a collection of images that relate to the quote. Then, add captions or messages that help express the quote. Lastly, connect images and create a comic strip.

Challenge Seven:
Complete the following sentence fragment with three or more separate statements. Figure out a way to incorporate a quotation, adage, or joke.(Application)

Artistic expression...

Example:

The last movie that I saw...
1.) ...caused my mind to reflect on the possibilities of humans having superpowers. For instance, by combining advanced nanotechnology with our understanding of genetics, we could modify ourselves into more supercharged people.

2.) ...agitated me because it depicted the cruelties of mankind. However, I then reflected on an anonymous quote that "Unfortunately, the road to progress can have various levels of bumpiness".

3.) ...frightened me because it was a creepy horror film. Now, I want to sleep with the lights on, but my parents disagree. Even though, I don't pay the electric bill. I feel that I should be able to make this decision!

Chapter 11
Section 4

Exploration of Adages, Aphorisms, Proverbs, and Maxims:

Common Core State Standards:
- CCSS.ELA-LITERACY.WHST.6-8.6
- CCSS.ELA-LITERACY.WHST.6-8.8
- CCSS.ELA-LITERACY.WHST.6-8.10
- CCSS.ELA-LITERACY.RH.6-8.4
- CCSS.ELA-LITERACY.RH.6-8.7

Learning Objectives:
- A. Experience perceptive sayings from various cultures
- B. Examine beliefs and understandings of various individuals and groups

Adages, Aphorisms, Proverbs, and Maxims

Instructions:
Place your answers to each challenge into a journal or folder

Challenge One:
Select an adage, aphorism, proverb, or maxim. Research the origin of the adage, aphorism, proverb, or maxim. Cite source(s).(Knowledge)

Challenge Two:
Translate your chosen adage, aphorism, proverb, or maxim into your own words.(Comprehension)

Challenge Three:
Compose a small paragraph or a short segment of dialogue that includes your chosen adage, aphorism, proverb, or maxim.(Application)

Challenge Four:
Do you agree or disagree with the message of your chosen adage, aphorism, proverb, or maxim. Defend your response. Cite sources.(Evaluation)

Suggested Start:
1. Reflect on your chosen adage, aphorism, proverb, or maxim.
2. Identify problems, if any.

Potential Resources:
1.) En.wikiquote.org
2.) Thinkexist.com

Challenge Five:
Select at least three pictures based on your selected adage, aphorism, proverb, or maxim. Next, build three posters by adding text to the chosen pictures. (Synthesis)

Suggested Start:
"If One does not Plow, There will be no Harvest"
1. Make sure you understand the adage, aphorism, proverb, or maxim.
2. Reflect on the meaning(s) of your chosen adage, aphorism, proverb, or maxim.
3. Search for images that symbolize or reflect the adage, aphorism, proverb, or maxim.
4. Construct posters.

If one does not plow,
there will be no harvest.

Challenge Six:

Is it better to <u>placate</u> or <u>agitate</u>?

In this exercise, consider possible scenarios when it is better to do one or the other underlined options. Next, find scenarios that benefit from each underlined option. Then, try to find scenarios that do not benefit from each underlined option. Create a chart that represents your conclusions. Lastly, compose statements using historical examples or scientific data that validate each item inside your chart. (Evaluation)

Example: Is it better to <u>spark</u> or <u>spur</u>?

Neither	Spark	Spur	Both
malice	critical thoughts	truthfulness	healthy behavior
hatred	cooperation	obedience	innovations
ignorance	motivation	horse	inventions
	confidence		imagination
			students
			self-control

A. <u>Hatred</u> can <u>spark</u> destructive behavior such as... (insert historical example).
B. Although, at times effective, spurred obedience has a limited shelf life; eventually, the spurred will rebel or revolt such as a child or colony...
C. According to _____(author/researcher/expert), sparking confidence can boost students' comprehension.

Chapter 11
Section 5

Exploration of Business

Common Core State Standards:
- CCSS.ELA-LITERACY.WHST.6-8.6
- CCSS.ELA-LITERACY.WHST.6-8.7
- CCSS.ELA-LITERACY.WHST.6-8.8
- CCSS.ELA-LITERACY.WHST.6-8.9
- CCSS.ELA-LITERACY.WHST.6-8.10
- CCSS.ELA-LITERACY.RH.6-8.4
- CCSS.ELA-LITERACY.RH.6-8.7

Learning Objectives:
- A. Examine business costs and opportunities
- B. Communicate information through graphics and text such as diagrams and charts

Organization Path

Instructions:
Place your answers to each challenge into a journal or folder

Challenge One:
Name a business or organization that you patronize on a monthly basis. Classify the type of business it is. Identify its main product.(Knowledge)

Challenge Two:
Identify three competitors of this business.(Comprehension)

Challenge Three:
Identify three products or services of your chosen company. Create a chart that displays the relationship among the main product and the additional products. Determine if these products are:
- Integrated and necessary for the main product to operate such as gasoline or motor oil for cars
- Complementary to the product and enhances product like air conditioning and power windows for cars
- Vital to the business such as their brand brake pads and spark plugs for cars(Application)

Main Product(Windows Operating System)			
	Integrated and Necessary	Enhances Main Product	Vital to Business
Microsoft Office	No	Yes	Yes
Internet Explorer	Yes	Yes	Yes
Xbox 360	No	No	No

Challenge Four:

Categorize the four chosen products by popularity among consumers, history of the products, revenue, profit, target audience(name their main customers), and strongest direct competitor, quasi-competitor and indirect competitor. Use a scale from 4 to 1, 4 being highest, to grade each category. Then, based on your chart, describe the growth potential (or lack of future potential) of each product. Which product is the strongest? Which product would you focus more resources on for the future of the company. Defend your decision. Cite sources.(Analysis)

Strengths and Weaknesses				
	Windows OS	Microsoft Office	Internet Explorer	Xbox 360
Popularity	3	4	2	1
Revenue	3	4	2	1
Profitabil-ity	3	4	2	1

Strengths and Weaknesses by Details				
	Windows OS	Microsoft Office	Internet Explorer	Xbox 360
Years Available	28 yrs.	23 yrs.	19 yrs.	8 yrs.
Direct Competitor	Mac OS X	LibreOf-fice	Chrome	Playsta-tion 3
Quasi-Competitor	Android OS	QuickOf-fice	Smart-TVs	Gameboy Advance
Indirect Competitor	Pen and Paper	Typewriter	Library Card	Mobile Device
Rankings among direct Com-petitors	#1	#1	#2	#1

Challenge Five:

Choose one of your chosen company's most popular or well-known products or services. Research this product or service and build a diagram that displays the fabrication process of the product or service. Cite sources.(Synthesis)

Your diagram or chart should display the work that goes into producing a product or service.

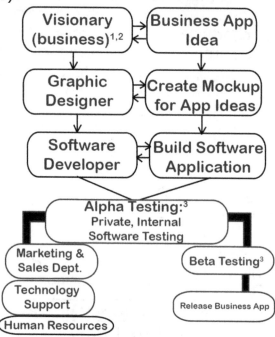

1 Does the app solve a problem?
2 Can it be profitable?
3 Testing may require restarts or revisions.

Challenge Six:

Create a chart that explains two of the product's major features. For example, an alarm clock normally has a minimum of two features, the time display and the alarm function. Use graphics, if possible. Cite sources.(Analysis)

Alarm Radio	
Radio	converts radio waves...
Alarm Buzzer	is a feature of the...

Challenge Seven:
Based on your gathered research and your product choice, create a visual flowchart or graphical diagram that demonstrates the interaction between human resources and non-human resources to produce the product or service. Start with the necessary (raw) materials required to produce the product or service. For example, an organic farmer needs supplies, materials, equipment, and workers. Then, your flowchart should display the interactions between the workforce and resources until the end-product reaches consumers. (Synthesis)

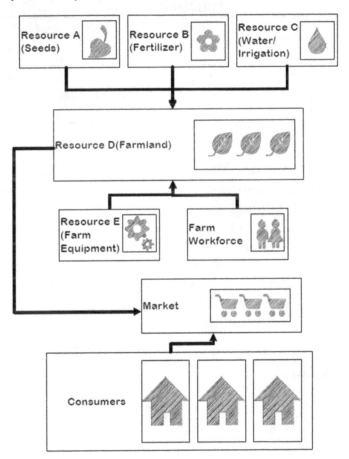

Challenge Eight:

Identify three individuals that had a major impact on your chosen company's industry. Create a multi-media chart to describe their impact. Based on your research of these three individuals, which individual had the biggest impact on their industry. Defend your argument. Cite sources.(Evaluation)

Industry: Telecommunications		
insert image	John Doe	was an inventor whose radical and unorthodox methods produced the first....
insert image	Jane Doe	was an amazing engineer who invented the first....
insert image	Dr. Cooper	was a well-known and well-respected physician that accidentally invented....

Potential Resources:
- www.bls.gov/ooh
- www.bls.gov/iag
- howstuffworks.com
- visual.merriam-webster.com
- finance.yahoo.com
- ehow.com
- sba.gov
- entrepreneur.com

Rubric for Chapter
See Appendix A

Reflective Questions for Chapter
See Appendix B

Chapter 12

Connections to Common Core State Standards:

CCSS.ELA-LITERACY.WHST.6-8.6
Use technology, including the Internet, to produce and publish writing and present the relationships between information and ideas clearly and efficiently.(2010)

CCSS.ELA-LITERACY.WHST.6-8.7
Conduct short research projects to answer a question(including a self-generated question), drawing on several sources and generating additional related, focused questions that allow for multiple avenues of exploration.(2010)

CCSS.ELA-LITERACY.WHST.6-8.8
Gather relevant information from multiple print and digital sources, using search terms effectively; assess the credibility and accuracy of each source; and quote or paraphrase the data and conclusions of others while avoiding plagiarism and following a standard form of citation.(2010)

CCSS.ELA-LITERACY.WHST.6-8.9
Draw evidence from informational texts to support analysis, reflection, and research.(2010)

Connections to
Common Core State Standards:

CCSS.ELA-LITERACY.WHST.6-8.10
Write routinely over extended time frames(time for revision and reflection) and shorter time frames(a single sitting or a day or two) for a range of discipline-specific tasks, purposes, and audiences.(2010)

CCSS.ELA-LITERACY.RH.6-8.1
Cite specific textual evidence to support analysis of primary and secondary sources.(2010)

CCSS.ELA-LITERACY.RH.6-8.4
Determine the meaning of words and phrases as they are used in a text, including vocabulary specific to domains related to history/social studies.(2010)

CCSS.ELA-LITERACY.RH.6-8.7
Integrate visual information(e.g., in charts, graphs, photographs, videos, or maps) with other information in print and digital text.(2010)

CCSS.ELA-LITERACY.RST.6-8.1
Cite specific textual evidence to support analysis of science and technical texts.(2010)

CCSS.ELA-LITERACY.RST.6-8.2
Determine the central ideas or conclusions of a text; provide an accurate summary of the text distinct from prior knowledge or opinions.(2010)

CCSS.ELA-LITERACY.RST.6-8.
Distinguish among facts, reasoned judgment based on research findings, and speculation in text.(2010)

Chapter 12
Section 1

Exploration of the Idiom:
Go the Extra Mile

Common Core State Standards:
- CCSS.ELA-LITERACY.WHST.6-8.8
- CCSS.ELA-LITERACY.WHST.6-8.10
- CCSS.ELA-LITERACY.RH.6-8.4
- CCSS.ELA-LITERACY.RH.6-8.7

Learning Objectives:
- A. Understand the figurative meaning of idioms
- B. Comprehend the problematic issues with literal translations of idioms

Go the Extra Mile

Instructions:
Place your answers to each challenge into a journal or folder

Challenge One:
Translate "Go the extra mile" **into your own words**. (Comprehension)

Challenge Two:
Create two separate sentences using the idiom "Go the extra mile".(Application)

Challenge Three:
Identify another idiom that is similar to "Go the extra mile".(Analysis)

Challenge Four:
Name groups that might use the idiomatic phrase "Go the extra mile".(Analysis)

Challenge Five:
Recall and list **fictional** characters that "Went the extra mile". Explain their motivation or environment that caused the character to go the extra mile.(Evaluation)

Suggested Start:
Using an American English Idiom dictionary, define the figurative meaning of "Go the extra mile".

Potential Resources:
    1.) Idioms.thefreedictionary.com
    2.) Dictionary.reference.com/idioms

Challenge Six:

Create, draw or sketch three **individual** objects that represent the word "Prudent". Based on your images, explain the connection(s) to the subject.(Synthesis)

Example 1:
Humbled

Example 2:
Driven

Challenge Seven:

Create two or more images that express the question "What does negativity accomplish?" But, use as few images and letters as possible. Then, repeat this process with the thought, "Am I conservative with money?" Communicate the subtle or overt meaning of the objects inside your images.(Synthesis)

Example One: *I dislike tomatoes.*

Example Two: *I love tomatoes.*

Chapter 12
Section 2

Perspectives on:
Styles and Methods

Common Core State Standards:
- CCSS.ELA-LITERACY.WHST.6-8.7
- CCSS.ELA-LITERACY.WHST.6-8.8
- CCSS.ELA-LITERACY.WHST.6-8.10
- CCSS.ELA-LITERACY.RST.6-8.1
- CCSS.ELA-LITERACY.RST.6-8.2

Learning Objectives:
- A. Gain perspective on vague writing
- B. Gain awareness of potential problems with "absolute" statements in writing
- C. Gain perspective on multiple answers

How Many Ways Can Shoe Laces Be Tied?

Instructions:
Place your answers to each challenge into a journal or folder

Challenge One:
Answer the question, "How many ways can shoe laces be tied?" (Analysis)

Challenge Two:
Answer the question, "How many ways can you tie your shoes?"(Analysis)

Here are recommendations to keep in mind when answering the above questions:
1. Consider the meaning of "tied shoe laces".
2. Consider the length of the shoe laces.
3. Is there more than one type of shoe lace?
4. Cite sources that defend your argument.

Suggested Start:
1. Pause before answering the question.
2. Define "Tied".
3. Define "Shoe".

Potential Resources:
1.) Merriam-Webster.com
2.) Bartleby.com

Challenge Three:
Create a joke that you must answer in a figurative way and a literal way. Remember, keep it clean and respectful. NO PRACTICAL JOKES!(Analysis)

Example:
Joke(the setup): *They say "failure is a part of learning".*
Figurative answer (punchline): *Could someone please explain that to my parents.*
Literal answer: *This quote translates more often into "We learn from our mistakes". Whether a person is completing a quiz or learning to ride a bike, mistakes may occur, and they have the option to grow from their small failures.*

The secret to creating jokes is to ask questions about the world. In other words, analyze the world around you. If it doesn't make sense, question it. Then, research it.

To help, start with a statement like:
    Why is it that...............
    Ever notice that...........
    Whose idea was it to make...
    One day, there was a.................
    Why does....
    Where's the......
    How is it that....

Don't forget to explore and explain the answer in a figurative and literal way. Creating jokes can be challenging. Worst case scenario, find and use a joke that you can answer in a figurative and literal way. Explain, why it is funny. Give credit to the comedian.

Challenge Four:

First, **define** the word, "Adept". Second, create a two column chart with a "negative factors" side and a "positive factors" side. Third, contrast the positive factors and negative issues of the word, "Adept". (Analysis)

Example:

According to _____'s dictionary, **failure** is....

Failure	
Negative Factors	**Positive Factors**
May spark negative emotions	Mistakes and failings are a part of the creation process
May affect interpersonal relationships	"When you quit that is true failure"
	Don't make failing a habit; however, if it happens, learn from your failure

Challenge Five:

Find an image. Then, create a chart that lists the directly observable features versus the not-visible, but inferable features of the image.(Analysis)

Example: Submarine	
Observable and Visible	**Not Visible, but Inferable**
is a vehicle	holds crew
is submersible	holds weapons
	has instruments

Chapter 12
Section 3

Exploring Quotations on: Greed

Common Core State Standards:
- CCSS.ELA-LITERACY.WHST.6-8.6
- CCSS.ELA-LITERACY.WHST.6-8.8
- CCSS.ELA-LITERACY.WHST.6-8.10
- CCSS.ELA-LITERACY.RH.6-8.1
- CCSS.ELA-LITERACY.RH.6-8.4
- CCSS.ELA-LITERACY.RH.6-8.7

Learning Objectives:
- A. Gain knowledge on the topic of "greed"
- B. Experience other perspectives on "greed"

Quotations on Greed

Instructions:
Place your answers to each challenge into a journal or folder

Challenge One:
Locate a quotation on the topic of "greed".(Knowledge)

Challenge Two:
Translate your selected quotation on "greed" into your own words.(Comprehension)

Challenge Three:
Compose a biographical statement using your chosen quotation on "greed".(Application)

Challenge Four:
Create your own quote on "greed".(Synthesis)

Challenge Five:
Select or create a poem on "greed".(Synthesis)

Suggested Start:
1. Reflect on "greedy" fictional characters.
2. Quotation resources are available at your local library.

Potential Resources:
1.) Quoteland.com
2.) Brainyquote.com
3.) Quotationspage.com
4.) En.wikiquote.org

Challenge Six:

Using a quotation on "greed", discover a way to express the meaning through pictures and words. Then, create a comic strip that explains the quotation.(Synthesis)

Example:
"Hunger"

"Thou shouldst eat to live; not live to eat."

Socrates

Create a collection of images that relate to the quote. Then, add captions or messages that help express the quote. Lastly, connect images and create a comic strip.

Challenge Seven:

Complete the following sentence fragment with three or more separate statements. Figure out a way to incorporate a quotation, adage, or joke.(Application)

The dollar symbol...

Example:

The last movie that I saw...

1.) ...caused my mind to reflect on the possibilities of humans having superpowers. For instance, by combining advanced nanotechnology with our understanding of genetics, we could modify ourselves into more supercharged people.

2.) ...agitated me because it depicted the cruelties of mankind. However, I then reflected on an anonymous quote that "Unfortunately, the road to progress can have various levels of bumpiness".

3.) ...frightened me because it was a creepy horror film. Now, I want to sleep with the lights on, but my parents disagree. Even though, I don't pay the electric bill. I feel that I should be able to make this decision!

Chapter 12
Section 4

Exploration of Adages, Aphorisms, Proverbs, and Maxims:

Common Core State Standards:
- CCSS.ELA-LITERACY.WHST.6-8.6
- CCSS.ELA-LITERACY.WHST.6-8.8
- CCSS.ELA-LITERACY.WHST.6-8.10
- CCSS.ELA-LITERACY.RH.6-8.4
- CCSS.ELA-LITERACY.RH.6-8.7

Learning Objectives:
- A. Experience perceptive sayings from various cultures
- B. Examine beliefs and understandings of various individuals and groups

Adages, Aphorisms, Proverbs, and Maxims

Instructions:
Place your answers to each challenge into a journal or folder

Challenge One:
Select an adage, aphorism, proverb, or maxim. Research the origin of the adage, aphorism, proverb, or maxim. Cite source(s).(Knowledge)

Challenge Two:
Translate your chosen adage, aphorism, proverb, or maxim into your own words.(Comprehension)

Challenge Three:
Compose a small paragraph or a short segment of dialogue that includes your chosen adage, aphorism, proverb, or maxim.(Application)

Challenge Four:
Do you agree or disagree with the message of your chosen adage, aphorism, proverb, or maxim. Defend your response. Cite sources.(Evaluation)

Suggested Start:
1. Reflect on your chosen adage, aphorism, proverb, or maxim.
2. Identify problems, if any.

Potential Resources:
1.) En.wikiquote.org
2.) Thinkexist.com

Challenge Five:
Select at least three pictures based on your selected adage, aphorism, proverb, or maxim. Next, build three posters by adding text to the chosen pictures. (Synthesis)

Suggested Start:
"If One does not Plow, There will be no Harvest"
1. Make sure you understand the adage, aphorism, proverb, or maxim.
2. Reflect on the meaning(s) of your chosen adage, aphorism, proverb, or maxim.
3. Search for images that symbolize or reflect the adage, aphorism, proverb, or maxim.
4. Construct posters.

If one does not plow,
    there will be no harvest.

Challenge Six:

Is it better to <u>emulate</u> or <u>imitate</u>?

In this exercise, consider possible scenarios when it is better to do one or the other underlined options. Next, find scenarios that benefit from each underlined option. Then, try to find scenarios that do not benefit from each underlined option. Create a chart that represents your conclusions. Lastly, compose statements using historical examples or scientific data that validate each item inside your chart. (Evaluation)

Example: Is it better to <u>spark</u> or <u>spur</u>?

Neither	Spark	Spur	Both
malice	critical thoughts	truthfulness	healthy behavior
hatred	cooperation	obedience	innovations
ignorance	motivation	horse	inventions
	confidence		imagination
			students
			self-control

  A. <u>Hatred</u> can <u>spark</u> destructive behavior such as... (insert historical example).

  B. Although, at times effective, spurred obedience has a limited shelf life; eventually, the spurred will rebel or revolt such as a child or colony...

  C. According to _____(author/researcher/expert), sparking confidence can boost students' comprehension.

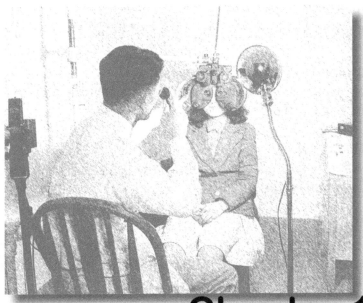

Chapter 12
Section 5

Exploration of Business

Common Core State Standards:
- CCSS.ELA-LITERACY.WHST.6-8.6
- CCSS.ELA-LITERACY.WHST.6-8.7
- CCSS.ELA-LITERACY.WHST.6-8.8
- CCSS.ELA-LITERACY.WHST.6-8.9
- CCSS.ELA-LITERACY.WHST.6-8.10
- CCSS.ELA-LITERACY.RH.6-8.4
- CCSS.ELA-LITERACY.RH.6-8.7

Learning Objectives:
- A. Examine products and services from the view of an organizational entity such as a business
- B. Communicate information through graphics and text such as diagrams and charts

Product and Service Path

Instructions:
Place your answers to each challenge into a journal or folder

Challenge One:
Identify a product or service that you use on a weekly basis.(Knowledge)

Challenge Two:
Identify the type of companies that produce your chosen product or service. Classify their industry.(Comprehension)

Challenge Three:
Identify three direct competitors of your chosen product or service. Describe and chart the competition based on market share, business size (by employees), years available, marketing reach(local, regional, national, global), revenue and profits. Research and use industry averages if your chosen company or its competitors are not publicly traded.(Analysis)

Main Product (Web Browsers)				
	Market Share	**Business Size**	**Marketing Reach**	**Years Available**
Internet Explorer (product)	2	large enterprise	global	19
Chrome (competitor)	1	large enterprise	global	6
Firefox (competitor)	3	mid-size	global	12
Opera (competitor)	4	mid-size	global	18

Challenge four:

Create a diagram that displays the major parts or sequences of your chosen product or service. Next explain two of the product's major parts. For example, an Xbox 360 has multiple, specialized parts such as the central processing unit, the graphics processing unit and the hard drive. Use graphics. Cite sources. (Analysis)

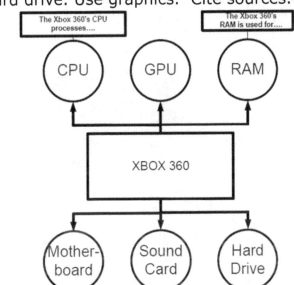

Challenge Five:

Based on your chosen product or service, identify three influential people that had a major impact on this industry through improvements, innovations, or inventions. Describe their effects on the industry. Cite sources.(Analysis)

Industry: Telecommunications		
insert image	John Doe	was an inventor whose radical and unorthodox methods produced the first....
insert image	Jane Doe	was an amazing engineer who invented the first....
insert image	Dr. Cooper	was a well-known and well-respected physician that accidentally invented....

Challenge Six:

Create an organizational chart (unofficial) of a company that offers your chosen product or service. Next, pinpoint the areas where your three previously chosen influential people would work. For example, if one of your selected influential people is a visionary executive leader, then they would fit somewhere at the top of the organizational chart(org chart).(Synthesis)

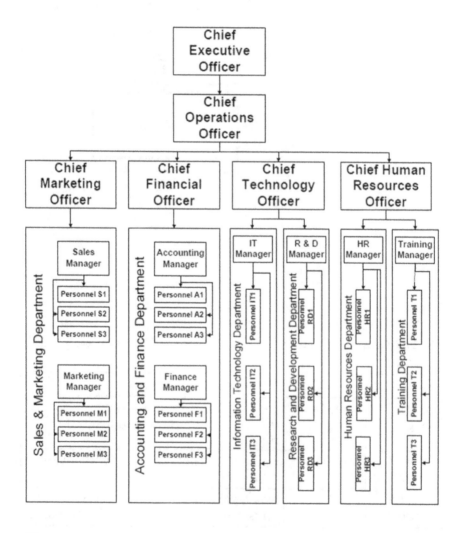

Challenge Seven:
Based on your gathered research and your product choice, create a visual flowchart or graphical diagram that demonstrates the interaction between human resources and non-human resources to produce the product or service. Start with the necessary (raw) materials required to produce the product or service. For example, an organic farmer needs supplies, materials, equipment, and workers. Then, your flowchart should display the interactions between the workforce and resources until the end-product reaches consumers. (Synthesis)

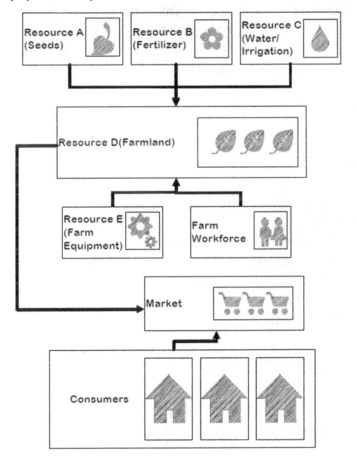

Challenge Eight:

Based on your product choice or service selection,

- Identify two supplemental/complementary products or services such as computer applications complement computer operating systems
- Identify two required/necessary products (computer operating system are necessary to operate computers)
- Identify two separate or indirectly connected products or services that the company produces(Xbox 360 or Zune)

Discover which product(s) is your strongest seller(s). Why? Would you eliminate any products or services from the company's product lineup? Explain. Which product or service deserves the most research and development? Elaborate. Lastly, which product or service deserves the most marketing. Explain. Cite sources.(Evaluation)

Potential Resources:

- www.bls.gov/ooh
- www.bls.gov/iag
- howstuffworks.com
- visual.merriam-webster.com
- finance.yahoo.com
- ehow.com
- sba.gov
- entrepreneur.com

Rubric for Chapter
See Appendix A

Reflective Questions for Chapter
See Appendix B

Chapter 13

Connections to
Common Core State Standards:

CCSS.ELA-LITERACY.WHST.6-8.6
Use technology, including the Internet, to produce and publish writing and present the relationships between information and ideas clearly and efficiently.(2010)

CCSS.ELA-LITERACY.WHST.6-8.7
Conduct short research projects to answer a question(including a self-generated question), drawing on several sources and generating additional related, focused questions that allow for multiple avenues of exploration.(2010)

CCSS.ELA-LITERACY.WHST.6-8.8
Gather relevant information from multiple print and digital sources, using search terms effectively; assess the credibility and accuracy of each source; and quote or paraphrase the data and conclusions of others while avoiding plagiarism and following a standard form of citation.(2010)

CCSS.ELA-LITERACY.WHST.6-8.9
Draw evidence from informational texts to support analysis, reflection, and research.(2010)

Connections to
Common Core State Standards:
(continued)

CCSS.ELA-LITERACY.WHST.6-8.10
Write routinely over extended time frames(time for revision and reflection) and shorter time frames(a single sitting or a day or two) for a range of discipline-specific tasks, purposes, and audiences.(2010)

CCSS.ELA-LITERACY.RH.6-8.1
Cite specific textual evidence to support analysis of primary and secondary sources.(2010)

CCSS.ELA-LITERACY.RH.6-8.4
Determine the meaning of words and phrases as they are used in a text, including vocabulary specific to domains related to history/social studies.(2010)

CCSS.ELA-LITERACY.RH.6-8.7
Integrate visual information(e.g., in charts, graphs, photographs, videos, or maps) with other information in print and digital text.(2010)

CCSS.ELA-LITERACY.RST.6-8.1
Cite specific textual evidence to support analysis of science and technical texts.(2010)

CCSS.ELA-LITERACY.RST.6-8.2
Determine the central ideas or conclusions of a text; provide an accurate summary of the text distinct from prior knowledge or opinions.(2010)

CCSS.ELA-LITERACY.RST.6-8.
Distinguish among facts, reasoned judgment based on research findings, and speculation in text.(2010)

Chapter 13
Section 1

Exploration of the Idiom:
Have a One-Track Mind

Common Core State Standards:
- CCSS.ELA-LITERACY.WHST.6-8.8
- CCSS.ELA-LITERACY.WHST.6-8.10
- CCSS.ELA-LITERACY.RH.6-8.4
- CCSS.ELA-LITERACY.RH.6-8.7

Learning Objectives:
- A. Understand the figurative meaning of idioms
- B. Comprehend the problematic issues with literal translations of idioms

Have a One-Track Mind

Instructions:
Place your answers to each challenge into a journal or folder

Challenge One:
Translate "Have a one-track mind" **into your own words.**(Comprehension)

Challenge Two:
Create two separate sentences using the idiom "Have a one-track mind".(Application)

Challenge Three:
Identify another idiom that is similar to "Have a one-track mind".(Analysis)

Challenge Four:
Recall and list fictional characters with "One-track minds". Provide examples of their behavior that illustrate the idiom.(Analysis)

Suggested Start:
Using an American English Idiom dictionary, define the figurative meaning of "Have a one-track mind".

Potential Resources:
1.) Idioms.thefreedictionary.com
2.) Dictionary.reference.com/idioms

Challenge Five:
Create, draw or sketch three **individual** objects that represent the word "Focused". Based on your images, explain the connection(s) to the subject.(Synthesis)

Example 1:
Humbled

Example 2:
Driven

Challenge Six:

Create two or more images that express the command "Take out the trash!" But, use as few images and letters as possible. Then, repeat this process with the thought, "Time to clean up!". Communicate the subtle or overt meaning of the objects inside your images.(Synthesis)

Example One: *I dislike bears.*

Example Two: *I love bears.*

Chapter 13
Section 2

Perspectives on:
Finite Methods

Common Core State Standards:
- CCSS.ELA-LITERACY.WHST.6-8.7
- CCSS.ELA-LITERACY.WHST.6-8.8
- CCSS.ELA-LITERACY.WHST.6-8.10
- CCSS.ELA-LITERACY.RST.6-8.1
- CCSS.ELA-LITERACY.RST.6-8.2

Learning Objectives:
- A. Gain perspective on vague writing
- B. Gain awareness of potential problems with "absolute" statements in writing
- C. Gain perspective on multiple answers

There are Only Two Ways to Multiply Two Numbers

Instructions:
Place your answers to each challenge into a journal or folder

Challenge One:
Respond to the statement, "There are only two ways to multiply two numbers". For example,

$$80 \times 5 = 400 \text{ or}$$
$$5 \times 80 = 400$$

Cite sources that defend your response. (Analysis)

Challenge Two:
Explain the concept of multiplication.(Analysis)

Here are recommendations to keep in mind when answering the above questions:
1. What is multiplication?
2. Define the process of multiplication?
3. Were you taught more than one way to multiple?
4. Cite sources that defend your argument.

Suggested Start:
   1. Pause before answering the question.
   2. Using a dictionary, define "Multiplication".
   3. Using an encyclopedia, research "Multiplication".

Potential Resources:
   1.) Merriam-Webster.com
   2.) Bartleby.com

Challenge Three:
Create a joke that you must answer in a figurative way and a literal way. Remember, keep it clean and respectful. NO PRACTICAL JOKES!(Analysis)

Example:
Joke(the setup): *They say "failure is a part of learning".*
Figurative answer (punchline): *Could someone please explain that to my parents.*
Literal answer: *This quote translates more often into "We learn from our mistakes". Whether a person is completing a quiz or learning to ride a bike, mistakes may occur, and they have the option to grow from their small failures.*

The secret to creating jokes is to ask questions about the world. In other words, analyze the world around you. If it doesn't make sense, question it. Then, research it.

To help, start with a statement like:
Why is it that...............
Ever notice that...........
Whose idea was it to make...
One day, there was a.................
Why does....
Where's the......
How is it that....

Don't forget to explore and explain the answer in a figurative and literal way. Creating jokes can be challenging. Worst case scenario, find and use a joke that you can answer in a figurative and literal way. Explain, why it is funny. Give credit to the comedian.

Challenge Four:
First, **define** the word, "Sagacious". Second, create a two column chart with a "negative factors" side and a "positive factors" side. Third, contrast the positive factors and negative issues of the word, "Sagacious". (Analysis)

Example:
According to _____'s dictionary, **failure** is....

Failure	
Negative Factors	**Positive Factors**
May spark negative emotions	Mistakes and failings are a part of the creation process
May affect interpersonal relationships	"When you quit that is true failure"
	Don't make failing a habit; however, if it happens, learn from your failure

Challenge Five:
Find an image. Then, create a chart that lists the directly observable features versus the not-visible, but inferable features of the image.(Analysis)

Example: Ship	
Observable and Visible	**Not Visible, but Inferable**
is a vehicle	holds passengers
is in the ocean	holds cargo

Chapter 13
Section 3

Exploring Quotations on: Humility

Common Core State Standards:
- CCSS.ELA-LITERACY.WHST.6-8.6
- CCSS.ELA-LITERACY.WHST.6-8.8
- CCSS.ELA-LITERACY.WHST.6-8.10
- CCSS.ELA-LITERACY.RH.6-8.1
- CCSS.ELA-LITERACY.RH.6-8.4
- CCSS.ELA-LITERACY.RH.6-8.7

Learning Objectives:
- A. Gain knowledge on the topic of "humility"
- B. Experience other perspectives on "humility"

Quotations on Humility

Instructions:
Place your answers to each challenge into a journal or folder

Challenge One:
Locate a quotation on the topic of "humility".(Knowledge)

Challenge Two:
Translate your selected quotation on "humility" into your own words.(Comprehension)

Challenge Three:
Compose a biographical statement using your chosen quotation on "humility".(Application)

Challenge Four:
Create your own quote on "humility".(Synthesis)

Challenge Five:
Select or create a poem on "humility".(Synthesis)

Suggested Start:
1. Reflect on "humbling" experiences.
2. Quotation resources are available at your local library.

Potential Resources:
1.) Quoteland.com
2.) Brainyquote.com
3.) Quotationspage.com
4.) En.wikiquote.org

Challenge Six:

Using a quotation on "humility", discover a way to express the meaning through pictures and words. Then, create a comic strip that explains the quotation.(Synthesis)

Example:
"Hunger"
"Thou shouldst eat to live; not live to eat."
Socrates

Create a collection of images that relate to the quote. Then, add captions or messages that help express the quote. Lastly, connect images and create a comic strip.

Challenge Seven:
Complete the following sentence fragment with three or more separate statements. Figure out a way to incorporate a quotation, adage, or joke.(Application)

The Mojave Desert...

Example:

The last movie that I saw...
1.) ...caused my mind to reflect on the possibilities of humans having superpowers. For instance, by combining advanced nanotechnology with our understanding of genetics, we could modify ourselves into more supercharged people.

2.) ...agitated me because it depicted the cruelties of mankind. However, I then reflected on an anonymous quote that "Unfortunately, the road to progress can have various levels of bumpiness".

3.) ...frightened me because it was a creepy horror film. Now, I want to sleep with the lights on, but my parents disagree. Even though, I don't pay the electric bill. I feel that I should be able to make this decision!

Chapter 13
Section 4

Exploration of Adages, Aphorisms, Proverbs, and Maxims:

Common Core State Standards:
- CCSS.ELA-LITERACY.WHST.6-8.6
- CCSS.ELA-LITERACY.WHST.6-8.8
- CCSS.ELA-LITERACY.WHST.6-8.10
- CCSS.ELA-LITERACY.RH.6-8.4
- CCSS.ELA-LITERACY.RH.6-8.7

Learning Objectives:
- A. Experience perceptive sayings from various cultures
- B. Examine beliefs and understandings of various individuals and groups

Adages, Aphorisms, Proverbs, and Maxims

Instructions:
Place your answers to each challenge into a journal or folder

Challenge One:
Select an adage, aphorism, proverb, or maxim. Research the origin of the adage, aphorism, proverb, or maxim. Cite source(s).(Knowledge)

Challenge Two:
Translate your chosen adage, aphorism, proverb, or maxim into your own words.(Comprehension)

Challenge Three:
Compose a small paragraph or a short segment of dialogue that includes your chosen adage, aphorism, proverb, or maxim.(Application)

Challenge Four:
Do you agree or disagree with the message of your chosen adage, aphorism, proverb, or maxim. Defend your response. Cite sources.(Evaluation)

Suggested Start:
1. Reflect on your chosen adage, aphorism, proverb, or maxim.
2. Identify problems, if any.

Potential Resources:
1.) En.wikiquote.org
2.) Thinkexist.com

Challenge Five:
Select at least three pictures based on your selected adage, aphorism, proverb, or maxim. Next, build three posters by adding text to the chosen pictures. (Synthesis)

Suggested Start:
"If One does not Plow, There will be no Harvest"
1. Make sure you understand the adage, aphorism, proverb, or maxim.
2. Reflect on the meaning(s) of your chosen adage, aphorism, proverb, or maxim.
3. Search for images that symbolize or reflect the adage, aphorism, proverb, or maxim.
4. Construct posters.

If one does not plow, there will be no harvest.

Challenge Six:

Is it better to <u>record</u> or <u>erase</u>?

In this exercise, consider possible scenarios when it is better to do one or the other underlined options. Next, find scenarios that benefit from each underlined option. Then, try to find scenarios that do not benefit from each underlined option. Create a chart that represents your conclusions. Lastly, compose statements using historical examples or scientific data that validate each item inside your chart. (Evaluation)

Example: Is it better to <u>spark</u> or <u>spur</u>?

Neither	Spark	Spur	Both
malice	critical thoughts	truthfulness	healthy behavior
hatred	cooperation	obedience	innovations
ignorance	motivation	horse	inventions
	confidence		imagination
			students
			self-control

A. <u>Hatred</u> can <u>spark</u> destructive behavior such as... (insert historical example).
B. Although, at times effective, spurred obedience has a limited shelf life; eventually, the spurred will rebel or revolt such as a child or colony...
C. According to _____(author/researcher/expert), sparking confidence can boost students' comprehension.

Chapter 13
Section 5

Exploration of Business

Common Core State Standards:
- CCSS.ELA-LITERACY.WHST.6-8.6
- CCSS.ELA-LITERACY.WHST.6-8.7
- CCSS.ELA-LITERACY.WHST.6-8.8
- CCSS.ELA-LITERACY.WHST.6-8.9
- CCSS.ELA-LITERACY.WHST.6-8.10
- CCSS.ELA-LITERACY.RH.6-8.4
- CCSS.ELA-LITERACY.RH.6-8.7

Learning Objectives:
- A. Examine business costs and opportunities
- B. Communicate information through graphics and text such as diagrams and charts

Organization Path

Instructions:
Place your answers to each challenge into a journal or folder

Challenge One:
Name a business or organization that you patronize on an infrequent basis such as every 6-12 months. Classify the type of business it is. Identify its main product.(Knowledge)

Challenge Two:
Identify three competitors of this business.(Comprehension)

Challenge Three:
Identify three products or services of your chosen company. Create a chart that displays the relationship among the main product and the additional products. Determine if these products are:
- Integrated and necessary for the main product to operate such as gasoline or motor oil for cars
- Complementary to the product and enhances product like air conditioning and power windows for cars
- Vital to the business such as their brand brake pads and spark plugs for cars

Main Product(Windows Operating System)			
	Integrated and Necessary	Enhances Main Product	Vital to Business
Microsoft Office	No	Yes	Yes
Internet Explorer	Yes	Yes	Yes
Xbox 360	No	No	No

Challenge Four:

Categorize the four chosen products by popularity among consumers, history of the products, revenue, profit, target audience(name their main customers), and strongest direct competitor, quasi-competitor and indirect competitor. Use a scale from 4 to 1, 4 being highest, to grade each category. Then, based on your chart, describe the growth potential (or lack of future potential) of each product. Which product is the strongest? Which product would you focus more resources on for the future of the company. Defend your decision. Cite sources.(Analysis)

Strengths and Weaknesses				
	Windows OS	Microsoft Office	Internet Explorer	Xbox 360
Popularity	3	4	2	1
Revenue	3	4	2	1
Profitabil-ity	3	4	2	1

Strengths and Weaknesses by Details				
	Windows OS	Microsoft Office	Internet Explorer	Xbox 360
Years Available	28 yrs.	23 yrs.	19 yrs.	8 yrs.
Direct Competitor	Mac OS X	LibreOffice	Chrome	Playstation 3
Quasi-Competitor	Android OS	QuickOffice	Smart-TVs	Gameboy Advance
Indirect Competitor	Pen and Paper	Typewriter	Library Card	Mobile Device
Rankings among direct Competitors	#1	#1	#2	#1

Challenge Five:

Choose one of your chosen company's most popular or well-known products or services. Research this product or service and build a diagram that displays the fabrication process of the product or service. Cite sources.(Synthesis)

Your diagram or chart should display the work that goes into producing a product or service.

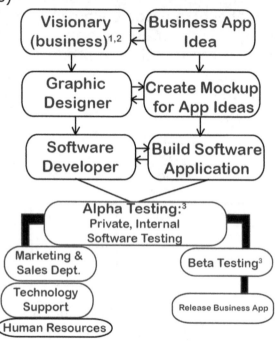

1 Does the app solve a problem?
2 Can it be profitable?
3 Testing may require restarts or revisions.

Challenge Six:

Create a chart that explains two of the product's major features. For example, an alarm clock normally has a minimum of two features, the time display and the alarm function. Use graphics, if possible. Cite sources.(Analysis)

Alarm Radio	
Radio	converts radio waves...
Alarm Buzzer	is a feature of the...

Challenge Seven:

Based on your gathered research and your product choice, create a visual flowchart or graphical diagram that demonstrates the interaction between human resources and non-human resources to produce the product or service. Start with the necessary (raw) materials required to produce the product or service. For example, an organic farmer needs supplies, materials, equipment, and workers. Then, your flowchart should display the interactions between the workforce and resources until the end-product reaches consumers. (Synthesis)

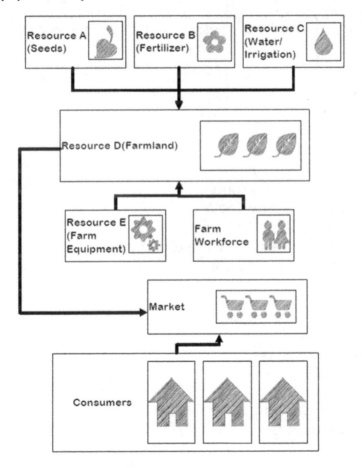

Challenge Eight:

Identify three individuals that had a major impact on your chosen company's industry. Create a multimedia chart to describe their impact. Based on your research of these three individuals, which individual had the biggest impact on their industry. Defend your argument. Cite sources.(Evaluation)

Industry: Telecommunications		
insert image	John Doe	was an inventor whose radical and unorthodox methods produced the first....
insert image	Jane Doe	was an amazing engineer who invented the first....
insert image	Dr. Cooper	was a well-known and well-respected physician that accidentally invented....

Potential Resources:
- www.bls.gov/ooh
- www.bls.gov/iag
- howstuffworks.com
- visual.merriam-webster.com
- finance.yahoo.com
- ehow.com
- sba.gov
- entrepreneur.com

Rubric for Chapter
See Appendix A

Reflective Questions for Chapter
See Appendix B

Chapter 14

Connections to
Common Core State Standards:

CCSS.ELA-LITERACY.WHST.6-8.6
Use technology, including the Internet, to produce and publish writing and present the relationships between information and ideas clearly and efficiently.(2010)

CCSS.ELA-LITERACY.WHST.6-8.7
Conduct short research projects to answer a question(including a self-generated question), drawing on several sources and generating additional related, focused questions that allow for multiple avenues of exploration.(2010)

CCSS.ELA-LITERACY.WHST.6-8.8
Gather relevant information from multiple print and digital sources, using search terms effectively; assess the credibility and accuracy of each source; and quote or paraphrase the data and conclusions of others while avoiding plagiarism and following a standard form of citation.(2010)

CCSS.ELA-LITERACY.WHST.6-8.9
Draw evidence from informational texts to support analysis, reflection, and research.(2010)

Connections to
Common Core State Standards:
(continued)

CCSS.ELA-LITERACY.WHST.6-8.10
Write routinely over extended time frames(time for revision and reflection) and shorter time frames(a single sitting or a day or two) for a range of discipline-specific tasks, purposes, and audiences.(2010)

CCSS.ELA-LITERACY.RH.6-8.1
Cite specific textual evidence to support analysis of primary and secondary sources.(2010)

CCSS.ELA-LITERACY.RH.6-8.4
Determine the meaning of words and phrases as they are used in a text, including vocabulary specific to domains related to history/social studies.(2010)

CCSS.ELA-LITERACY.RH.6-8.7
Integrate visual information(e.g., in charts, graphs, photographs, videos, or maps) with other information in print and digital text.(2010)

CCSS.ELA-LITERACY.RST.6-8.1
Cite specific textual evidence to support analysis of science and technical texts.(2010)

CCSS.ELA-LITERACY.RST.6-8.2
Determine the central ideas or conclusions of a text; provide an accurate summary of the text distinct from prior knowledge or opinions.(2010)

CCSS.ELA-LITERACY.RST.6-8.
Distinguish among facts, reasoned judgment based on research findings, and speculation in text.(2010)

Chapter 14
Section 1

Exploration of the Idiom:
All in Good Time

Common Core State Standards:
- CCSS.ELA-LITERACY.WHST.6-8.8
- CCSS.ELA-LITERACY.WHST.6-8.10
- CCSS.ELA-LITERACY.RH.6-8.4
- CCSS.ELA-LITERACY.RH.6-8.7

Learning Objectives:
- A. Understand the figurative meaning of idioms
- B. Comprehend the problematic issues with literal translations of idioms

All in Good Time

Instructions:
Place your answers to each challenge into a journal or folder

Challenge One:
Translate "All in Good Time" **into your own words**. (Comprehension)

Challenge Two:
Create two separate sentences using the idiom "All in Good Time".(Application)

Challenge Three:
Identify another idiom that is similar to "All in Good Time".(Analysis)

Challenge Four:
Identify an idiom that has the opposite meaning of "All in Good Time".(Analysis)

Challenge Five:
Recall and list **fictional** characters that would recommend "All in Good Time" as a guiding principle.

Suggested Start:
Using an American English Idiom dictionary, define the figurative meaning of "All in Good Time".

Potential Resources:
    1.) Idioms.thefreedictionary.com
    2.) Dictionary.reference.com/idioms

Challenge Six:

Create, draw or sketch three **individual** objects that represent the word "Efficiency". Based on your images, explain the connection(s) to the subject.(Synthesis)

Example 1:
Humbled

Example 2:
Driven

Challenge Seven:

Create two or more images that express the command "Be Cooperative!" But, use as few images and letters as possible. Then, repeat this process with the thought, "Things would go easier if we cooperated!" Communicate the subtle or overt meaning of the objects inside your images.(Synthesis)

Example One: *I dislike bees.*

Example Two: *I love bees.*

Chapter 14
Section 2

Perspectives on:
Time and Place

Common Core State Standards:
- CCSS.ELA-LITERACY.WHST.6-8.7
- CCSS.ELA-LITERACY.WHST.6-8.8
- CCSS.ELA-LITERACY.WHST.6-8.10
- CCSS.ELA-LITERACY.RST.6-8.1
- CCSS.ELA-LITERACY.RST.6-8.2

Learning Objectives:
- A. Gain perspective on vague writing
- B. Gain awareness of potential problems with "absolute" statements in writing
- C. Gain perspective on multiple answers

The Sahara Desert has Always Been a Desert

Instructions:
Place your answers to each challenge into a journal or folder

Challenge One:
Respond to the following statement, "The Sahara Desert has always been a desert". Defend your response through research.(Analysis)

Challenge Two:
Respond to the following statement, "The Sahara Desert is an anomaly." Explain.(Evaluation)

Challenge Three:
Respond to the following statement. "The Sahara Desert was never affected by the last ice age". Cite sources that defend your research.(Analysis)

Here are recommendations to keep in mind when answering the above questions:
1. Consider the land?
2. Consider time?
3. Cite sources that defend your argument.

Suggested Start:
   1. Pause before answering the question.
   2. Using a dictionary, define "desert".

Potential Resources:
      1.) Merriam-Webster.com
      2.) Bartleby.com

Challenge Four:
Create a joke that you must answer in a figurative way and a literal way. Remember, keep it clean and respectful. NO PRACTICAL JOKES!(Analysis)

Example:
Joke(the setup): *They say "failure is a part of learning".*
Figurative answer (punchline): *Could someone please explain that to my parents.*
Literal answer: *This quote translates more often into "We learn from our mistakes". Whether a person is completing a quiz or learning to ride a bike, mistakes may occur, and they have the option to grow from their small failures.*

The secret to creating jokes is to ask questions about the world. In other words, analyze the world around you. If it doesn't make sense, question it. Then, research it.

To help, start with a statement like:
    Why is it that...............
    Ever notice that...........
    Whose idea was it to make...
    One day, there was a.................
    Why does....
    Where's the......
    How is it that....

Don't forget to explore and explain the answer in a figurative and literal way. Creating jokes can be challenging. Worst case scenario, find and use a joke that you can answer in a figurative and literal way. Explain, why it is funny. Give credit to the comedian.

Challenge Five:

First, **define** the word, "Capricious". Second, create a two column chart with a "negative factors" side and a "positive factors" side. Third, contrast the positive factors and negative issues of the word, "Capricious". (Analysis)

Example:

According to _____'s dictionary, **failure** is....

Failure	
Negative Factors	**Positive Factors**
May spark negative emotions	Mistakes and failings are a part of the creation process
May affect interpersonal relationships	"When you quit that is true failure"
	Don't make failing a habit; however, if it happens, learn from your failure

Challenge Six:

Find an image. Then, create a chart that lists the directly observable features versus the not-visible, but inferable features of the image.(Analysis)

Example: Bulldozer	
Observable and Visible	**Not Visible, but Inferable**
is a vehicle	holds driver
	has controls

Chapter 14
Section 3

Exploring Quotations on: Knowledge

Common Core State Standards:
- CCSS.ELA-LITERACY.WHST.6-8.6
- CCSS.ELA-LITERACY.WHST.6-8.8
- CCSS.ELA-LITERACY.WHST.6-8.10
- CCSS.ELA-LITERACY.RH.6-8.1
- CCSS.ELA-LITERACY.RH.6-8.4
- CCSS.ELA-LITERACY.RH.6-8.7

Learning Objectives:
- A. Gain insight on "knowledge"
- B. Experience other perspectives on "knowledge"

Quotations on Knowledge

Instructions:
Place your answers to each challenge into a journal or folder

Challenge One:
Locate a quotation on the topic of "knowledge". (Knowledge)

Challenge Two:
Translate your selected quotation on "knowledge" into your own words.(Comprehension)

Challenge Three:
Compose a biographical statement using your chosen quotation on "knowledge".(Application)

Challenge Four:
Create your own quote on "knowledge".(Synthesis)

Challenge Five:
Select or create a poem on "knowledge".(Synthesis)

Suggested Start:
1. Reflect on knowledgeable people.
2. Quotation resources are available at your local library.

Potential Resources:
1.) Quoteland.com
2.) Brainyquote.com
3.) Quotationspage.com
4.) En.wikiquote.org

Challenge Six:
Using a quotation on "knowledge", discover a way
to express the meaning through pictures and words.
Then, create a comic strip that explains the quotation.
(Synthesis)

Example:
> "Hunger"
> "Thou shouldst eat to live; not live to eat."
> Socrates

Create a collection of images that relate to the
quote. Then, add captions or messages that help
express the quote. Lastly, connect images and
create a comic strip.

Challenge Seven:
Complete the following sentence fragment with three or more separate statements. Figure out a way to incorporate a quotation, adage, or joke.(Application)

I like to invest my time...

Example:

The last movie that I saw...
1.) ...caused my mind to reflect on the possibilities of humans having superpowers. For instance, by combining advanced nanotechnology with our understanding of genetics, we could modify ourselves into more supercharged people.

2.) ...agitated me because it depicted the cruelties of mankind. However, I then reflected on an anonymous quote that "Unfortunately, the road to progress can have various levels of bumpiness".

3.) ...frightened me because it was a creepy horror film. Now, I want to sleep with the lights on, but my parents disagree. Even though, I don't pay the electric bill. I feel that I should be able to make this decision!

Chapter 14
Section 4

Exploration of Adages, Aphorisms, Proverbs, and Maxims:

Common Core State Standards:
- CCSS.ELA-LITERACY.WHST.6-8.6
- CCSS.ELA-LITERACY.WHST.6-8.8
- CCSS.ELA-LITERACY.WHST.6-8.10
- CCSS.ELA-LITERACY.RH.6-8.4
- CCSS.ELA-LITERACY.RH.6-8.7

Learning Objectives:
- A. Experience perceptive sayings from various cultures
- B. Examine beliefs and understandings of various individuals and groups

Adages, Aphorisms, Proverbs, and Maxims

Instructions:
Place your answers to each challenge into a journal or folder

Challenge One:
Select an adage, aphorism, proverb, or maxim. Research the origin of the adage, aphorism, proverb, or maxim. Cite source(s).(Knowledge)

Challenge Two:
Translate your chosen adage, aphorism, proverb, or maxim into your own words.(Comprehension)

Challenge Three:
Compose a small paragraph or a short segment of dialogue that includes your chosen adage, aphorism, proverb, or maxim.(Application)

Challenge Four:
Do you agree or disagree with the message of your chosen adage, aphorism, proverb, or maxim. Defend your response. Cite sources.(Evaluation)

Suggested Start:
1. Reflect on your chosen adage, aphorism, proverb, or maxim.
2. Identify problems, if any.

Potential Resources:
1.) En.wikiquote.org
2.) Thinkexist.com

Challenge Five:

Select at least three pictures based on your selected adage, aphorism, proverb, or maxim. Next, build three posters by adding text to the chosen pictures. (Synthesis)

Suggested Start:
"If One does not Plow, There will be no Harvest"

1. Make sure you understand the adage, aphorism, proverb, or maxim.
2. Reflect on the meaning(s) of your chosen adage, aphorism, proverb, or maxim.
3. Search for images that symbolize or reflect the adage, aphorism, proverb, or maxim.
4. Construct posters.

If one does not plow, there will be no harvest.

Challenge Six:

Is it better to <u>rebel</u> or <u>revolt</u>?

In this exercise, consider possible scenarios when it is better to do one or the other underlined options. Next, find scenarios that benefit from each underlined option. Then, try to find scenarios that do not benefit from each underlined option. Create a chart that represents your conclusions. Lastly, compose statements using historical examples or scientific data that validate each item inside your chart. (Evaluation)

Example: Is it better to <u>spark</u> or <u>spur</u>?

Neither	Spark	Spur	Both
malice	critical thoughts	truthfulness	healthy behavior
hatred	cooperation	obedience	innovations
ignorance	motivation	horse	inventions
	confidence		imagination
			students
			self-control

A. <u>Hatred</u> can <u>spark</u> destructive behavior such as... (insert historical example).
B. Although, at times effective, spurred obedience has a limited shelf life; eventually, the spurred will rebel or revolt such as a child or colony...
C. According to _____(author/researcher/expert), sparking confidence can boost students' comprehension.

Chapter 14
Section 5

Exploration of Business

Common Core State Standards:
- CCSS.ELA-LITERACY.WHST.6-8.6
- CCSS.ELA-LITERACY.WHST.6-8.7
- CCSS.ELA-LITERACY.WHST.6-8.8
- CCSS.ELA-LITERACY.WHST.6-8.9
- CCSS.ELA-LITERACY.WHST.6-8.10
- CCSS.ELA-LITERACY.RH.6-8.4
- CCSS.ELA-LITERACY.RH.6-8.7

Learning Objectives:
- A. Examine products and services from the view of an organizational entity such as a business
- B. Communicate information through graphics and text such as diagrams and charts

Product and Service Path

Instructions:
Place your answers to each challenge into a journal or folder

Challenge One:
Identify a product or service that was once very popular but now is on the verge of extinction.(Knowledge)

Challenge Two:
Identify the type of companies that produce your chosen product or service. Classify their industry.(Comprehension)

Challenge Three:
Identify three direct competitors of your chosen product or service. Describe and chart the competition based on market share, business size (by employees), years available, marketing reach(local, regional, national, global), revenue and profits. Research and use industry averages if your chosen company or its competitors are not publicly traded.(Analysis)

Main Product (Web Browsers)				
	Market Share	**Business Size**	**Marketing Reach**	**Years Available**
Internet Explorer (product)	2	large enterprise	global	19
Chrome (competitor)	1	large enterprise	global	6
Firefox (competitor)	3	mid-size	global	12
Opera (competitor)	4	mid-size	global	18

Challenge four:

Create a diagram that displays the major parts or sequences of your chosen product or service. Next explain two of the product's major parts. For example, an Xbox 360 has multiple, specialized parts such as the central processing unit, the graphics processing unit and the hard drive. Use graphics. Cite sources. (Analysis)

Challenge Five:

Based on your chosen product or service, identify three influential people that had a major impact on this industry through improvements, innovations, or inventions. Describe their effects on the industry. Cite sources.(Analysis)

Industry: Telecommunications		
insert image	John Doe	was an inventor whose radical and unorthodox methods produced the first....
insert image	Jane Doe	was an amazing engineer who invented the first....
insert image	Dr. Cooper	was a well-known and well-respected physician that accidentally invented....

Challenge Six:

Create an organizational chart (unofficial) of a company that offers your chosen product or service. Next, pinpoint the areas where your three previously chosen influential people would work. For example, if one of your selected influential people is a visionary executive leader, then they would fit somewhere at the top of the organizational chart(org chart).(Synthesis)

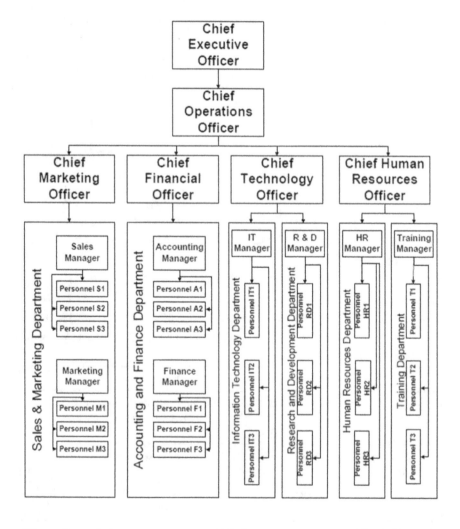

Challenge Seven:
Based on your gathered research and your product choice, create a visual flowchart or graphical diagram that demonstrates the interaction between human resources and non-human resources to produce the product or service. Start with the necessary (raw) materials required to produce the product or service. For example, an organic farmer needs supplies, materials, equipment, and workers. Then, your flowchart should display the interactions between the workforce and resources until the end-product reaches consumers. (Synthesis)

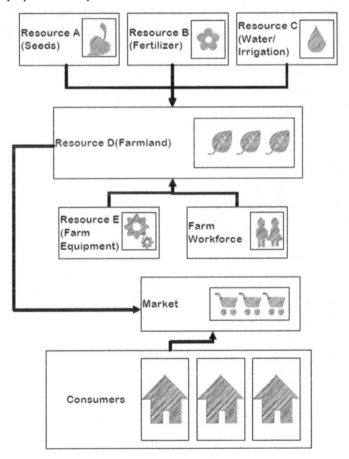

Challenge Eight:

Based on your product choice or service selection,

- Identify two supplemental/complementary products or services such as computer applications complement computer operating systems
- Identify two required/necessary products (computer operating system are necessary to operate computers)
- Identify two separate or indirectly connected products or services that the company produces(Xbox 360 or Zune)

Discover which product(s) is your strongest seller(s). Why? Would you eliminate any products or services from the company's product lineup? Explain. Which product or service deserves the most research and development? Elaborate. Lastly, which product or service deserves the most marketing. Explain. Cite sources.(Evaluation)

Potential Resources:

- www.bls.gov/ooh
- www.bls.gov/iag
- howstuffworks.com
- visual.merriam-webster.com
- finance.yahoo.com
- ehow.com
- sba.gov
- entrepreneur.com

Rubric for Chapter
See Appendix A

Reflective Questions for Chapter
See Appendix B

Chapter 15

Connections to Common Core State Standards:

CCSS.ELA-LITERACY.WHST.6-8.6
Use technology, including the Internet, to produce and publish writing and present the relationships between information and ideas clearly and efficiently.(2010)

CCSS.ELA-LITERACY.WHST.6-8.7
Conduct short research projects to answer a question(including a self-generated question), drawing on several sources and generating additional related, focused questions that allow for multiple avenues of exploration.(2010)

CCSS.ELA-LITERACY.WHST.6-8.8
Gather relevant information from multiple print and digital sources, using search terms effectively; assess the credibility and accuracy of each source; and quote or paraphrase the data and conclusions of others while avoiding plagiarism and following a standard form of citation.(2010)

CCSS.ELA-LITERACY.WHST.6-8.9
Draw evidence from informational texts to support analysis, reflection, and research.(2010)

Connections to
Common Core State Standards:
(continued)

CCSS.ELA-LITERACY.WHST.6-8.10
Write routinely over extended time frames(time for revision and reflection) and shorter time frames(a single sitting or a day or two) for a range of discipline-specific tasks, purposes, and audiences.(2010)

CCSS.ELA-LITERACY.RH.6-8.1
Cite specific textual evidence to support analysis of primary and secondary sources.(2010)

CCSS.ELA-LITERACY.RH.6-8.4
Determine the meaning of words and phrases as they are used in a text, including vocabulary specific to domains related to history/social studies.(2010)

CCSS.ELA-LITERACY.RH.6-8.7
Integrate visual information(e.g., in charts, graphs, photographs, videos, or maps) with other information in print and digital text.(2010)

CCSS.ELA-LITERACY.RST.6-8.1
Cite specific textual evidence to support analysis of science and technical texts.(2010)

CCSS.ELA-LITERACY.RST.6-8.2
Determine the central ideas or conclusions of a text; provide an accurate summary of the text distinct from prior knowledge or opinions.(2010)

CCSS.ELA-LITERACY.RST.6-8.
Distinguish among facts, reasoned judgment based on research findings, and speculation in text.(2010)

Chapter 15
Section 1

Exploration of the Idiom:
Time is Money

Common Core State Standards:
- CCSS.ELA-LITERACY.WHST.6-8.8
- CCSS.ELA-LITERACY.WHST.6-8.10
- CCSS.ELA-LITERACY.RH.6-8.4
- CCSS.ELA-LITERACY.RH.6-8.7

Learning Objectives:
A. Understand the figurative meaning of idioms
B. Comprehend the problematic issues with literal translations of idioms

Time is Money

Instructions:
Place your answers to each challenge into a journal or folder

Challenge One:
Translate "Time is Money" **into your own words**. (Comprehension)

Challenge Two:
Create two separate sentences using the idiom "Time is Money".(Application)

Challenge Three:
Identify another idiom that is similar to "Time is Money".(Analysis)

Challenge Four:
Locate an idiom that expresses the opposite meaning of "Time is Money".(Analysis)

Challenge Five:
Recall and list **fictional** characters that symbolize the idiomatic expression "Time is Money". Explain.(Evaluation)

Suggested Start:
Using an American English Idiom dictionary, define the figurative meaning of "Time is Money".

Potential Resources:
    1.) Idioms.thefreedictionary.com
    2.) Dictionary.reference.com/idioms

Challenge Six:

Create, draw or sketch three **individual** objects that represent the word "Malleable". Based on your images, explain the connection(s) to the subject.(Synthesis)

Example 1:
Humbled

Example 2:
Driven

Challenge Seven:

Create two or more images that express the command "Change your attitude!" But, use as few images and letters as possible. Then, repeat this process with the thought, "His leadership style is negatively affecting the group!" Communicate the subtle or overt meaning of the objects inside your images.(Synthesis)

Example One: *I dislike frogs.*

Example Two: *I love frogs.*

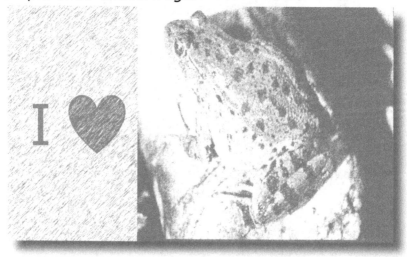

Chapter 15
Section 2

Perspectives on:
Prehistoric Time

Common Core State Standards:
- CCSS.ELA-LITERACY.WHST.6-8.7
- CCSS.ELA-LITERACY.WHST.6-8.8
- CCSS.ELA-LITERACY.WHST.6-8.10
- CCSS.ELA-LITERACY.RST.6-8.1
- CCSS.ELA-LITERACY.RST.6-8.2

Learning Objectives:
- A. Gain perspective on vague writing
- B. Gain awareness of potential problems with "absolute" statements in writing
- C. Gain perspective on multiple answers

All Dinosaurs are Extinct

Instructions:
Place your answers to each challenge into a journal or folder

Challenge One:
Respond to the statement, "All Dinosaurs are Extinct". Cite sources that defend your response.(Analysis)

Challenge Two:
How many known mass extinction events took place on earth? (Comprehension)

Here are recommendations to keep in mind when answering the above questions:
1. What is a dinosaur?
2. What is a mass extinction?
3. Cite sources that defend your argument.

Suggested Start:
1. Pause before answering the question.
2. Using a dictionary, define "era".
3. Using an encyclopedia, research "dinosaur".

Potential Resources:
1.) Merriam-Webster.com
2.) Bartleby.com

Challenge Three:
Create a joke that you must answer in a figurative way and a literal way. Remember, keep it clean and respectful. NO PRACTICAL JOKES!(Analysis)

Example:
Joke(the setup): *They say "failure is a part of learning".*
Figurative answer (punchline): *Could someone please explain that to my parents.*
Literal answer: *This quote translates more often into "We learn from our mistakes". Whether a person is completing a quiz or learning to ride a bike, mistakes may occur, and they have the option to grow from their small failures.*

The secret to creating jokes is to ask questions about the world. In other words, analyze the world around you. If it doesn't make sense, question it. Then, research it.

To help, start with a statement like:
    Why is it that...............
    Ever notice that...........
    Whose idea was it to make...
    One day, there was a.................
    Why does....
    Where's the......
    How is it that....

Don't forget to explore and explain the answer in a figurative and literal way. Creating jokes can be challenging. Worst case scenario, find and use a joke that you can answer in a figurative and literal way. Explain, why it is funny. Give credit to the comedian.

Challenge Four:

First, **define** the word, "Charismatic". Second, create a two column chart with a "negative factors" side and a "positive factors" side. Third, contrast the positive factors and negative issues of the word, "Charismatic". (Analysis)

Example:

According to _____'s dictionary, **failure** is....

Failure	
Negative Factors	**Positive Factors**
May spark negative emotions	Mistakes and failings are a part of the creation process
May affect interpersonal relationships	"When you quit that is true failure"
	Don't make failing a habit; however, if it happens, learn from your failure

Challenge Five:

Find an image. Then, create a chart that lists the directly observable features versus the not-visible, but inferable features of the image.(Analysis)

Example: Crane	
Observable and Visible	**Not Visible, but Inferable**
is a vehicle	has driver
is on the ground	has controls
has a hook	

Chapter 15
Section 3

Exploring Quotations on: Experience

Common Core State Standards:
- CCSS.ELA-LITERACY.WHST.6-8.6
- CCSS.ELA-LITERACY.WHST.6-8.8
- CCSS.ELA-LITERACY.WHST.6-8.10
- CCSS.ELA-LITERACY.RH.6-8.1
- CCSS.ELA-LITERACY.RH.6-8.4
- CCSS.ELA-LITERACY.RH.6-8.7

Learning Objectives:
- A. Gain knowledge on the topic of "experience"
- B. Experience other perspectives on "experience"

Quotations on Experience

Instructions:
Place your answers to each challenge into a journal or folder

Challenge One:
Locate a quotation on the topic of "experience". (Knowledge)

Challenge Two:
Translate your selected quotation on "experience" into your own words.(Comprehension)

Challenge Three:
Compose a biographical statement using your chosen quotation on "experience".(Application)

Challenge Four:
Create your own quote on "experience".(Synthesis)

Challenge Five:
Find or create a poem on "experience".(Synthesis)

Suggested Start:
1. Reflect on "experience".
2. Quotation resources are available at your local library.

Potential Resources:
1.) Quoteland.com
2.) Brainyquote.com
3.) Quotationspage.com
4.) En.wikiquote.org

Challenge Six:

Using a quotation on "experience", discover a way to express the meaning through pictures and words. Then, create a comic strip that explains the quotation. (Synthesis)

Example:
"Hunger"
"Thou shouldst eat to live; not live to eat."
Socrates

Create a collection of images that relate to the quote. Then, add captions or messages that help express the quote. Lastly, connect images and create a comic strip.

Challenge Seven:

Complete the following sentence fragment with three or more separate statements. Figure out a way to incorporate a quotation, adage, or joke.(Application)

Knowledge and Experience...

Example:

The last movie that I saw...

1.) ...caused my mind to reflect on the possibilities of humans having superpowers. For instance, by combining advanced nanotechnology with our understanding of genetics, we could modify ourselves into more supercharged people.

2.) ...agitated me because it depicted the cruelties of mankind. However, I then reflected on an anonymous quote that "Unfortunately, the road to progress can have various levels of bumpiness".

3.) ...frightened me because it was a creepy horror film. Now, I want to sleep with the lights on, but my parents disagree. Even though, I don't pay the electric bill. I feel that I should be able to make this decision!

Chapter 15
Section 4

Exploration of Adages,
Aphorisms, Proverbs, and Maxims:

Common Core State Standards:
- CCSS.ELA-LITERACY.WHST.6-8.6
- CCSS.ELA-LITERACY.WHST.6-8.8
- CCSS.ELA-LITERACY.WHST.6-8.10
- CCSS.ELA-LITERACY.RH.6-8.4
- CCSS.ELA-LITERACY.RH.6-8.7

Learning Objectives:
- A. Experience perceptive sayings from various cultures
- B. Examine beliefs and understandings of various individuals and groups

Adages, Aphorisms, Proverbs, and Maxims

Instructions:
Place your answers to each challenge into a journal or folder

Challenge One:
Select an adage, aphorism, proverb, or maxim. Research the origin of the adage, aphorism, proverb, or maxim. Cite source(s).(Knowledge)

Challenge Two:
Translate your chosen adage, aphorism, proverb, or maxim into your own words.(Comprehension)

Challenge Three:
Compose a small paragraph or a short segment of dialogue that includes your chosen adage, aphorism, proverb, or maxim.(Application)

Challenge Four:
Do you agree or disagree with the message of your chosen adage, aphorism, proverb, or maxim. Defend your response. Cite sources.(Evaluation)

Suggested Start:
1. Reflect on your chosen adage, aphorism, proverb, or maxim.
2. Identify problems, if any.

Potential Resources:
1.) En.wikiquote.org
2.) Thinkexist.com

Challenge Five:
Select at least three pictures based on your selected adage, aphorism, proverb, or maxim. Next, build three posters by adding text to the chosen pictures. (Synthesis)

Suggested Start:
"If One does not Plow, There will be no Harvest"
1. Make sure you understand the adage, aphorism, proverb, or maxim.
2. Reflect on the meaning(s) of your chosen adage, aphorism, proverb, or maxim.
3. Search for images that symbolize or reflect the adage, aphorism, proverb, or maxim.
4. Construct posters.

If one does not plow, there will be no harvest.

Challenge Six:

Is it better to <u>memorize</u> or <u>improvise</u>?

In this exercise, consider possible scenarios when it is better to do one or the other underlined options. Next, find scenarios that benefit from each underlined option. Then, try to find scenarios that do not benefit from each underlined option. Create a chart that represents your conclusions. Lastly, compose statements using historical examples or scientific data that validate each item inside your chart. (Evaluation)

Example: Is it better to <u>spark</u> or <u>spur</u>?

Neither	Spark	Spur	Both
malice	critical thoughts	truthfulness	healthy behavior
hatred	cooperation	obedience	innovations
ignorance	motivation	horse	inventions
	confidence		imagination
			students
			self-control

    A. <u>Hatred</u> can <u>spark</u> destructive behavior such as... (insert historical example).
    B. Although, at times effective, spurred obedience has a limited shelf life; eventually, the spurred will rebel or revolt such as a child or colony...
    C. According to _____(author/researcher/expert), sparking confidence can boost students' comprehension.

Chapter 15
Section 5

Exploration of Business

Common Core State Standards:
- CCSS.ELA-LITERACY.WHST.6-8.6
- CCSS.ELA-LITERACY.WHST.6-8.7
- CCSS.ELA-LITERACY.WHST.6-8.8
- CCSS.ELA-LITERACY.WHST.6-8.9
- CCSS.ELA-LITERACY.WHST.6-8.10
- CCSS.ELA-LITERACY.RH.6-8.4
- CCSS.ELA-LITERACY.RH.6-8.7

Learning Objectives:
- A. Examine business costs and opportunities
- B. Communicate information through graphics and text such as diagrams and charts

Organization Path

Instructions:
Place your answers to each challenge into a journal or folder

Challenge One:
Name a business or organization that provides a vital service. Classify the type of organization it is. Identify its main product or service.(Knowledge)

Challenge Two:
Identify three competitors of this business.(Comprehension)

Challenge Three:
Identify three products or services of your chosen company. Create a chart that displays the relationship among the main product and the additional products. Determine if these products are:
- Integrated and necessary for the main product to operate such as gasoline or motor oil for cars
- Complementary to the product and enhances product like air conditioning and power windows for cars
- Vital to the business such as their brand brake pads and spark plugs for cars(Application)

Main Product(Windows Operating System)			
	Integrated and Necessary	Enhances Main Product	Vital to Business
Microsoft Office	No	Yes	Yes
Internet Explorer	Yes	Yes	Yes
Xbox 360	No	No	No

Challenge Four:

Categorize the four chosen products by popularity among consumers, history of the products, revenue, profit, target audience(name their main customers), and strongest direct competitor, quasi-competitor and indirect competitor. Use a scale from 4 to 1, 4 being highest, to grade each category. Then, based on your chart, describe the growth potential (or lack of future potential) of each product. Which product is the strongest? Which product would you focus more resources on for the future of the company. Defend your decision. Cite sources.(Analysis)

Strengths and Weaknesses				
	Windows OS	Microsoft Office	Internet Explorer	Xbox 360
Popularity	3	4	2	1
Revenue	3	4	2	1
Profitabil- ity	3	4	2	1

Strengths and Weaknesses by Details				
	Windows OS	Microsoft Office	Internet Explorer	Xbox 360
Years Available	28 yrs.	23 yrs.	19 yrs.	8 yrs.
Direct Competitor	Mac OS X	LibreOf- fice	Chrome	Playsta- tion 3
Quasi- Competitor	Android OS	QuickOf- fice	Smart- TVs	Gameboy Advance
Indirect Competitor	Pen and Paper	Typewriter	Library Card	Mobile Device
Rankings among direct Com- petitors	#1	#1	#2	#1

Challenge Five:
Choose one of your chosen company's most popular or well-known products or services. Research this product or service and build a diagram that displays the fabrication process of the product or service. Cite sources.(Synthesis)

Your diagram or chart should display the work that goes into producing a product or service.

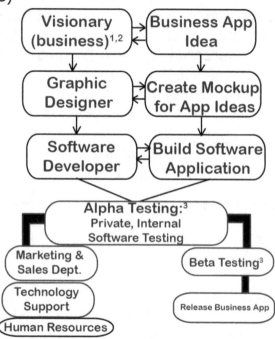

1 Does the app solve a problem?
2 Can it be profitable?
3 Testing may require restarts or revisions.

Challenge Six:
Create a chart that explains two of the product's major features. For example, an alarm clock normally has a minimum of two features, the time display and the alarm function. Use graphics, if possible. Cite sources.(Analysis)

Alarm Radio	
Radio	converts radio waves...
Alarm Buzzer	is a feature of the...

Challenge Seven:

Based on your gathered research and your product choice, create a visual flowchart or graphical diagram that demonstrates the interaction between human resources and non-human resources to produce the product or service. Start with the necessary (raw) materials required to produce the product or service. For example, an organic farmer needs supplies, materials, equipment, and workers. Then, your flowchart should display the interactions between the workforce and resources until the end-product reaches consumers. (Synthesis)

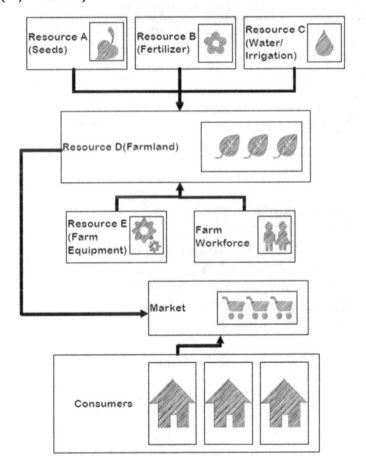

Challenge Eight:

Identify three individuals that had a major impact on your chosen company's industry. Create a multimedia chart to describe their impact. Based on your research of these three individuals, which individual had the biggest impact on their industry. Defend your argument. Cite sources.(Evaluation)

Industry: Telecommunications		
insert image	John Doe	was an inventor whose radical and unorthodox methods produced the first....
insert image	Jane Doe	was an amazing engineer who invented the first....
insert image	Dr. Cooper	was a well-known and well-respected physician that accidentally invented....

Potential Resources:

- www.bls.gov/ooh
- www.bls.gov/iag
- howstuffworks.com
- visual.merriam-webster.com
- finance.yahoo.com
- ehow.com
- sba.gov
- entrepreneur.com

Rubric for Chapter
See Appendix A

Reflective Questions for Chapter
See Appendix B

Chapter 16

Connections to
Common Core State Standards:

CCSS.ELA-LITERACY.WHST.6-8.6
Use technology, including the Internet, to produce and publish writing and present the relationships between information and ideas clearly and efficiently.(2010)

CCSS.ELA-LITERACY.WHST.6-8.7
Conduct short research projects to answer a question(including a self-generated question), drawing on several sources and generating additional related, focused questions that allow for multiple avenues of exploration.(2010)

CCSS.ELA-LITERACY.WHST.6-8.8
Gather relevant information from multiple print and digital sources, using search terms effectively; assess the credibility and accuracy of each source; and quote or paraphrase the data and conclusions of others while avoiding plagiarism and following a standard form of citation.(2010)

CCSS.ELA-LITERACY.WHST.6-8.9
Draw evidence from informational texts to support analysis, reflection, and research.(2010)

Connections to
Common Core State Standards:
(continued)

CCSS.ELA-LITERACY.WHST.6-8.10
Write routinely over extended time frames(time for revision and reflection) and shorter time frames(a single sitting or a day or two) for a range of discipline-specific tasks, purposes, and audiences.(2010)

CCSS.ELA-LITERACY.RH.6-8.1
Cite specific textual evidence to support analysis of primary and secondary sources.(2010)

CCSS.ELA-LITERACY.RH.6-8.4
Determine the meaning of words and phrases as they are used in a text, including vocabulary specific to domains related to history/social studies.(2010)

CCSS.ELA-LITERACY.RH.6-8.7
Integrate visual information(e.g., in charts, graphs, photographs, videos, or maps) with other information in print and digital text.(2010)

CCSS.ELA-LITERACY.RST.6-8.1
Cite specific textual evidence to support analysis of science and technical texts.(2010)

CCSS.ELA-LITERACY.RST.6-8.2
Determine the central ideas or conclusions of a text; provide an accurate summary of the text distinct from prior knowledge or opinions.(2010)

CCSS.ELA-LITERACY.RST.6-8.
Distinguish among facts, reasoned judgment based on research findings, and speculation in text.(2010)

Chapter 16
Section 1

Exploration of the Idiom: Work Like a Horse

Common Core State Standards:
- CCSS.ELA-LITERACY.WHST.6-8.8
- CCSS.ELA-LITERACY.WHST.6-8.10
- CCSS.ELA-LITERACY.RH.6-8.4
- CCSS.ELA-LITERACY.RH.6-8.7

Learning Objectives:
- A. Understand the figurative meaning of idioms
- B. Comprehend the problematic issues with literal translations of idioms

Work Like a Horse

Instructions:
Place your answers to each challenge into a journal or folder

Challenge One:
Translate "Work Like a Horse" **into your own words**. (Comprehension)

Challenge Two:
Create two separate sentences using the idiom "Work Like a Horse".(Application)

Challenge Three:
Identify another idiom that is similar to "Work Like a Horse"(Analysis).

Challenge Four:
Identify an idiom that is the opposite of "Work Like a Horse"(Analysis).

Challenge Five:
Recall and list **fictional** characters that could represent the idiom "Works Like a Horse".(Evaluation)

Suggested Start:
Using an American English Idiom dictionary, define the figurative meaning of "Work Like a Horse".

Potential Resources:
    1.) Idioms.thefreedictionary.com
    2.) Dictionary.reference.com/idioms

Challenge Six:

Create, draw or sketch three **individual** objects that represent the word "Measurable". Based on your images, explain the connection(s) to the subject.(Synthesis)

Example 1:
Humbled

Example 2:
Driven

Challenge Seven:

Create two or more images that express the statement "I forgot!" But, use as few images and letters as possible. Then, repeat this process with the thought, "Why do I always forget to do my homework!" Communicate the subtle or overt meaning of the objects inside your images.(Synthesis)

Example One: *I dislike lions.*

Example Two: *I love lions.*

Chapter 16
Section 2

Perspectives on:
Possibilities

Common Core State Standards:
- CCSS.ELA-LITERACY.WHST.6-8.7
- CCSS.ELA-LITERACY.WHST.6-8.8
- CCSS.ELA-LITERACY.WHST.6-8.10
- CCSS.ELA-LITERACY.RST.6-8.1
- CCSS.ELA-LITERACY.RST.6-8.2

Learning Objectives:
- A. Gain perspective on vague writing
- B. Gain awareness of potential problems with "absolute" statements in writing
- C. Gain perspective on multiple answers

Four Leaf Clovers are Very Difficult to Find

Instructions:
Place your answers to each challenge into a journal or folder

Challenge One:
Respond to the statement, "Four leaf clovers are very difficult to find".   Explain.(Analysis)

Challenge Two:
Answer the question, "Is it possible to produce four leaf clovers every time?" Cite sources that defend your answer.(Evaluation)

Here are recommendations to keep in mind when answering the above questions:
1. What are clovers?
2. What are four leaf clovers?
3. Cite sources that defend your argument.

Suggested Start:
1. Pause before answering the question.
2. Using a dictionary, define "difficult".
3. Operationalize the word "four leaf clover".

Potential Resources:
1.) Merriam-Webster.com
2.) Bartleby.com

Challenge Three:
Create a joke that you must answer in a figurative way and a literal way. Remember, keep it clean and respectful. NO PRACTICAL JOKES!(Analysis)

Example:
Joke(the setup): *They say "failure is a part of learning".*
Figurative answer (punchline): *Could someone please explain that to my parents.*
Literal answer: *This quote translates more often into "We learn from our mistakes". Whether a person is completing a quiz or learning to ride a bike, mistakes may occur, and they have the option to grow from their small failures.*

The secret to creating jokes is to ask questions about the world. In other words, analyze the world around you. If it doesn't make sense, question it. Then, research it.

To help, start with a statement like:
    Why is it that...............
    Ever notice that...........
    Whose idea was it to make...
    One day, there was a.................
    Why does....
    Where's the......
    How is it that....

Don't forget to explore and explain the answer in a figurative and literal way. Creating jokes can be challenging. Worst case scenario, find and use a joke that you can answer in a figurative and literal way. Explain, why it is funny. Give credit to the comedian.

Challenge Four:
First, **define** the word, "Epic". Second, create a two column chart with a "negative factors" side and a "positive factors" side. Third, contrast the positive factors and negative issues of the word, "Epic".(Analysis)

Example:
According to _____'s dictionary, **failure** is....

Failure	
Negative Factors	**Positive Factors**
May spark negative emotions	Mistakes and failings are a part of the creation process
May affect interpersonal relationships	"When you quit that is true failure"
	Don't make failing a habit; however, if it happens, learn from your failure

Challenge Five:
Find an image. Then, create a chart that lists the directly observable features versus the not-visible, but inferable features of the image.(Analysis)

Example: Dump Truck	
Observable and Visible	**Not Visible, but Inferable**
is a vehicle	has driver
has tires	has controls
carries materials	

Chapter 16
Section 3

Exploring Quotations on:
Education

Common Core State Standards:
- CCSS.ELA-LITERACY.WHST.6-8.6
- CCSS.ELA-LITERACY.WHST.6-8.8
- CCSS.ELA-LITERACY.WHST.6-8.10
- CCSS.ELA-LITERACY.RH.6-8.1
- CCSS.ELA-LITERACY.RH.6-8.4
- CCSS.ELA-LITERACY.RH.6-8.7

Learning Objectives:
- A. Gain knowledge on the topic of "education"
- B. Experience other perspectives on "education"

Quotations on Education

Instructions:
Place your answers to each challenge into a journal or folder

Challenge One:
Locate a quotation on the topic of "education".(Knowledge)

Challenge Two:
Translate your selected quotation on "education" into your own words.(Comprehension)

Challenge Three:
Compose a biographical statement using your chosen quotation on "education".(Application)

Challenge Four:
Create your own quote on "education".(Synthesis)

Challenge Five:
Locate or create a poem on "education".(Synthesis)

Suggested Start:
1. Reflect on "education".
2. Quotation resources are available at your local library.

Potential Resources:
1.) Quoteland.com
2.) Brainyquote.com
3.) Quotationspage.com
4.) En.wikiquote.org

Challenge Six:

Using a quotation on "education", discover a way to express the meaning through pictures and words. Then, create a comic strip that explains the quotation. (Synthesis)

Example:
                "Hunger"
"Thou shouldst eat to live; not live to eat."
                                Socrates

Create a collection of images that relate to the quote. Then, add captions or messages that help express the quote. Lastly, connect images and create a comic strip.

Challenge Seven:
Complete the following sentence fragment with three or more separate statements. Figure out a way to incorporate a quotation, adage, or joke.(Application)

My portfolio demonstrates...

Example:

The last movie that I saw...
1.) ...caused my mind to reflect on the possibilities of humans having superpowers. For instance, by combining advanced nanotechnology with our understanding of genetics, we could modify ourselves into more supercharged people.

2.) ...agitated me because it depicted the cruelties of mankind. However, I then reflected on an anonymous quote that "Unfortunately, the road to progress can have various levels of bumpiness".

3.) ...frightened me because it was a creepy horror film. Now, I want to sleep with the lights on, but my parents disagree. Even though, I don't pay the electric bill. I feel that I should be able to make this decision!

Chapter 16
Section 4

Exploration of Adages, Aphorisms, Proverbs, and Maxims:

Common Core State Standards:
- CCSS.ELA-LITERACY.WHST.6-8.6
- CCSS.ELA-LITERACY.WHST.6-8.8
- CCSS.ELA-LITERACY.WHST.6-8.10
- CCSS.ELA-LITERACY.RH.6-8.4
- CCSS.ELA-LITERACY.RH.6-8.7

Learning Objectives:
- A. Experience perceptive sayings from various cultures
- B. Examine beliefs and understandings of various individuals and groups

Adages, Aphorisms, Proverbs, and Maxims

Instructions:
Place your answers to each challenge into a journal or folder

Challenge One:
Select an adage, aphorism, proverb, or maxim. Research the origin of the adage, aphorism, proverb, or maxim. Cite source(s).(Knowledge)

Challenge Two:
Translate your chosen adage, aphorism, proverb, or maxim into your own words.(Comprehension)

Challenge Three:
Compose a small paragraph or a short segment of dialogue that includes your chosen adage, aphorism, proverb, or maxim.(Application)

Challenge Four:
Do you agree or disagree with the message of your chosen adage, aphorism, proverb, or maxim. Defend your response. Cite sources.(Evaluation)

Suggested Start:
1. Reflect on your chosen adage, aphorism, proverb, or maxim.
2. Identify problems, if any.

Potential Resources:
1.) En.wikiquote.org
2.) Thinkexist.com

Challenge Five:
Select at least three pictures based on your selected adage, aphorism, proverb, or maxim. Next, build three posters by adding text to the chosen pictures. (Synthesis)

Suggested Start:
"Truth is Stranger than Fiction"
1. Make sure you understand the adage, aphorism, proverb, or maxim.
2. Reflect on the meaning(s) of your chosen adage, aphorism, proverb, or maxim.
3. Search for images that symbolize or reflect the adage, aphorism, proverb, or maxim.
4. Construct posters.

Challenge Six:

Is it better to <u>trade</u> or <u>barter</u>?

In this exercise, consider possible scenarios when it is better to do one or the other underlined options. Next, find scenarios that benefit from each underlined option. Then, try to find scenarios that do not benefit from each underlined option. Create a chart that represents your conclusions. Lastly, compose statements using historical examples or scientific data that validate each item inside your chart. (Evaluation)

Example: Is it better to <u>spark</u> or <u>spur</u>?

Neither	Spark	Spur	Both
malice	critical thoughts	truthfulness	healthy behavior
hatred	cooperation	obedience	innovations
ignorance	motivation	horse	inventions
	confidence		imagination
			students
			self-control

    A. <u>Hatred</u> can <u>spark</u> destructive behavior such as... (insert historical example).
    B. Although, at times effective, spurred obedience has a limited shelf life; eventually, the spurred will rebel or revolt such as a child or colony...
    C. According to _____(author/researcher/expert), sparking confidence can boost students' comprehension.

Chapter 16
Section 5

Exploration of Business

Common Core State Standards:
- CCSS.ELA-LITERACY.WHST.6-8.6
- CCSS.ELA-LITERACY.WHST.6-8.7
- CCSS.ELA-LITERACY.WHST.6-8.8
- CCSS.ELA-LITERACY.WHST.6-8.9
- CCSS.ELA-LITERACY.WHST.6-8.10
- CCSS.ELA-LITERACY.RH.6-8.4
- CCSS.ELA-LITERACY.RH.6-8.7

Learning Objectives:
- A. Examine products and services from the view of an organizational entity such as a business
- B. Communicate information through graphics and text such as diagrams and charts

Product and Service Path

Instructions:
Place your answers to each challenge into a journal or folder

Challenge One:
Identify a popular 20+ year old technology product or service.(Knowledge)

Challenge Two:
Identify the type of companies that produce your chosen product or service. Classify their industry.(Comprehension)

Challenge Three:
Identify three direct competitors of your chosen product or service. Describe and chart the competition based on market share, business size (by employees), years available, marketing reach(local, regional, national, global), revenue and profits. Research and use industry averages if your chosen company or its competitors are not publicly traded.(Analysis)

Main Product (Web Browsers)				
	Market Share	**Business Size**	**Marketing Reach**	**Years Available**
Internet Explorer (product)	2	large enterprise	global	19
Chrome (competitor)	1	large enterprise	global	6
Firefox (competitor)	3	mid-size	global	12
Opera (competitor)	4	mid-size	global	18

Challenge four:

Create a diagram that displays the major parts or sequences of your chosen product or service. Next explain two of the product's major parts. For example, an Xbox 360 has multiple, specialized parts such as the central processing unit, the graphics processing unit and the hard drive. Use graphics. Cite sources. (Analysis)

Challenge Five:

Based on your chosen product or service, identify three influential people that had a major impact on this industry through improvements, innovations, or inventions. Describe their effects on the industry. Cite sources.(Analysis)

Industry: Telecommunications		
insert image	John Doe	was an inventor whose radical and unorthodox methods produced the first....
insert image	Jane Doe	was an amazing engineer who invented the first....
insert image	Dr. Cooper	was a well-known and well-respected physician that accidentally invented....

Challenge Six:

Create an organizational chart (unofficial) of a company that offers your chosen product or service. Next, pinpoint the areas where your three previously chosen influential people would work. For example, if one of your selected influential people is a visionary executive leader, then they would fit somewhere at the top of the organizational chart(org chart).(Synthesis)

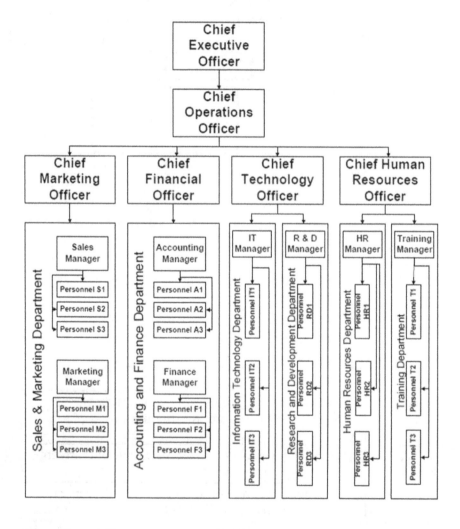

Challenge Seven:

Based on your gathered research and your product choice, create a visual flowchart or graphical diagram that demonstrates the interaction between human resources and non-human resources to produce the product or service. Start with the necessary (raw) materials required to produce the product or service. For example, an organic farmer needs supplies, materials, equipment, and workers. Then, your flowchart should display the interactions between the workforce and resources until the end-product reaches consumers. (Synthesis)

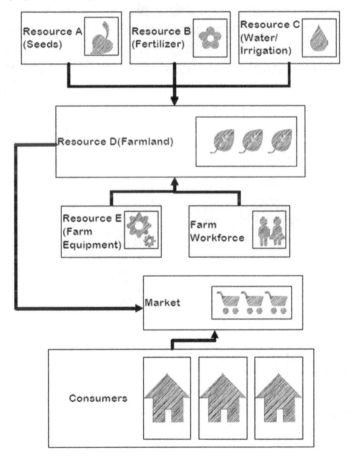

Challenge Eight:
Based on your product choice or service selection,
- Identify two supplemental/complementary products or services such as computer applications complement computer operating systems
- Identify two required/necessary products (computer operating system are necessary to operate computers)
- Identify two separate or indirectly connected products or services that the company produces(Xbox 360 or Zune)

Discover which product(s) is your strongest seller(s). Why? Would you eliminate any products or services from the company's product lineup? Explain. Which product or service deserves the most research and development? Elaborate. Lastly, which product or service deserves the most marketing. Explain. Cite sources.(Evaluation)

Potential Resources:
- www.bls.gov/ooh
- www.bls.gov/iag
- howstuffworks.com
- visual.merriam-webster.com
- finance.yahoo.com
- ehow.com
- sba.gov
- entrepreneur.com

Rubric for Chapter
See Appendix A

Reflective Questions for Chapter
See Appendix B

Chapter 17

Connections to
Common Core State Standards:

CCSS.ELA-LITERACY.WHST.6-8.6
Use technology, including the Internet, to produce and publish writing and present the relationships between information and ideas clearly and efficiently.(2010)

CCSS.ELA-LITERACY.WHST.6-8.7
Conduct short research projects to answer a question(including a self-generated question), drawing on several sources and generating additional related, focused questions that allow for multiple avenues of exploration.(2010)

CCSS.ELA-LITERACY.WHST.6-8.8
Gather relevant information from multiple print and digital sources, using search terms effectively; assess the credibility and accuracy of each source; and quote or paraphrase the data and conclusions of others while avoiding plagiarism and following a standard form of citation.(2010)

CCSS.ELA-LITERACY.WHST.6-8.9
Draw evidence from informational texts to support analysis, reflection, and research.(2010)

Connections to
Common Core State Standards:
(continued)

CCSS.ELA-LITERACY.WHST.6-8.10
Write routinely over extended time frames(time for revision and reflection) and shorter time frames(a single sitting or a day or two) for a range of discipline-specific tasks, purposes, and audiences.(2010)

CCSS.ELA-LITERACY.RH.6-8.1
Cite specific textual evidence to support analysis of primary and secondary sources.(2010)

CCSS.ELA-LITERACY.RH.6-8.4
Determine the meaning of words and phrases as they are used in a text, including vocabulary specific to domains related to history/social studies.(2010)

CCSS.ELA-LITERACY.RH.6-8.7
Integrate visual information(e.g., in charts, graphs, photographs, videos, or maps) with other information in print and digital text.(2010)

CCSS.ELA-LITERACY.RST.6-8.1
Cite specific textual evidence to support analysis of science and technical texts.(2010)

CCSS.ELA-LITERACY.RST.6-8.2
Determine the central ideas or conclusions of a text; provide an accurate summary of the text distinct from prior knowledge or opinions.(2010)

CCSS.ELA-LITERACY.RST.6-8.
Distinguish among facts, reasoned judgment based on research findings, and speculation in text.(2010)

Chapter 17
Section 1

Exploration of the Idiom:
Close Call

Common Core State Standards:
- CCSS.ELA-LITERACY.WHST.6-8.8
- CCSS.ELA-LITERACY.WHST.6-8.10
- CCSS.ELA-LITERACY.RH.6-8.4
- CCSS.ELA-LITERACY.RH.6-8.7

Learning Objectives:
A. Understand the figurative meaning of idioms
B. Comprehend the problematic issues with literal translations of idioms

Close Call

Instructions:
Place your answers to each challenge into a journal or folder

Challenge One:
Translate "Close Call" **into your own words.**(Comprehension)

Challenge Two:
Create two separate sentences using the idiom "Close Call".(Application)

Challenge Three:
Identify another idiom that is similar to "Close Call". (Analysis)

Challenge Four:
Recall and list **fictional** characters that had "Close Calls". Describe and defend your list of characters. (Analysis)

Challenge Five:
Recall and list **fictional** characters that had the opposite of a close call. Describe and defend. your list of characters.(Analysis)

Suggested Start:
Using an American English Idiom dictionary, define the figurative meaning of "Close Call".

Potential Resources:
    1.) Idioms.thefreedictionary.com
    2.) Dictionary.reference.com/idioms

Challenge Six:

Create, draw or sketch three **individual** objects that represent the word "fluctuating". Based on your images, explain the connection(s) to the subject.(Synthesis)

Example 1:
Humbled

Example 2:
Driven

Challenge Seven:
Create two or more images that express the command "Rotate!" But, use as few images and letters as possible. Then, repeat this process with the thought, "Their opinion has swung to the other direction". Communicate the subtle or overt meaning of the objects inside your images.(Synthesis)
Example One: *I dislike lizards.*

Example Two: *I love lizards.*

Chapter 17
Section 2

Perspectives on:
Expressions

Common Core State Standards:
- CCSS.ELA-LITERACY.WHST.6-8.7
- CCSS.ELA-LITERACY.WHST.6-8.8
- CCSS.ELA-LITERACY.WHST.6-8.10
- CCSS.ELA-LITERACY.RST.6-8.1
- CCSS.ELA-LITERACY.RST.6-8.2

Learning Objectives:
- A. Gain perspective on vague writing
- B. Gain awareness of potential problems with "absolute" statements in writing
- C. Gain perspective on multiple answers

Is there another way to Mathematically express "25 + 25 + 25"?

Instructions:
Place your answers to each challenge into a journal or folder

Challenge One:
Answer the question, "Is there another way to mathematically express 25 + 25 + 25?" Explain.(Analysis)

Challenge Two:
If possible, list various ways to mathematically express "25+25+25". Explain each possibility.(Evaluation)

Here are recommendations to keep in mind when answering the above questions:
1. Is there more than one answer?
2. Is there more than one question?
3. Cite sources that defend your argument.

Suggested Start:
   1. Pause before answering the question.
   2. Visualize the problem through drawing images.
   3. Operationalize the word 'Mathematically'

Potential Resources:
   1.) Merriam-Webster.com
   2.) Bartleby.com

Challenge Three:
Create a joke that you must answer in a figurative way and a literal way. Remember, keep it clean and respectful. NO PRACTICAL JOKES!(Analysis)

Example:
Joke(the setup):   *They say "failure is a part of learning".*
Figurative answer (punchline): *Could someone please explain that to my parents.*
Literal answer: *This quote translates more often into "We learn from our mistakes". Whether a person is completing a quiz or learning to ride a bike, mistakes may occur, and they have the option to grow from their small failures.*

The secret to creating jokes is to ask questions about the world. In other words, analyze the world around you. If it doesn't make sense, question it. Then, research it.

To help, start with a statement like:
 Why is it that...............
 Ever notice that...........
 Whose idea was it to make...
 One day, there was a.................
 Why does....
 Where's the......
 How is it that....

Don't forget to explore and explain the answer in a figurative and literal way. Creating jokes can be challenging. Worst case scenario, find and use a joke that you can answer in a figurative and literal way. Explain, why it is funny. Give credit to the comedian.

Challenge Four:

First, **define** the word, "Definitive". Second, create a two column chart with a "negative factors" side and a "positive factors" side. Third, contrast the positive factors and negative issues of the word, "Definitive". (Analysis)

Example:

According to _____'s dictionary, **failure** is....

Failure	
Negative Factors	**Positive Factors**
May spark negative emotions	Mistakes and failings are a part of the creation process
May affect interpersonal relationships	"When you quit that is true failure"
	Don't make failing a habit; however, if it happens, learn from your failure

Challenge Five:

Find an image. Then, create a chart that lists the directly observable features versus the not-visible, but inferable features of the image.(Analysis)

Example: Steam Shovel	
Observable and Visible	**Not Visible, but Inferable**
is a vehicle	has a construction worker
is on the ground	has an engine
has a mechanical shovel	

Chapter 17
Section 3

Exploring Quotations on: Pride

Common Core State Standards:
- CCSS.ELA-LITERACY.WHST.6-8.6
- CCSS.ELA-LITERACY.WHST.6-8.8
- CCSS.ELA-LITERACY.WHST.6-8.10
- CCSS.ELA-LITERACY.RH.6-8.1
- CCSS.ELA-LITERACY.RH.6-8.4
- CCSS.ELA-LITERACY.RH.6-8.7

Learning Objectives:
- A. Gain knowledge on the topic of "pride"
- B. Experience other perspectives on "pride"

Quotations on Pride

Instructions:
Place your answers to each challenge into a journal or folder

Challenge One:
Locate a quotation on the topic of "pride".(Knowledge)

Challenge Two:
Translate your selected quotation on "pride" into your own words.(Comprehension)

Challenge Three:
Compose a biographical statement using your chosen quotation on "pride".(Application)

Challenge Four:
Create your own quote on "pride".(Synthesis)

Challenge Five:
Find or create a poem on "pride".(Synthesis)

Suggested Start:
1. Define "pride".
2. Quotation resources are available at your local library.

Potential Resources:
1.) Quoteland.com
2.) Brainyquote.com
3.) Quotationspage.com
4.) En.wikiquote.org

Challenge Six:
Using a quotation on "pride", discover a way to express the meaning through pictures and words. Then, create a comic strip that explains the quotation.(Synthesis)

Example:
"Hunger"

"Thou shouldst eat to live; not live to eat."

Socrates

Create a collection of images that relate to the quote. Then, add captions or messages that help express the quote. Lastly, connect images and create a comic strip.

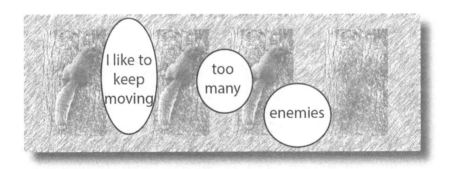

Challenge Seven:
Complete the following sentence fragment with three
or more separate statements. Figure out a way to incorporate a quotation, adage, or joke.(Application)

The multimedia presentation...

Example:

The last movie that I saw...
1.) ...caused my mind to reflect on the possibilities of humans having superpowers. For
instance, by combining advanced nanotechnology with our understanding of genetics, we
could modify ourselves into more supercharged
people.

2.) ...agitated me because it depicted the cruelties of mankind. However, I then reflected on an
anonymous quote that "Unfortunately, the road
to progress can have various levels of bumpiness".

3.) ...frightened me because it was a creepy
horror film. Now, I want to sleep with the lights
on, but my parents disagree. Even though, I
don't pay the electric bill. I feel that I should be
able to make this decision!

Chapter 17
Section 4

Exploration of Adages,
Aphorisms, Proverbs, and Maxims:

Common Core State Standards:
- CCSS.ELA-LITERACY.WHST.6-8.6
- CCSS.ELA-LITERACY.WHST.6-8.8
- CCSS.ELA-LITERACY.WHST.6-8.10
- CCSS.ELA-LITERACY.RH.6-8.4
- CCSS.ELA-LITERACY.RH.6-8.7

Learning Objectives:
- A. Experience perceptive sayings from various cultures
- B. Examine beliefs and understandings of various individuals and groups

Adages, Aphorisms, Proverbs, and Maxims

Instructions:
Place your answers to each challenge into a journal or folder

Challenge One:
Select an adage, aphorism, proverb, or maxim. Research the origin of the adage, aphorism, proverb, or maxim. Cite source(s).(Knowledge)

Challenge Two:
Translate your chosen adage, aphorism, proverb, or maxim into your own words.(Comprehension)

Challenge Three:
Compose a small paragraph or a short segment of dialogue that includes your chosen adage, aphorism, proverb, or maxim.(Application)

Challenge Four:
Do you agree or disagree with the message of your chosen adage, aphorism, proverb, or maxim. Defend your response. Cite sources.(Evaluation)

Suggested Start:
1. Reflect on your chosen adage, aphorism, proverb, or maxim.
2. Identify problems, if any.

Potential Resources:
1.) En.wikiquote.org
2.) Thinkexist.com

Challenge Five:
Select at least three pictures based on your selected adage, aphorism, proverb, or maxim. Next, build three posters by adding text to the chosen pictures. (Synthesis)

Suggested Start:
"Truth is Stranger than Fiction"
1. Make sure you understand the adage, aphorism, proverb, or maxim.
2. Reflect on the meaning(s) of your chosen adage, aphorism, proverb, or maxim.
3. Search for images that symbolize or reflect the adage, aphorism, proverb, or maxim.
4. Construct posters.

Challenge Six:

Is it better to <u>sell</u> or <u>buy</u>?

In this exercise, consider possible scenarios when it is better to do one or the other underlined options. Next, find scenarios that benefit from each underlined option. Then, try to find scenarios that do not benefit from each underlined option. Create a chart that represents your conclusions. Lastly, compose statements using historical examples or scientific data that validate each item inside your chart. (Evaluation)

Example: Is it better to <u>spark</u> or <u>spur</u>?

Neither	Spark	Spur	Both
malice	critical thoughts	truthfulness	healthy behavior
hatred	cooperation	obedience	innovations
ignorance	motivation	horse	inventions
	confidence		imagination
			students
			self-control

   A. <u>Hatred</u> can <u>spark</u> destructive behavior such as... (insert historical example).

   B. Although, at times effective, spurred obedience has a limited shelf life; eventually, the spurred will rebel or revolt such as a child or colony...

   C. According to _____(author/researcher/expert), sparking confidence can boost students' comprehension.

Chapter 17
Section 5

Exploration of Business

Common Core State Standards:
- CCSS.ELA-LITERACY.WHST.6-8.6
- CCSS.ELA-LITERACY.WHST.6-8.7
- CCSS.ELA-LITERACY.WHST.6-8.8
- CCSS.ELA-LITERACY.WHST.6-8.9
- CCSS.ELA-LITERACY.WHST.6-8.10
- CCSS.ELA-LITERACY.RH.6-8.4
- CCSS.ELA-LITERACY.RH.6-8.7

Learning Objectives:
- A. Examine business costs and opportunities
- B. Communicate information through graphics and text such as diagrams and charts

Organization Path

Instructions:
Place your answers to each challenge into a journal or folder

Challenge One:
Brainstorm a list of four financially strong businesses. Choose one of the businesses. Then, classify the type of organization it is. Identify its main product. (Knowledge)

Challenge Two:
Identify three competitors of this business.(Comprehension)

Challenge Three:
Identify three products or services of your chosen company. Create a chart that displays the relationship among the main product and the additional products. Determine if these products are:
- Integrated and necessary for the main product to operate such as gasoline or motor oil for cars
- Complementary to the product and enhances product like air conditioning and power windows for cars
- Vital to the business such as their brand brake pads and spark plugs for cars(Application)

Main Product(Windows Operating System)			
	Integrated and Necessary	Enhances Main Product	Vital to Business
Microsoft Office	No	Yes	Yes
Internet Explorer	Yes	Yes	Yes
Xbox 360	No	No	No

Challenge Four:

Categorize the four chosen products by popularity among consumers, history of the products, revenue, profit, target audience(name their main customers), and strongest direct competitor, quasi-competitor and indirect competitor. Use a scale from 4 to 1, 4 being highest, to grade each category. Then, based on your chart, describe the growth potential (or lack of future potential) of each product. Which product is the strongest? Which product would you focus more resources on for the future of the company. Defend your decision. Cite sources.(Analysis)

Strengths and Weaknesses				
	Windows OS	Microsoft Office	Internet Explorer	Xbox 360
Popularity	3	4	2	1
Revenue	3	4	2	1
Profitabil-ity	3	4	2	1

Strengths and Weaknesses by Details				
	Windows OS	Microsoft Office	Internet Explorer	Xbox 360
Years Available	28 yrs.	23 yrs.	19 yrs.	8 yrs.
Direct Competitor	Mac OS X	LibreOf-fice	Chrome	Playsta-tion 3
Quasi-Competitor	Android OS	QuickOf-fice	Smart-TVs	Gameboy Advance
Indirect Competitor	Pen and Paper	Typewriter	Library Card	Mobile Device
Rankings among direct Com-petitors	#1	#1	#2	#1

Challenge Five:
Choose one of your chosen company's most popular or well-known products or services. Research this product or service and build a diagram that displays the fabrication process of the product or service. Cite sources.(Synthesis)

Your diagram or chart should display the work that goes into producing a product or service.

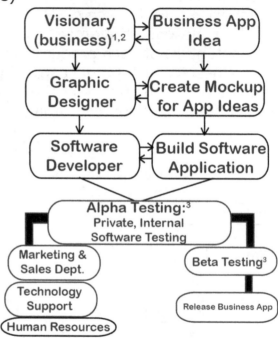

1 Does the app solve a problem?
2 Can it be profitable?
3 Testing may require restarts or revisions.

Challenge Six:
Create a chart that explains two of the product's major features. For example, an alarm clock normally has a minimum of two features, the time display and the alarm function. Use graphics, if possible. Cite sources.(Analysis)

Alarm Radio	
Radio	converts radio waves...
Alarm Buzzer	is a feature of the...

Challenge Seven:

Based on your gathered research and your product choice, create a visual flowchart or graphical diagram that demonstrates the interaction between human resources and non-human resources to produce the product or service. Start with the necessary (raw) materials required to produce the product or service. For example, an organic farmer needs supplies, materials, equipment, and workers. Then, your flowchart should display the interactions between the workforce and resources until the end-product reaches consumers. (Synthesis)

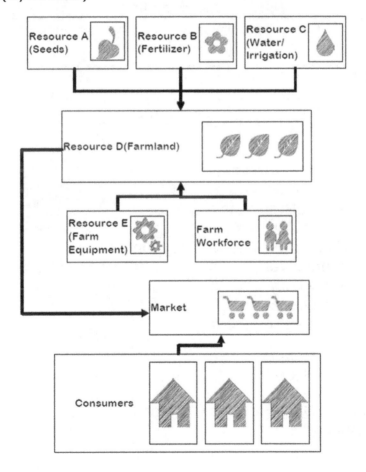

Challenge Eight:
Identify three individuals that had a major impact on your chosen company's industry. Create a multi-media chart to describe their impact. Based on your research of these three individuals, which individual had the biggest impact on their industry. Defend your argument. Cite sources.(Evaluation)

Industry: Telecommunications		
insert image	John Doe	was an inventor whose radical and unorthodox methods produced the first....
insert image	Jane Doe	was an amazing engineer who invented the first....
insert image	Dr. Cooper	was a well-known and well-respected physician that accidentally invented....

Potential Resources:
- www.bls.gov/ooh
- www.bls.gov/iag
- howstuffworks.com
- visual.merriam-webster.com
- finance.yahoo.com
- ehow.com
- sba.gov
- entrepreneur.com

Rubric for Chapter
See Appendix A

Reflective Questions for Chapter
See Appendix B

Chapter 18

Connections to
Common Core State Standards:

CCSS.ELA-LITERACY.WHST.6-8.6
Use technology, including the Internet, to produce and publish writing and present the relationships between information and ideas clearly and efficiently.(2010)

CCSS.ELA-LITERACY.WHST.6-8.7
Conduct short research projects to answer a question(including a self-generated question), drawing on several sources and generating additional related, focused questions that allow for multiple avenues of exploration.(2010)

CCSS.ELA-LITERACY.WHST.6-8.8
Gather relevant information from multiple print and digital sources, using search terms effectively; assess the credibility and accuracy of each source; and quote or paraphrase the data and conclusions of others while avoiding plagiarism and following a standard form of citation.(2010)

CCSS.ELA-LITERACY.WHST.6-8.9
Draw evidence from informational texts to support analysis, reflection, and research.(2010)

Connections to
Common Core State Standards:
(continued)

CCSS.ELA-LITERACY.WHST.6-8.10
Write routinely over extended time frames(time for revision and reflection) and shorter time frames(a single sitting or a day or two) for a range of discipline-specific tasks, purposes, and audiences.(2010)

CCSS.ELA-LITERACY.RH.6-8.1
Cite specific textual evidence to support analysis of primary and secondary sources.(2010)

CCSS.ELA-LITERACY.RH.6-8.4
Determine the meaning of words and phrases as they are used in a text, including vocabulary specific to domains related to history/social studies.(2010)

CCSS.ELA-LITERACY.RH.6-8.7
Integrate visual information(e.g., in charts, graphs, photographs, videos, or maps) with other information in print and digital text.(2010)

CCSS.ELA-LITERACY.RST.6-8.1
Cite specific textual evidence to support analysis of science and technical texts.(2010)

CCSS.ELA-LITERACY.RST.6-8.2
Determine the central ideas or conclusions of a text; provide an accurate summary of the text distinct from prior knowledge or opinions.(2010)

CCSS.ELA-LITERACY.RST.6-8.
Distinguish among facts, reasoned judgment based on research findings, and speculation in text.(2010)

Chapter 18
Section 1

Exploration of the Idiom:
Ahead of Time

Common Core State Standards:
- CCSS.ELA-LITERACY.WHST.6-8.8
- CCSS.ELA-LITERACY.WHST.6-8.10
- CCSS.ELA-LITERACY.RH.6-8.4
- CCSS.ELA-LITERACY.RH.6-8.7

Learning Objectives:
A. Understand the figurative meaning of idioms
B. Comprehend the problematic issues with literal translations of idioms

Ahead of (their) Time

Instructions:
Place your answers to each challenge into a journal or folder

Challenge One:
Translate "Ahead of their Time" **into your own words**.(Comprehension)

Challenge Two:
Create two separate sentences using the idiom "Ahead of their Time".(Application)

Challenge Three:
Identify another idiom that is similar to "Ahead of their Time".(Analysis)

Challenge Four:
Recall and list **fictional** characters that symbolize "Ahead of their Time".(Analysis)

Challenge Five:
Recall or research historical figures that were "ahead of their time"? Illustrate the reason(s) your historical figures were "Ahead of their Time".(Analysis)

Suggested Start:
1. Using an American English Idiom dictionary, define the figurative meaning of "Ahead of time".
2. Define "Ahead of his (or her) time".

Potential Resources:
1.) Idioms.thefreedictionary.com
2.) Dictionary.reference.com/idioms

Challenge Six:

Create, draw or sketch three **individual** objects that represent the word "Forward". Based on your images, explain the connection(s) to the subject.(Synthesis)

Example 1:
Humbled

Example 2:
Driven

Challenge Seven:

Create two or more images that express the feeling "I dislike brussel sprouts!" But, use as few images and letters as possible. Then, repeat this process with the thought, "I love brussel sprouts". Communicate the subtle or overt meaning of the objects inside your images.(Synthesis)

Example One: *I dislike mice.*

Example Two: *I love mice.*

Chapter 18
Section 2

Perspectives on:
Nothing

Common Core State Standards:
- CCSS.ELA-LITERACY.WHST.6-8.7
- CCSS.ELA-LITERACY.WHST.6-8.8
- CCSS.ELA-LITERACY.WHST.6-8.10
- CCSS.ELA-LITERACY.RST.6-8.1
- CCSS.ELA-LITERACY.RST.6-8.2

Learning Objectives:
- A. Gain perspective on vague writing
- B. Gain awareness of potential problems with "absolute" statements in writing
- C. Gain perspective on multiple answers

Is Nothing Something?

Instructions:
Place your answers to each challenge into a journal or folder

Challenge One:
Respond to the question, "Is nothing something?" Cite sources that defend your argument.(Analysis)

Challenge Two:
Respond to the question "Can something exist inside of nothing?" Provide example, if possible.(Analysis)

Here are recommendations to keep in mind when answering the above questions:
1. What is nothing?
2. What is something?
3. Is there more than one type of nothing?
4. Cite sources that defend your argument.

Suggested Start:
1. Pause before answering the question.
2. Using a dictionary, define "nothing".
3. Using a dictionary, define "something".
4. Operationalize "exist".

Potential Resources:
1.) Merriam-Webster.com
2.) Bartleby.com

Challenge Three:
Create a joke that you must answer in a figurative way and a literal way. Remember, keep it clean and respectful. NO PRACTICAL JOKES!(Analysis)

Example:
Joke(the setup): *They say "failure is a part of learning".*
Figurative answer (punchline): *Could someone please explain that to my parents.*
Literal answer: *This quote translates more often into "We learn from our mistakes". Whether a person is completing a quiz or learning to ride a bike, mistakes may occur, and they have the option to grow from their small failures.*

The secret to creating jokes is to ask questions about the world. In other words, analyze the world around you. If it doesn't make sense, question it. Then, research it.

To help, start with a statement like:
Why is it that..............
Ever notice that...........
Whose idea was it to make...
One day, there was a.................
Why does....
Where's the......
How is it that....

Don't forget to explore and explain the answer in a figurative and literal way. Creating jokes can be challenging. Worst case scenario, find and use a joke that you can answer in a figurative and literal way. Explain, why it is funny. Give credit to the comedian.

Challenge Four:
First, **define** the word, "Dilettante". Second, create a two column chart with a "negative factors" side and a "positive factors" side. Third, contrast the positive factors and negative issues of the word, "Dilettante". (Analysis)

Example:
According to _____'s dictionary, **failure** is....

Failure	
Negative Factors	**Positive Factors**
May spark negative emotions	Mistakes and failings are a part of the creation process
May affect interpersonal relationships	"When you quit that is true failure"
	Don't make failing a habit; however, if it happens, learn from your failure

Challenge Five:
Find an image. Then, create a chart that lists the directly observable features versus the not-visible, but inferable features of the image.(Analysis)

Example: Truck	
Observable and Visible	**Not Visible, but Inferable**
is a vehicle	has a driver
has tires	has steering wheel

Chapter 18
Section 3

Exploring Quotations on:
Perception

Common Core State Standards:
- CCSS.ELA-LITERACY.WHST.6-8.6
- CCSS.ELA-LITERACY.WHST.6-8.8
- CCSS.ELA-LITERACY.WHST.6-8.10
- CCSS.ELA-LITERACY.RH.6-8.1
- CCSS.ELA-LITERACY.RH.6-8.4
- CCSS.ELA-LITERACY.RH.6-8.7

Learning Objectives:
- A. Gain knowledge on the topic of "perception"
- B. Experience other perspectives on "perception"

Quotations on Perception

Instructions:
Place your answers to each challenge into a journal or folder

Challenge One:
Locate a quotation on the topic of "perception". (Knowledge)

Challenge Two:
Translate your selected quotation on "perception" into your own words.(Comprehension)

Challenge Three:
Compose a biographical statement using your chosen quotation on "perception".(Application)

Challenge Four:
Select or create a quote on "perception".(Synthesis)

Challenge Five:
Select or create a poem on "perception".(Synthesis)

Suggested Start:
1. Reflect on "perception".
2. Quotation resources are available at your local library.

Potential Resources:
1.) En.wikiquote.org
2.) Brainyquote.com
3.) Quotationspage.com

Challenge Six:
Using a quotation on "perception", discover a way to express the meaning through pictures and words. Then, create a comic strip that explains the quotation. (Synthesis)

Example:
"Hunger"
"Thou shouldst eat to live; not live to eat."
Socrates

Create a collection of images that relate to the quote. Then, add captions or messages that help express the quote. Lastly, connect images and create a comic strip.

Challenge Seven:
Complete the following sentence fragment with three or more separate statements. Figure out a way to incorporate a quotation, adage, or joke.(Application)

The documentary on perception...

Example:

The last movie that I saw...
1.) ...caused my mind to reflect on the possibilities of humans having superpowers. For instance, by combining advanced nanotechnology with our understanding of genetics, we could modify ourselves into more supercharged people.

2.) ...agitated me because it depicted the cruelties of mankind. However, I then reflected on an anonymous quote that "Unfortunately, the road to progress can have various levels of bumpiness".

3.) ...frightened me because it was a creepy horror film. Now, I want to sleep with the lights on, but my parents disagree. Even though, I don't pay the electric bill. I feel that I should be able to make this decision!

Chapter 18
Section 4

Exploration of Adages,
Aphorisms, Proverbs, and Maxims:

Common Core State Standards:
- CCSS.ELA-LITERACY.WHST.6-8.6
- CCSS.ELA-LITERACY.WHST.6-8.8
- CCSS.ELA-LITERACY.WHST.6-8.10
- CCSS.ELA-LITERACY.RH.6-8.4
- CCSS.ELA-LITERACY.RH.6-8.7

Learning Objectives:
- A. Experience perceptive sayings from various cultures
- B. Examine beliefs and understandings of various individuals and groups

Adages, Aphorisms, Proverbs, and Maxims

Instructions:
Place your answers to each challenge into a journal or folder

Challenge One:
Select an adage, aphorism, proverb, or maxim. Research the origin of the adage, aphorism, proverb, or maxim. Cite source(s).(Knowledge)

Challenge Two:
Translate your chosen adage, aphorism, proverb, or maxim into your own words.(Comprehension)

Challenge Three:
Compose a small paragraph or a short segment of dialogue that includes your chosen adage, aphorism, proverb, or maxim.(Application)

Challenge Four:
Do you agree or disagree with the message of your chosen adage, aphorism, proverb, or maxim. Defend your response. Cite sources.(Evaluation)

Suggested Start:
1. Reflect on your chosen adage, aphorism, proverb, or maxim.
2. Identify problems, if any.

Potential Resources:
   1.) En.wikiquote.org
   2.) Thinkexist.com

Challenge Five:

Select at least three pictures based on your selected adage, aphorism, proverb, or maxim. Next, build three posters by adding text to the chosen pictures. (Synthesis)

Suggested Start:
"Truth is Stranger than Fiction"

1. Make sure you understand the adage, aphorism, proverb, or maxim.
2. Reflect on the meaning(s) of your chosen adage, aphorism, proverb, or maxim.
3. Search for images that symbolize or reflect the adage, aphorism, proverb, or maxim.
4. Construct posters.

Challenge Six:

Is it better to <u>mimic</u> or <u>mock</u>?

In this exercise, consider possible scenarios when it is better to do one or the other underlined options. Next, find scenarios that benefit from each underlined option. Then, try to find scenarios that do not benefit from each underlined option. Create a chart that represents your conclusions. Lastly, compose statements using historical examples or scientific data that validate each item inside your chart. (Evaluation)

Example: Is it better to <u>spark</u> or <u>spur</u>?

Neither	Spark	Spur	Both
malice	critical thoughts	truthfulness	healthy behavior
hatred	cooperation	obedience	innovations
ignorance	motivation	horse	inventions
	confidence		imagination
			students
			self-control

    A. <u>Hatred</u> can <u>spark</u> destructive behavior such as... (insert historical example).

    B. Although, at times effective, spurred obedience has a limited shelf life; eventually, the spurred will rebel or revolt such as a child or colony...

    C. According to _____(author/researcher/expert), sparking confidence can boost students' comprehension.

Chapter 18
Section 5

Exploration of Business

Common Core State Standards:
- CCSS.ELA-LITERACY.WHST.6-8.6
- CCSS.ELA-LITERACY.WHST.6-8.7
- CCSS.ELA-LITERACY.WHST.6-8.8
- CCSS.ELA-LITERACY.WHST.6-8.9
- CCSS.ELA-LITERACY.WHST.6-8.10
- CCSS.ELA-LITERACY.RH.6-8.4
- CCSS.ELA-LITERACY.RH.6-8.7

Learning Objectives:
- A. Examine products and services from the view of an organizational entity such as a business
- B. Communicate information through graphics and text such as diagrams and charts

Product and Service Path

Instructions:
Place your answers to each challenge into a journal or folder

Challenge One:
Brainstorm a list of four discontinued products or services. Select one of the products or services.(Knowledge)

Challenge Two:
Identify the type of companies that produced your chosen product or service. Classify their industry. (Comprehension)

Challenge Three:
Identify three previous direct competitors of your chosen product or service. Describe and chart the competition based on business size (by employees), years available, marketing reach(local, regional, national, global), revenue and profits.(Analysis)

Main Product (Web Browsers)				
	Market Share	Business Size	Marketing Reach	Years Available
Internet Explorer (product)	2	large enterprise	global	19
Chrome (competitor)	1	large enterprise	global	6
Firefox (competitor)	3	mid-size	global	12
Opera (competitor)	4	mid-size	global	18

Challenge four:

Create a diagram that displays the major parts or sequences of your chosen product or service. Next explain two of the product's major parts. For example, an Xbox 360 has multiple, specialized parts such as the central processing unit, the graphics processing unit and the hard drive. Use graphics. Cite sources. (Analysis)

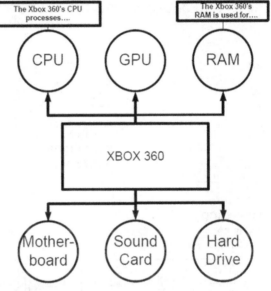

Challenge Five:

Based on your chosen product or service, identify three influential people that had a major impact on this industry through improvements, innovations, or inventions. Describe their effects on the industry. Cite sources.(Analysis)

Industry: Telecommunications		
insert image	John Doe	was an inventor whose radical and unorthodox methods produced the first....
insert image	Jane Doe	was an amazing engineer who invented the first....
insert image	Dr. Cooper	was a well-known and well-respected physician that accidentally invented....

Challenge Six:

Create an organizational chart (unofficial) of a company that offers your chosen product or service. Next, pinpoint the areas where your three previously chosen influential people would work. For example, if one of your selected influential people is a visionary executive leader, then they would fit somewhere at the top of the organizational chart(org chart).(Synthesis)

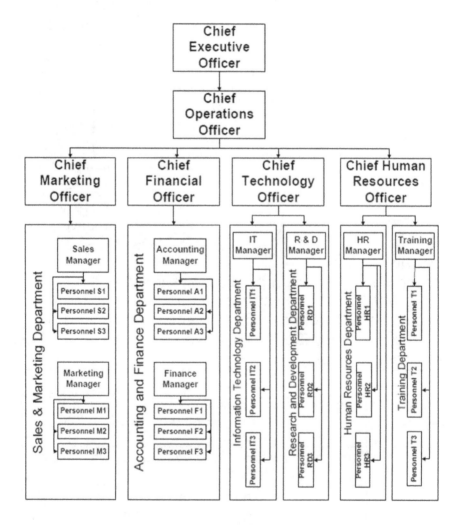

Challenge Seven:
Based on your gathered research and your product choice, create a visual flowchart or graphical diagram that demonstrates the interaction between human resources and non-human resources to produce the product or service. Start with the necessary (raw) materials required to produce the product or service. For example, an organic farmer needs supplies, materials, equipment, and workers. Then, your flowchart should display the interactions between the workforce and resources until the end-product reaches consumers. (Synthesis)

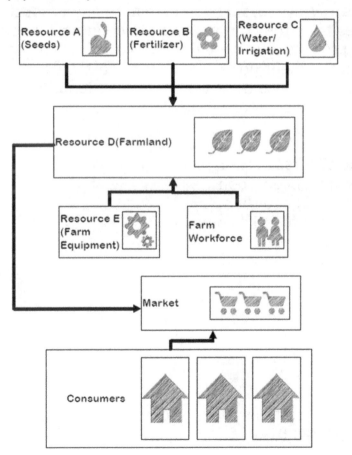

Challenge Eight:
Based on your product choice or service selection,
- Identify two supplemental/complementary products or services such as computer applications complement computer operating systems
- Identify two required/necessary products (computer operating system are necessary to operate computers)
- Identify two separate or indirectly connected products or services that the company produces(Xbox 360 or Zune)

Discover which product(s) was/is your strongest seller(s). Why? Would you eliminate any products or services from the company's product lineup? Explain. Which product or service deserves the most research and development now? Elaborate. Lastly, which product or service deserves the most marketing now. Explain. Cite sources.(Evaluation)

Potential Resources:
- www.bls.gov/ooh
- www.bls.gov/iag
- howstuffworks.com
- visual.merriam-webster.com
- finance.yahoo.com
- ehow.com
- sba.gov
- entrepreneur.com

Rubric for Chapter
See Appendix A

Reflective Questions for Chapter
See Appendix B

Chapter 19

Connections to Common Core State Standards:

CCSS.ELA-LITERACY.WHST.6-8.6
Use technology, including the Internet, to produce and publish writing and present the relationships between information and ideas clearly and efficiently.(2010)

CCSS.ELA-LITERACY.WHST.6-8.7
Conduct short research projects to answer a question(including a self-generated question), drawing on several sources and generating additional related, focused questions that allow for multiple avenues of exploration.(2010)

CCSS.ELA-LITERACY.WHST.6-8.8
Gather relevant information from multiple print and digital sources, using search terms effectively; assess the credibility and accuracy of each source; and quote or paraphrase the data and conclusions of others while avoiding plagiarism and following a standard form of citation.(2010)

CCSS.ELA-LITERACY.WHST.6-8.9
Draw evidence from informational texts to support analysis, reflection, and research.(2010)

Connections to
Common Core State Standards:
(continued)

CCSS.ELA-LITERACY.WHST.6-8.10
Write routinely over extended time frames(time for revision and reflection) and shorter time frames(a single sitting or a day or two) for a range of discipline-specific tasks, purposes, and audiences.(2010)

CCSS.ELA-LITERACY.RH.6-8.1
Cite specific textual evidence to support analysis of primary and secondary sources.(2010)

CCSS.ELA-LITERACY.RH.6-8.4
Determine the meaning of words and phrases as they are used in a text, including vocabulary specific to domains related to history/social studies.(2010)

CCSS.ELA-LITERACY.RH.6-8.7
Integrate visual information(e.g., in charts, graphs, photographs, videos, or maps) with other information in print and digital text.(2010)

CCSS.ELA-LITERACY.RST.6-8.1
Cite specific textual evidence to support analysis of science and technical texts.(2010)

CCSS.ELA-LITERACY.RST.6-8.2
Determine the central ideas or conclusions of a text; provide an accurate summary of the text distinct from prior knowledge or opinions.(2010)

CCSS.ELA-LITERACY.RST.6-8.
Distinguish among facts, reasoned judgment based on research findings, and speculation in text.(2010)

Chapter 19
Section 1

Exploration of the Idiom:
Have a Heart

Common Core State Standards:
- CCSS.ELA-LITERACY.WHST.6-8.8
- CCSS.ELA-LITERACY.WHST.6-8.10
- CCSS.ELA-LITERACY.RH.6-8.4
- CCSS.ELA-LITERACY.RH.6-8.7

Learning Objectives:
- A. Understand the figurative meaning of idioms
- B. Comprehend the problematic issues with literal translations of idioms

Have a Heart

Instructions:
Place your answers to each challenge into a journal or folder

Challenge One:
Translate "Have a Heart" **into your own words**. (Comprehension)

Challenge Two:
Create two separate sentences using the idiom "Have a Heart".(Application)

Challenge Three:
Identify another idiom that is similar to "Have a Heart".(Analysis)

Challenge Four:
List **fictional** characters that "Had a Heart" during their fictional work.(Analysis)

Challenge Five:
List **fictional** characters that had a "Change of Heart". Provide examples of their behavior before they had a "Change of Heart". Describe their behavior after they had a "Change of Heart".(Analysis)

Suggested Start:
Using an American English Idiom dictionary, define the figurative meaning of "Have a Heart".

Potential Resources:
      1.) Idioms.thefreedictionary.com
      2.) Dictionary.reference.com/idioms

Challenge Six:

Create, draw or sketch three **individual** objects that represent the word "Backward". Based on your images, explain the connection(s) to the subject.(Synthesis)

Example 1:
Humbled

Example 2:
Driven

Challenge Seven:
Create two or more images that express the statement "His heart was fluttering!" But, use as few images and letters as possible. Then, repeat this process with the thought, "Biomedical engineering is the future". Communicate the subtle or overt meaning of the objects inside your images.(Synthesis)
Example One: *I dislike pandas.*

Example Two: *I love pandas.*

Chapter 19
Section 2

Perspectives on:
Zero

Common Core State Standards:
- CCSS.ELA-LITERACY.WHST.6-8.7
- CCSS.ELA-LITERACY.WHST.6-8.8
- CCSS.ELA-LITERACY.WHST.6-8.10
- CCSS.ELA-LITERACY.RST.6-8.1
- CCSS.ELA-LITERACY.RST.6-8.2

Learning Objectives:
- A. Gain perspective on vague writing
- B. Gain awareness of potential problems with "absolute" statements in writing
- C. Gain perspective on multiple answers

Zero is a Recently Discovered Concept or Invention

Instructions:
Place your answers to each challenge into a journal or folder

Challenge One:
Respond to the statement, "Zero is a recently discovered concept or invention? Cite sources that defend your response.(Analysis)

Challenge Two:
Explain the concept of zero. Explain the historical invention of zero. Explain the first known usage of zero.(Evaluation)

Here are recommendations to keep in mind when answering the above questions:
1. What is zero?
2. What is the known history of zero?
3. What is the historical significance of zero?
4. Cite sources that defend your argument.

Suggested Start:
1. Pause before answering the question.
2. Using a dictionary, define "zero".
3. Using an encyclopedia, research "Mathematics".
4. Research "History of Mathematics"

Potential Resources:
1.) Bartleby.com

Challenge Three:
Create a joke that you must answer in a figurative way and a literal way. Remember, keep it clean and respectful. NO PRACTICAL JOKES!(Analysis)

Example:
Joke(the setup): *They say "failure is a part of learning".*
Figurative answer (punchline): *Could someone please explain that to my parents.*
Literal answer: *This quote translates more often into "We learn from our mistakes". Whether a person is completing a quiz or learning to ride a bike, mistakes may occur, and they have the option to grow from their small failures.*

The secret to creating jokes is to ask questions about the world. In other words, analyze the world around you. If it doesn't make sense, question it. Then, research it.

To help, start with a statement like:
Why is it that...............
Ever notice that...........
Whose idea was it to make...
One day, there was a.................
Why does....
Where's the......
How is it that....

Don't forget to explore and explain the answer in a figurative and literal way. Creating jokes can be challenging. Worst case scenario, find and use a joke that you can answer in a figurative and literal way. Explain, why it is funny. Give credit to the comedian.

Challenge Four:

First, **define** the word, "Insightful". Second, create a two column chart with a "negative factors" side and a "positive factors" side. Third, contrast the positive factors and negative issues of the word, "Insightful". (Analysis)

Example:

According to _____'s dictionary, **failure** is....

Failure	
Negative Factors	**Positive Factors**
May spark negative emotions	Mistakes and failings are a part of the creation process
May affect interpersonal relationships	"When you quit that is true failure"
	Don't make failing a habit; however, if it happens, learn from your failure

Challenge Five:

Find an image. Then, create a chart that lists the directly observable features versus the not-visible, but inferable features of the image.(Analysis)

Example: Train	
Observable and Visible	**Not Visible, but Inferable**
is a vehicle	holds passengers
is on railroad tracks	holds cargo

Chapter 19
Section 3

Exploring Quotations on:
Curiosity

Common Core State Standards:
- CCSS.ELA-LITERACY.WHST.6-8.6
- CCSS.ELA-LITERACY.WHST.6-8.8
- CCSS.ELA-LITERACY.WHST.6-8.10
- CCSS.ELA-LITERACY.RH.6-8.1
- CCSS.ELA-LITERACY.RH.6-8.4
- CCSS.ELA-LITERACY.RH.6-8.7

Learning Objectives:
- A. Gain knowledge on the topic of "curiosity"
- B. Experience other perspectives on "curiosity"

Quotations on Curiosity

Instructions:
Place your answers to each challenge into a journal or folder

Challenge One:
Locate a quotation on the topic of "curiosity".(Knowledge)

Challenge Two:
Translate your selected quotation on "curiosity" into your own words.(Comprehension)

Challenge Three:
Compose a biographical statement using your chosen quotation on "curiosity".(Application)

Challenge Four:
Create your own quote on "curiosity".(Synthesis)

Challenge Five:
Choose or create a poem on "curiosity".(Synthesis)

Suggested Start:
1. Reflect on "curiosity" and "learning".
2. Quotation resources are available at your local library.

Potential Resources:
1.) En.wikiquote.org
2.) Brainyquote.com
3.) Quotationspage.com

Challenge Six:
Using a quotation on "Curiosity", discover a way to express the meaning through pictures and words. Then, create a comic strip that explains the quotation.(Synthesis)

Example:
"Hunger"
"Thou shouldst eat to live; not live to eat."
Socrates

Create a collection of images that relate to the quote. Then, add captions or messages that help express the quote. Lastly, connect images and create a comic strip.

Challenge Seven:
Complete the following sentence fragment with three or more separate statements. Figure out a way to incorporate a quotation, adage, or joke.(Application)

Curiosity creates...

Example:

The last movie that I saw...
1.) ...caused my mind to reflect on the possibilities of humans having superpowers. For instance, by combining advanced nanotechnology with our understanding of genetics, we could modify ourselves into more supercharged people.

2.) ...agitated me because it depicted the cruelties of mankind. However, I then reflected on an anonymous quote that "Unfortunately, the road to progress can have various levels of bumpiness".

3.) ...frightened me because it was a creepy horror film. Now, I want to sleep with the lights on, but my parents disagree. Even though, I don't pay the electric bill. I feel that I should be able to make this decision!

Chapter 19
Section 4

Exploration of Adages,
Aphorisms, Proverbs, and Maxims:

Common Core State Standards:
- CCSS.ELA-LITERACY.WHST.6-8.6
- CCSS.ELA-LITERACY.WHST.6-8.8
- CCSS.ELA-LITERACY.WHST.6-8.10
- CCSS.ELA-LITERACY.RH.6-8.4
- CCSS.ELA-LITERACY.RH.6-8.7

Learning Objectives:
- A. Experience perceptive sayings from various cultures
- B. Examine beliefs and understandings of various individuals and groups

Adages, Aphorisms, Proverbs, and Maxims

Instructions:
Place your answers to each challenge into a journal or folder

Challenge One:
Select an adage, aphorism, proverb, or maxim. Research the origin of the adage, aphorism, proverb, or maxim. Cite source(s).(Knowledge)

Challenge Two:
Translate your chosen adage, aphorism, proverb, or maxim into your own words.(Comprehension)

Challenge Three:
Compose a small paragraph or a short segment of dialogue that includes your chosen adage, aphorism, proverb, or maxim.(Application)

Challenge Four:
Do you agree or disagree with the message of your chosen adage, aphorism, proverb, or maxim. Defend your response. Cite sources.(Evaluation)

Suggested Start:
1. Reflect on your chosen adage, aphorism, proverb, or maxim.
2. Identify problems, if any.

Potential Resources:
1.) En.wikiquote.org
2.) Thinkexist.com

Challenge Five:
Select at least three pictures based on your selected adage, aphorism, proverb, or maxim. Next, build three posters by adding text to the chosen pictures. (Synthesis)

Suggested Start:
"Truth is Stranger than Fiction"
1. Make sure you understand the adage, aphorism, proverb, or maxim.
2. Reflect on the meaning(s) of your chosen adage, aphorism, proverb, or maxim.
3. Search for images that symbolize or reflect the adage, aphorism, proverb, or maxim.
4. Construct posters.

Challenge Six:

Is it better to <u>force</u> or <u>coerce</u>?

In this exercise, consider possible scenarios when it is better to do one or the other underlined options. Next, find scenarios that benefit from each underlined option. Then, try to find scenarios that do not benefit from each underlined option. Create a chart that represents your conclusions. Lastly, compose statements using historical examples or scientific data that validate each item inside your chart. (Evaluation)

Example: Is it better to <u>spark</u> or <u>spur</u>?

Neither	Spark	Spur	Both
malice	critical thoughts	truthfulness	healthy behavior
hatred	cooperation	obedience	innovations
ignorance	motivation	horse	inventions
	confidence		imagination
			students
			self-control

   A. <u>Hatred</u> can <u>spark</u> destructive behavior such as... (insert historical example).
   B. Although, at times effective, spurred obedience has a limited shelf life; eventually, the spurred will rebel or revolt such as a child or colony...
   C. According to _____(author/researcher/expert), sparking confidence can boost students' comprehension.

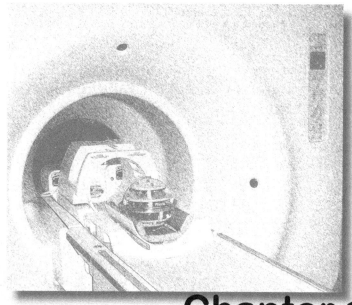

Chapter 19
Section 5

Exploration of Business

Common Core State Standards:
- CCSS.ELA-LITERACY.WHST.6-8.6
- CCSS.ELA-LITERACY.WHST.6-8.7
- CCSS.ELA-LITERACY.WHST.6-8.8
- CCSS.ELA-LITERACY.WHST.6-8.9
- CCSS.ELA-LITERACY.WHST.6-8.10
- CCSS.ELA-LITERACY.RH.6-8.4
- CCSS.ELA-LITERACY.RH.6-8.7

Learning Objectives:
A. Examine business costs and opportunities
B. Communicate information through graphics and text such as diagrams and charts

Organization Path

Instructions:
Place your answers to each challenge into a journal or folder

Challenge One:
Brainstorm a list of four businesses that offer fun products or services. Choose one of the businesses. Then, classify the business by type. Identify its main product.(Knowledge)

Challenge Two:
Identify three competitors of this business.(Comprehension)

Challenge Three:
Identify three products or services of your chosen company. Create a chart that displays the relationship among the main product and the additional products. Determine if these products are:
- Integrated and necessary for the main product to operate such as gasoline or motor oil for cars
- Complementary to the product and enhances product like air conditioning and power windows for cars
- Vital to the business such as their brand brake pads and spark plugs for cars(Application)

Main Product(Windows Operating System)			
	Integrated and Necessary	Enhances Main Product	Vital to Business
Microsoft Office	No	Yes	Yes
Internet Explorer	Yes	Yes	Yes
Xbox 360	No	No	No

Challenge Four:

Categorize the four chosen products by popularity among consumers, history of the products, revenue, profit, target audience(name their main customers), and strongest direct competitor, quasi-competitor and indirect competitor. Use a scale from 4 to 1, 4 being highest, to grade each category. Then, based on your chart, describe the growth potential (or lack of future potential) of each product. Which product is the strongest? Which product would you focus more resources on for the future of the company. Defend your decision. Cite sources.(Analysis)

Strengths and Weaknesses				
	Windows OS	Microsoft Office	Internet Explorer	Xbox 360
Popularity	3	4	2	1
Revenue	3	4	2	1
Profitabil-ity	3	4	2	1

Strengths and Weaknesses by Details				
	Windows OS	Microsoft Office	Internet Explorer	Xbox 360
Years Available	28 yrs.	23 yrs.	19 yrs.	8 yrs.
Direct Competitor	Mac OS X	LibreOf-fice	Chrome	Playsta-tion 3
Quasi-Competitor	Android OS	QuickOf-fice	Smart-TVs	Gameboy Advance
Indirect Competitor	Pen and Paper	Typewriter	Library Card	Mobile Device
Rankings among direct Competitors	#1	#1	#2	#1

Challenge Five:

Choose one of your chosen company's most popular or well-known products or services. Research this product or service and build a diagram that displays the fabrication process of the product or service. Cite sources.(Synthesis)

Your diagram or chart should display the work that goes into producing a product or service.

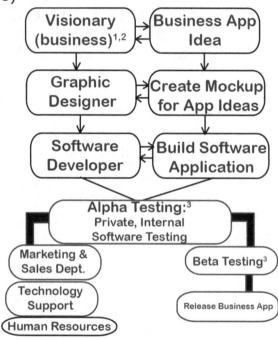

1 Does the app solve a problem?
2 Can it be profitable?
3 Testing may require restarts or revisions.

Challenge Six:

Create a chart that explains two of the product's major features. For example, an alarm clock normally has a minimum of two features, the time display and the alarm function. Use graphics, if possible. Cite sources.(Analysis)

Alarm Radio	
Radio	converts radio waves...
Alarm Buzzer	is a feature of the...

Challenge Seven:

Based on your gathered research and your product choice, create a visual flowchart or graphical diagram that demonstrates the interaction between human resources and non-human resources to produce the product or service. Start with the necessary (raw) materials required to produce the product or service. For example, an organic farmer needs supplies, materials, equipment, and workers. Then, your flowchart should display the interactions between the workforce and resources until the end-product reaches consumers. (Synthesis)

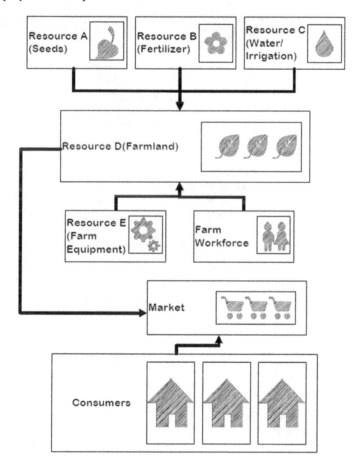

Challenge Eight:

Identify three individuals that had a major impact on your chosen company's industry. Create a multi-media chart to describe their impact. Based on your research of these three individuals, which individual had the biggest impact on their industry. Defend your argument. Cite sources.(Evaluation)

Industry: Telecommunications		
insert image	John Doe	was an inventor whose radical and unorthodox methods produced the first....
insert image	Jane Doe	was an amazing engineer who invented the first....
insert image	Dr. Cooper	was a well-known and well-respected physician that accidentally invented....

Potential Resources:
- www.bls.gov/ooh
- www.bls.gov/iag
- howstuffworks.com
- visual.merriam-webster.com
- finance.yahoo.com
- ehow.com
- sba.gov
- entrepreneur.com

Rubric for Chapter
See Appendix A

Reflective Questions for Chapter
See Appendix B

Chapter 20

Connections to Common Core State Standards:

CCSS.ELA-LITERACY.WHST.6-8.6
Use technology, including the Internet, to produce and publish writing and present the relationships between information and ideas clearly and efficiently.(2010)

CCSS.ELA-LITERACY.WHST.6-8.7
Conduct short research projects to answer a question(including a self-generated question), drawing on several sources and generating additional related, focused questions that allow for multiple avenues of exploration.(2010)

CCSS.ELA-LITERACY.WHST.6-8.8
Gather relevant information from multiple print and digital sources, using search terms effectively; assess the credibility and accuracy of each source; and quote or paraphrase the data and conclusions of others while avoiding plagiarism and following a standard form of citation.(2010)

CCSS.ELA-LITERACY.WHST.6-8.9
Draw evidence from informational texts to support analysis, reflection, and research.(2010)

Connections to
Common Core State Standards:
<u>(continued)</u>

CCSS.ELA-LITERACY.WHST.6-8.10
Write routinely over extended time frames(time for revision and reflection) and shorter time frames(a single sitting or a day or two) for a range of discipline-specific tasks, purposes, and audiences.(2010)

CCSS.ELA-LITERACY.RH.6-8.1
Cite specific textual evidence to support analysis of primary and secondary sources.(2010)

CCSS.ELA-LITERACY.RH.6-8.4
Determine the meaning of words and phrases as they are used in a text, including vocabulary specific to domains related to history/social studies.(2010)

CCSS.ELA-LITERACY.RH.6-8.7
Integrate visual information(e.g., in charts, graphs, photographs, videos, or maps) with other information in print and digital text.(2010)

CCSS.ELA-LITERACY.RST.6-8.1
Cite specific textual evidence to support analysis of science and technical texts.(2010)

CCSS.ELA-LITERACY.RST.6-8.2
Determine the central ideas or conclusions of a text; provide an accurate summary of the text distinct from prior knowledge or opinions.(2010)

CCSS.ELA-LITERACY.RST.6-8.
Distinguish among facts, reasoned judgment based on research findings, and speculation in text.(2010)

Chapter 20
Section 1

Exploration of the Idiom: Like a Fish out of Water

Common Core State Standards:
- CCSS.ELA-LITERACY.WHST.6-8.8
- CCSS.ELA-LITERACY.WHST.6-8.10
- CCSS.ELA-LITERACY.RH.6-8.4
- CCSS.ELA-LITERACY.RH.6-8.7

Learning Objectives:
A. Understand the figurative meaning of idioms
B. Comprehend the problematic issues with literal translations of idioms

Like a Fish out of Water

Instructions:
Place your answers to each challenge into a journal or folder

Challenge One:
Translate "Like a Fish out of Water" **into your own words**.(Comprehension)

Challenge Two:
Create two separate sentences using the idiom "Like a Fish out of Water".(Application)

Challenge Three:
Identify another idiom that is similar to "Like a Fish out of Water".(Analysis)

Challenge Four:
List **fictional** characters that were "fish out of water". Describe. Illustrate, why.(Analysis)

Challenge Five:
List historical figures that were "fish out of water". Describe and defend through research. Cite sources. (Analysis)

Suggested Start:
Using an American English Idiom dictionary, define the figurative meaning of "Like a Fish out of Water".

Potential Resources:
    1.) Idioms.thefreedictionary.com
    2.) Dictionary.reference.com/idioms

Challenge Six:

Create, draw or sketch three **individual** objects that represent the word "Unfathomable". Based on your images, explain the connection(s) to the subject.(Synthesis)

Example 1:
Humbled

Example 2:
Driven

Challenge Seven:

Create two or more images that express the feeling "These are my possessions!" But, use as few images and letters as possible. Then, repeat this process with the thought, "I need to improve my study habits!". Communicate the subtle or overt meaning of the objects inside your images.(Synthesis)

Example One: *I dislike pigeons.*

Example Two: *I love pigeons.*

Chapter 20
Section 2

Perspectives on:
Danger

Common Core State Standards:
- CCSS.ELA-LITERACY.WHST.6-8.7
- CCSS.ELA-LITERACY.WHST.6-8.8
- CCSS.ELA-LITERACY.WHST.6-8.10
- CCSS.ELA-LITERACY.RST.6-8.1
- CCSS.ELA-LITERACY.RST.6-8.2

Learning Objectives:
A. Gain perspective on vague writing
B. Gain awareness of potential problems with "absolute" statements in writing
C. Gain perspective on multiple answers

Nothing Can be Gained from Venom

Instructions:
Place your answers to each challenge into a journal or folder

Challenge One:
Respond to the statement, "Nothing can be gained from venom". Cite sources that defend your response.(Analysis)

Challenge Two:
Respond to the statement, "Nothing positive can be gained from venom". Cite sources that defend your response.(Evaluation)

Here are recommendations to keep in mind when answering the above questions:
1. What is venom?
2. What is the standard goal of venom?
3. Cite sources that defend your argument.

Suggested Start:
   1. Pause before answering the question.
   2. Using a dictionary, define "venom".
   3. Using an encyclopedia, research "venom".

Potential Resources:
   1.) Merriam-Webster.com
   2.) Bartleby.com

Challenge Three:
Create a joke that you must answer in a figurative way and a literal way. Remember, keep it clean and respectful. NO PRACTICAL JOKES!(Analysis)

Example:
Joke(the setup): *They say "failure is a part of learning".*
Figurative answer (punchline): *Could someone please explain that to my parents.*
Literal answer: *This quote translates more often into "We learn from our mistakes". Whether a person is completing a quiz or learning to ride a bike, mistakes may occur, and they have the option to grow from their small failures.*

The secret to creating jokes is to ask questions about the world. In other words, analyze the world around you. If it doesn't make sense, question it. Then, research it.

To help, start with a statement like:
   Why is it that...............
   Ever notice that...........
   Whose idea was it to make...
   One day, there was a.................
   Why does....
   Where's the......
   How is it that....

Don't forget to explore and explain the answer in a figurative and literal way. Creating jokes can be challenging. Worst case scenario, find and use a joke that you can answer in a figurative and literal way. Explain, why it is funny. Give credit to the comedian.

Challenge Four:

First, **define** the word, "Arrogant". Second, create a two column chart with a "negative factors" side and a "positive factors" side. Third, contrast the positive factors and negative issues of the word, "Arrogant". (Analysis)

Example:

According to _____'s dictionary, **failure** is....

Failure	
Negative Factors	**Positive Factors**
May spark negative emotions	Mistakes and failings are a part of the creation process
May affect interpersonal relationships	"When you quit that is true failure"
	Don't make failing a habit; however, if it happens, learn from your failure

Challenge Five:

Find an image. Then, create a chart that lists the directly observable features versus the not-visible, but inferable features of the image.(Analysis)

Example: Trolley	
Observable and Visible	**Not Visible, but Inferable**
is a vehicle	holds passengers
is on tracks	has conductor
is not jet propelled	has controls

Chapter 20
Section 3

Exploring Quotations on:
Motivation

Common Core State Standards:
- CCSS.ELA-LITERACY.WHST.6-8.6
- CCSS.ELA-LITERACY.WHST.6-8.8
- CCSS.ELA-LITERACY.WHST.6-8.10
- CCSS.ELA-LITERACY.RH.6-8.1
- CCSS.ELA-LITERACY.RH.6-8.4
- CCSS.ELA-LITERACY.RH.6-8.7

Learning Objectives:
- A. Gain knowledge on the topic of "motivation"
- B. Experience other perspectives on "motivation"

Quotations on Motivation

Instructions:
Place your answers to each challenge into a journal or folder

Challenge One:
Locate a quotation on the topic of "motivation". (knowledge)

Challenge Two:
Translate your selected quotation on "motivation" into your own words.(Comprehension)

Challenge Three:
Compose a biographical statement using your chosen quotation on "motivation".(Application)

Challenge Four:
Create your own quote on "motivation".(Synthesis)

Challenge Five:
Choose or create a poem on "motivation".(Synthesis)

Suggested Start:
1. Reflect on motivational experiences.
2. Quotation resources are available at your local library.

Potential Resources:
1.) En.wikiquote.org
2.) Brainyquote.com
3.) Quotationspage.com

Challenge Six:

Using a quotation on "motivation", discover a way to express the meaning through pictures and words. Then, create a comic strip that explains the quotation. (Synthesis)

Example:
"Hunger"
"Thou shouldst eat to live; not live to eat."
Socrates

Create a collection of images that relate to the quote. Then, add captions or messages that help express the quote. Lastly, connect images and create a comic strip.

Challenge Seven:

Complete the following sentence fragment with three or more separate statements. Figure out a way to incorporate a quotation, adage, or joke.(Application)

Motivational seminars...

Example:

The last movie that I saw...

1.) ...caused my mind to reflect on the possibilities of humans having superpowers. For instance, by combining advanced nanotechnology with our understanding of genetics, we could modify ourselves into more supercharged people.

2.) ...agitated me because it depicted the cruelties of mankind. However, I then reflected on an anonymous quote that "Unfortunately, the road to progress can have various levels of bumpiness".

3.) ...frightened me because it was a creepy horror film. Now, I want to sleep with the lights on, but my parents disagree. Even though, I don't pay the electric bill. I feel that I should be able to make this decision!

Chapter 20
Section 4

Exploration of Adages,
Aphorisms, Proverbs, and Maxims:

Common Core State Standards:
- CCSS.ELA-LITERACY.WHST.6-8.6
- CCSS.ELA-LITERACY.WHST.6-8.8
- CCSS.ELA-LITERACY.WHST.6-8.10
- CCSS.ELA-LITERACY.RH.6-8.4
- CCSS.ELA-LITERACY.RH.6-8.7

Learning Objectives:
- A. Experience perceptive sayings from various cultures
- B. Examine beliefs and understandings of various individuals and groups

Adages, Aphorisms, Proverbs, and Maxims

Instructions:
Place your answers to each challenge into a journal or folder

Challenge One:
Select an adage, aphorism, proverb, or maxim. Research the origin of the adage, aphorism, proverb, or maxim. Cite source(s).(Knowledge)

Challenge Two:
Translate your chosen adage, aphorism, proverb, or maxim into your own words.(Comprehension)

Challenge Three:
Compose a small paragraph or a short segment of dialogue that includes your chosen adage, aphorism, proverb, or maxim.(Application)

Challenge Four:
Do you agree or disagree with the message of your chosen adage, aphorism, proverb, or maxim. Defend your response. Cite sources.(Evaluation)

Suggested Start:
1. Reflect on your chosen adage, aphorism, proverb, or maxim.
2. Identify problems, if any.

Potential Resources:
1.) En.wikiquote.org
2.) Thinkexist.com

Challenge Five:
Select at least three pictures based on your selected adage, aphorism, proverb, or maxim. Next, build three posters by adding text to the chosen pictures. (Synthesis)

Suggested Start:
"Truth is Stranger than Fiction"
1. Make sure you understand the adage, aphorism, proverb, or maxim.
2. Reflect on the meaning(s) of your chosen adage, aphorism, proverb, or maxim.
3. Search for images that symbolize or reflect the adage, aphorism, proverb, or maxim.
4. Construct posters.

Challenge Six:

Is it better to <u>enjoy</u> or <u>exploit</u>?

In this exercise, consider possible scenarios when it is better to do one or the other underlined options. Next, find scenarios that benefit from each underlined option. Then, try to find scenarios that do not benefit from each underlined option. Create a chart that represents your conclusions. Lastly, compose statements using historical examples or scientific data that validate each item inside your chart. (Evaluation)

Example: Is it better to <u>spark</u> or <u>spur</u>?

Neither	Spark	Spur	Both
malice	critical thoughts	truthfulness	healthy behavior
hatred	cooperation	obedience	innovations
ignorance	motivation	horse	inventions
	confidence		imagination
			students
			self-control

  A. <u>Hatred</u> can <u>spark</u> destructive behavior such as... (insert historical example).
  B. Although, at times effective, spurred obedience has a limited shelf life; eventually, the spurred will rebel or revolt such as a child or colony...
  C. According to _____(author/researcher/expert), sparking confidence can boost students' comprehension.

Chapter 20
Section 5

Exploration of Business

Common Core State Standards:
- CCSS.ELA-LITERACY.WHST.6-8.6
- CCSS.ELA-LITERACY.WHST.6-8.7
- CCSS.ELA-LITERACY.WHST.6-8.8
- CCSS.ELA-LITERACY.WHST.6-8.9
- CCSS.ELA-LITERACY.WHST.6-8.10
- CCSS.ELA-LITERACY.RH.6-8.4
- CCSS.ELA-LITERACY.RH.6-8.7

Learning Objectives:
- A. Examine products and services from the view of an organizational entity such as a business
- B. Communicate information through graphics and text such as diagrams and charts

Product and Service Path

Instructions:
Place your answers to each challenge into a journal or folder

Challenge One:
Identify the greatest product or service ever invented. (Knowledge)

Challenge Two:
Identify the type of companies that produce your chosen product or service. Classify their industry.(Comprehension)

Challenge Three:
Identify three direct competitors of your chosen product or service. Describe and chart the competition based on market share, business size (by employees), years available, marketing reach(local, regional, national, global), revenue and profits. Research and use industry averages if your chosen company or its competitors are not publicly traded.(Analysis)

Main Product (Web Browsers)				
	Market Share	**Business Size**	**Marketing Reach**	**Years Available**
Internet Explorer (product)	2	large enterprise	global	19
Chrome (competitor)	1	large enterprise	global	6
Firefox (competitor)	3	mid-size	global	12
Opera (competitor)	4	mid-size	global	18

Challenge four:

Create a diagram that displays the major parts or sequences of your chosen product or service. Next explain two of the product's major parts. For example, an Xbox 360 has multiple, specialized parts such as the central processing unit, the graphics processing unit and the hard drive. Use graphics. Cite sources. (Analysis)

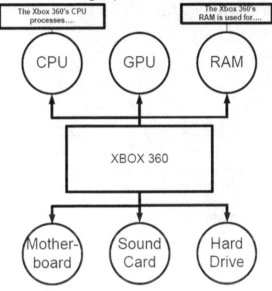

Challenge Five:

Based on your chosen product or service, identify three influential people that had a major impact on this industry through improvements, innovations, or inventions. Describe their effects on the industry. Cite sources.(Analysis)

Industry: Telecommunications		
insert image	John Doe	was an inventor whose radical and unorthodox methods produced the first....
insert image	Jane Doe	was an amazing engineer who invented the first....
insert image	Dr. Cooper	was a well-known and well-respected physician that accidentally invented....

Challenge Six:
Create an organizational chart (unofficial) of a company that offers your chosen product or service. Next, pinpoint the areas where your three previously chosen influential people would work. For example, if one of your selected influential people is a visionary executive leader, then they would fit somewhere at the top of the organizational chart(org chart).(Synthesis)

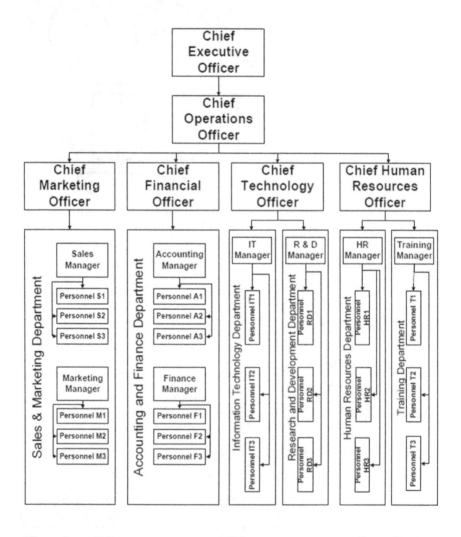

Challenge Seven:

Based on your gathered research and your product choice, create a visual flowchart or graphical diagram that demonstrates the interaction between human resources and non-human resources to produce the product or service. Start with the necessary (raw) materials required to produce the product or service. For example, an organic farmer needs supplies, materials, equipment, and workers. Then, your flowchart should display the interactions between the workforce and resources until the end-product reaches consumers. (Synthesis)

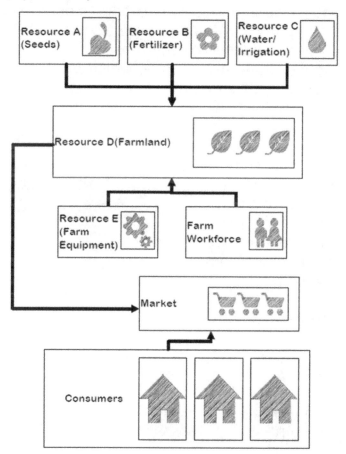

Challenge Eight:

Based on your product choice or service selection,

- Identify two supplemental/complementary products or services such as computer applications complement computer operating systems
- Identify two required/necessary products (computer operating system are necessary to operate computers)
- Identify two separate or indirectly connected products or services that the company produces(Xbox 360 or Zune)

Discover which product(s) is your strongest seller(s). Why? Would you eliminate any products or services from the company's product lineup? Explain. Which product or service deserves the most research and development? Elaborate. Lastly, which product or service deserves the most marketing. Explain. Cite sources.(Evaluation)

Potential Resources:

- www.bls.gov/ooh
- www.bls.gov/iag
- howstuffworks.com
- visual.merriam-webster.com
- finance.yahoo.com
- ehow.com
- sba.gov
- entrepreneur.com

Rubric for Chapter
See Appendix A

Reflective Questions for Chapter
See Appendix B

Chapter 21

Connections to Common Core State Standards:

CCSS.ELA-LITERACY.WHST.6-8.6
Use technology, including the Internet, to produce and publish writing and present the relationships between information and ideas clearly and efficiently.(2010)

CCSS.ELA-LITERACY.WHST.6-8.7
Conduct short research projects to answer a question(including a self-generated question), drawing on several sources and generating additional related, focused questions that allow for multiple avenues of exploration.(2010)

CCSS.ELA-LITERACY.WHST.6-8.8
Gather relevant information from multiple print and digital sources, using search terms effectively; assess the credibility and accuracy of each source; and quote or paraphrase the data and conclusions of others while avoiding plagiarism and following a standard form of citation.(2010)

CCSS.ELA-LITERACY.WHST.6-8.9
Draw evidence from informational texts to support analysis, reflection, and research.(2010)

Connections to
Common Core State Standards:
(continued)

CCSS.ELA-LITERACY.WHST.6-8.10
Write routinely over extended time frames(time for revision and reflection) and shorter time frames(a single sitting or a day or two) for a range of discipline-specific tasks, purposes, and audiences.(2010)

CCSS.ELA-LITERACY.RH.6-8.1
Cite specific textual evidence to support analysis of primary and secondary sources.(2010)

CCSS.ELA-LITERACY.RH.6-8.4
Determine the meaning of words and phrases as they are used in a text, including vocabulary specific to domains related to history/social studies.(2010)

CCSS.ELA-LITERACY.RH.6-8.7
Integrate visual information(e.g., in charts, graphs, photographs, videos, or maps) with other information in print and digital text.(2010)

CCSS.ELA-LITERACY.RST.6-8.1
Cite specific textual evidence to support analysis of science and technical texts.(2010)

CCSS.ELA-LITERACY.RST.6-8.2
Determine the central ideas or conclusions of a text; provide an accurate summary of the text distinct from prior knowledge or opinions.(2010)

CCSS.ELA-LITERACY.RST.6-8.
Distinguish among facts, reasoned judgment based on research findings, and speculation in text.(2010)

Chapter 21
Section 1

Exploration of the Idiom: As Quiet as a Mouse

Common Core State Standards:
- CCSS.ELA-LITERACY.WHST.6-8.8
- CCSS.ELA-LITERACY.WHST.6-8.10
- CCSS.ELA-LITERACY.RH.6-8.4
- CCSS.ELA-LITERACY.RH.6-8.7

Learning Objectives:
- A. Understand the figurative meaning of idioms
- B. Comprehend the problematic issues with literal translations of idioms

As Quiet as a Mouse

Instructions:
Place your answers to each challenge into a journal or folder

Challenge One:
Translate "As Quiet as a Mouse" **into your own words**.(Comprehension)

Challenge Two:
Create two separate sentences using the idiom "As Quiet as a Mouse".(Application)

Challenge Three:
Identify another idiom that is similar to "As Quiet as a Mouse".(Analysis)

Challenge Four:
List **fictional** characters that were "Quiet as a Mouse". Provide examples of their behavior. Illustrate, why. (Analysis)

Challenge Five:
List **fictional** characters that were the opposite of this idiom. Provide examples of their behavior. If possible, explain the reasoning for their behavior. Defend your answer through events from their fictional works. (Evaluation)

Suggested Start:
Using an American English Idiom dictionary, define the figurative meaning of "Quiet as a Mouse".

Potential Resource:
    1.) Dictionary.reference.com/idioms

Challenge Six:
Create, draw or sketch three **individual** objects that represent the word "Monolithic". Based on your images, explain the connection(s) to the subject.(Synthesis)

Example 1:
Humbled

Example 2:
Driven

Challenge Seven:
Create two or more images that express the statement "What is the connection!" But, use as few images and letters as possible. Then, repeat this process with the thought, "I can't disguise my feelings!". Communicate the subtle or overt meaning of the objects inside your images.(Synthesis)
Example One: *I dislike snakes.*

Example Two: *I love snakes.*

Chapter 21
Section 2

Perspectives on:
Radiation

Common Core State Standards:
- CCSS.ELA-LITERACY.WHST.6-8.7
- CCSS.ELA-LITERACY.WHST.6-8.8
- CCSS.ELA-LITERACY.WHST.6-8.10
- CCSS.ELA-LITERACY.RST.6-8.1
- CCSS.ELA-LITERACY.RST.6-8.2

Learning Objectives:
- A. Gain perspective on vague writing
- B. Gain awareness of potential problems with "absolute" statements in writing
- C. Gain perspective on multiple answers

Radiation Does Not Have Any Benefits.

Instructions:
Place your answers to each challenge into a journal or folder

Challenge One:
"Radiation does not have any benefits". Respond to this statement.(Analysis)

Challenge Two:
Research two or more uncontrollable sources of radiation. Illustrate, why these sources are considered uncontrollable.(Analysis)

Here are recommendations to keep in mind when answering the above questions:
1. What is radiation?
2. Explore the types of radiation?
3. Cite sources that defend your argument.

Suggested Start:
   1. Pause before answering the question.
   2. Using a dictionary, define "radiation".
   3. Using an encyclopedia, explore "radiation".

Potential Resources:
   1.) Merriam-Webster.com
   2.) Bartleby.com

Challenge Three:
Create a joke that you must answer in a figurative way and a literal way. Remember, keep it clean and respectful. NO PRACTICAL JOKES!(Analysis)

Example:
Joke(the setup): *They say "failure is a part of learning".*
Figurative answer (punchline): *Could someone please explain that to my parents.*
Literal answer: *This quote translates more often into "We learn from our mistakes". Whether a person is completing a quiz or learning to ride a bike, mistakes may occur, and they have the option to grow from their small failures.*

The secret to creating jokes is to ask questions about the world. In other words, analyze the world around you. If it doesn't make sense, question it. Then, research it.

To help, start with a statement like:
　　Why is it that...............
　　Ever notice that...........
　　Whose idea was it to make...
　　One day, there was a.................
　　Why does....
　　Where's the......
　　How is it that....

Don't forget to explore and explain the answer in a figurative and literal way. Creating jokes can be challenging. Worst case scenario, find and use a joke that you can answer in a figurative and literal way. Explain, why it is funny. Give credit to the comedian.

Challenge Four:
First, **define** the word, "Static". Second, create a two column chart with a "negative factors" side and a "positive factors" side. Third, contrast the positive factors and negative issues of the word, "Static". (Analysis)
Example:
According to _____'s dictionary, **failure** is....

Failure	
Negative Factors	**Positive Factors**
May spark negative emotions	Mistakes and failings are a part of the creation process
May affect interpersonal relationships	"When you quit that is true failure"
	Don't make failing a habit; however, if it happens, learn from your failure

Challenge Five:
Find an image. Then, create a chart that lists the directly observable features versus the not-visible, but inferable features of the image.(Analysis)

Example: Subway Train	
Observable and Visible	**Not Visible, but Inferable**
is a vehicle	holds passengers
is underground	has lights

Chapter 21
Section 3

Exploring Quotations on:
Traditions

Common Core State Standards:
- CCSS.ELA-LITERACY.WHST.6-8.6
- CCSS.ELA-LITERACY.WHST.6-8.8
- CCSS.ELA-LITERACY.WHST.6-8.10
- CCSS.ELA-LITERACY.RH.6-8.1
- CCSS.ELA-LITERACY.RH.6-8.4
- CCSS.ELA-LITERACY.RH.6-8.7

Learning Objectives:
- A. Gain knowledge on the topic of "traditions"
- B. Experience other perspectives on "traditions"

Quotations on Traditions

Instructions:
Place your answers to each challenge into a journal or folder

Challenge One:
Locate a quotation on the topic of "traditions".(Knowledge)

Challenge Two:
Translate your selected quotation on "traditions" into your own words.(Comprehension)

Challenge Three:
Compose a biographical statement using your chosen quotation on "traditions".(Application)

Challenge Four:
Create your own quote on "traditions".(Synthesis)

Challenge Five:
Choose or create a poem on "traditions".(Synthesis)

Suggested Start:
1. Reflect on "traditions".
2. Quotation resources are available at your local library.

Potential Resources:
1.) En.wikiquote.org
2.) Brainyquote.com
3.) Quotationspage.com

Challenge Six:
Using a quotation on "traditions", discover a way to express the meaning through pictures and words. Then, create a comic strip that explains the quotation. (Synthesis)

Example:
"Hunger"
"Thou shouldst eat to live; not live to eat."
Socrates

Create a collection of images that relate to the quote. Then, add captions or messages that help express the quote. Lastly, connect images and create a comic strip.

Challenge Seven:
Complete the following sentence fragment with three or more separate statements. Figure out a way to incorporate a quotation, adage, or joke.(Application)

Traditions become...

Example:

The last movie that I saw...
1.) ...caused my mind to reflect on the possibilities of humans having superpowers. For instance, by combining advanced nanotechnology with our understanding of genetics, we could modify ourselves into more supercharged people.

2.) ...agitated me because it depicted the cruelties of mankind. However, I then reflected on an anonymous quote that "Unfortunately, the road to progress can have various levels of bumpiness".

3.) ...frightened me because it was a creepy horror film. Now, I want to sleep with the lights on, but my parents disagree. Even though, I don't pay the electric bill. I feel that I should be able to make this decision!

Chapter 21
Section 4

Exploration of Adages, Aphorisms, Proverbs, and Maxims:

Common Core State Standards:
- CCSS.ELA-LITERACY.WHST.6-8.6
- CCSS.ELA-LITERACY.WHST.6-8.8
- CCSS.ELA-LITERACY.WHST.6-8.10
- CCSS.ELA-LITERACY.RH.6-8.4
- CCSS.ELA-LITERACY.RH.6-8.7

Learning Objectives:
A. Experience perceptive sayings from various cultures
B. Examine beliefs and understandings of various individuals and groups

Adages, Aphorisms, Proverbs, and Maxims

Instructions:
Place your answers to each challenge into a journal or folder

Challenge One:
Select an adage, aphorism, proverb, or maxim. Research the origin of the adage, aphorism, proverb, or maxim. Cite source(s).(Knowledge)

Challenge Two:
Translate your chosen adage, aphorism, proverb, or maxim into your own words.(Comprehension)

Challenge Three:
Compose a small paragraph or a short segment of dialogue that includes your chosen adage, aphorism, proverb, or maxim.(Application)

Challenge Four:
Do you agree or disagree with the message of your chosen adage, aphorism, proverb, or maxim. Defend your response. Cite sources.(Evaluation)

Suggested Start:
1. Reflect on your chosen adage, aphorism, proverb, or maxim.
2. Identify problems, if any.

Potential Resources:
1.) En.wikiquote.org
2.) Thinkexist.com

Challenge Five:

Select at least three pictures based on your selected adage, aphorism, proverb, or maxim. Next, build three posters by adding text to the chosen pictures. (Synthesis)

Suggested Start:
"Keep your Mouth Shut, and your Eyes Open"

1. Make sure you understand the adage, aphorism, proverb, or maxim.
2. Reflect on the meaning(s) of your chosen adage, aphorism, proverb, or maxim.
3. Search for images that symbolize or reflect the adage, aphorism, proverb, or maxim.
4. Construct posters.

Challenge Six:

Is it better to <u>train</u> or <u>educate</u>?

In this exercise, consider possible scenarios when it is better to do one or the other underlined options. Next, find scenarios that benefit from each underlined option. Then, try to find scenarios that do not benefit from each underlined option. Create a chart that represents your conclusions. Lastly, compose statements using historical examples or scientific data that validate each item inside your chart. (Evaluation)

Example: Is it better to <u>spark</u> or <u>spur</u>?

Neither	Spark	Spur	Both
malice	critical thoughts	truthfulness	healthy behavior
hatred	cooperation	obedience	innovations
ignorance	motivation	horse	inventions
	confidence		imagination
			students
			self-control

A. <u>Hatred</u> can <u>spark</u> destructive behavior such as... (insert historical example).
B. Although, at times effective, spurred obedience has a limited shelf life; eventually, the spurred will rebel or revolt such as a child or colony...
C. According to _____(author/researcher/expert), sparking confidence can boost students' comprehension.

Chapter 21
Section 5

Exploration of Business

Common Core State Standards:
- CCSS.ELA-LITERACY.WHST.6-8.6
- CCSS.ELA-LITERACY.WHST.6-8.7
- CCSS.ELA-LITERACY.WHST.6-8.8
- CCSS.ELA-LITERACY.WHST.6-8.9
- CCSS.ELA-LITERACY.WHST.6-8.10
- CCSS.ELA-LITERACY.RH.6-8.4
- CCSS.ELA-LITERACY.RH.6-8.7

Learning Objectives:
- A. Examine business costs and opportunities
- B. Communicate information through graphics and text such as diagrams and charts

Organization Path

Instructions:
Place your answers to each challenge into a journal or folder

Challenge One:
Brainstorm a list of four organizations that offer vital products or services. Choose one of the organizations. Then, classify the business by type. Identify its main product.(Knowledge)

Challenge Two:
Identify three competitors of this business.(Comprehension)

Challenge Three:
Identify three products or services of your chosen company. Create a chart that displays the relationship among the main product and the additional products. Determine if these products are:
- Integrated and necessary for the main product to operate such as gasoline or motor oil for cars
- Complementary to the product and enhances product like air conditioning and power windows for cars
- Vital to the business such as their brand brake pads and spark plugs for cars(Application)

Main Product(Windows Operating System)			
	Integrated and Necessary	Enhances Main Product	Vital to Business
Microsoft Office	No	Yes	Yes
Internet Explorer	Yes	Yes	Yes
Xbox 360	No	No	No

Challenge Four:

Categorize the four chosen products by popularity among consumers, history of the products, revenue, profit, target audience(name their main customers), and strongest direct competitor, quasi-competitor and indirect competitor. Use a scale from 4 to 1, 4 being highest, to grade each category. Then, based on your chart, describe the growth potential (or lack of future potential) of each product. Which product is the strongest? Which product would you focus more resources on for the future of the company. Defend your decision. Cite sources.(Analysis)

Strengths and Weaknesses				
	Windows OS	Microsoft Office	Internet Explorer	Xbox 360
Popularity	3	4	2	1
Revenue	3	4	2	1
Profitabil- ity	3	4	2	1

Strengths and Weaknesses by Details				
	Windows OS	Microsoft Office	Internet Explorer	Xbox 360
Years Available	28 yrs.	23 yrs.	19 yrs.	8 yrs.
Direct Competitor	Mac OS X	LibreOf-fice	Chrome	Playsta-tion 3
Quasi-Competitor	Android OS	QuickOf-fice	Smart-TVs	Gameboy Advance
Indirect Competitor	Pen and Paper	Typewriter	Library Card	Mobile Device
Rankings among direct Com-petitors	#1	#1	#2	#1

Challenge Five:

Choose one of your chosen company's most popular or well-known products or services. Research this product or service and build a diagram that displays the fabrication process of the product or service. Cite sources.(Synthesis)

Your diagram or chart should display the work that goes into producing a product or service.

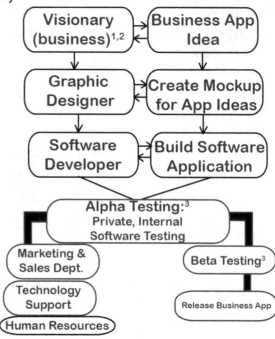

1 Does the app solve a problem?
2 Can it be profitable?
3 Testing may require restarts or revisions.

Challenge Six:

Create a chart that explains two of the product's major features. For example, an alarm clock normally has a minimum of two features, the time display and the alarm function. Use graphics, if possible. Cite sources.(Analysis)

Alarm Radio	
Radio	converts radio waves...
Alarm Buzzer	is a feature of the...

Challenge Seven:

Based on your gathered research and your product choice, create a visual flowchart or graphical diagram that demonstrates the interaction between human resources and non-human resources to produce the product or service. Start with the necessary (raw) materials required to produce the product or service. For example, an organic farmer needs supplies, materials, equipment, and workers. Then, your flowchart should display the interactions between the workforce and resources until the end-product reaches consumers. (Synthesis)

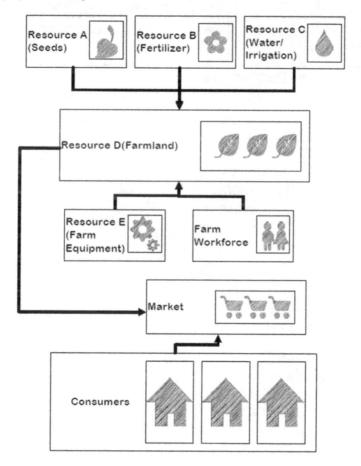

Challenge Eight:

Identify three individuals that had a major impact on your chosen company's industry. Create a multi-media chart to describe their impact. Based on your research of these three individuals, which individual had the biggest impact on their industry. Defend your argument. Cite sources.(Evaluation)

Industry: Telecommunications		
insert image	John Doe	was an inventor whose radical and unorthodox methods produced the first....
insert image	Jane Doe	was an amazing engineer who invented the first....
insert image	Dr. Cooper	was a well-known and well-respected physician that accidentally invented....

Potential Resources:

- www.bls.gov/ooh
- www.bls.gov/iag
- howstuffworks.com
- visual.merriam-webster.com
- finance.yahoo.com
- ehow.com
- sba.gov
- entrepreneur.com

Rubric for Chapter
See Appendix A

Reflective Questions for Chapter
See Appendix B

Chapter 22

Connections to
Common Core State Standards:

CCSS.ELA-LITERACY.WHST.6-8.6
Use technology, including the Internet, to produce and publish writing and present the relationships between information and ideas clearly and efficiently.(2010)

CCSS.ELA-LITERACY.WHST.6-8.7
Conduct short research projects to answer a question(including a self-generated question), drawing on several sources and generating additional related, focused questions that allow for multiple avenues of exploration.(2010)

CCSS.ELA-LITERACY.WHST.6-8.8
Gather relevant information from multiple print and digital sources, using search terms effectively; assess the credibility and accuracy of each source; and quote or paraphrase the data and conclusions of others while avoiding plagiarism and following a standard form of citation.(2010)

CCSS.ELA-LITERACY.WHST.6-8.9
Draw evidence from informational texts to support analysis, reflection, and research.(2010)

Connections to
Common Core State Standards:
(continued)

CCSS.ELA-LITERACY.WHST.6-8.10
Write routinely over extended time frames(time for revision and reflection) and shorter time frames(a single sitting or a day or two) for a range of discipline-specific tasks, purposes, and audiences.(2010)

CCSS.ELA-LITERACY.RH.6-8.1
Cite specific textual evidence to support analysis of primary and secondary sources.(2010)

CCSS.ELA-LITERACY.RH.6-8.4
Determine the meaning of words and phrases as they are used in a text, including vocabulary specific to domains related to history/social studies.(2010)

CCSS.ELA-LITERACY.RH.6-8.7
Integrate visual information(e.g., in charts, graphs, photographs, videos, or maps) with other information in print and digital text.(2010)

CCSS.ELA-LITERACY.RST.6-8.1
Cite specific textual evidence to support analysis of science and technical texts.(2010)

CCSS.ELA-LITERACY.RST.6-8.2
Determine the central ideas or conclusions of a text; provide an accurate summary of the text distinct from prior knowledge or opinions.(2010)

CCSS.ELA-LITERACY.RST.6-8.
Distinguish among facts, reasoned judgment based on research findings, and speculation in text.(2010)

Chapter 22
Section 1

Exploration of the Idiom:
Hopping Mad

Common Core State Standards:
- CCSS.ELA-LITERACY.WHST.6-8.8
- CCSS.ELA-LITERACY.WHST.6-8.10
- CCSS.ELA-LITERACY.RH.6-8.4
- CCSS.ELA-LITERACY.RH.6-8.7

Learning Objectives:
- A. Understand the figurative meaning of idioms
- B. Comprehend the problematic issues with literal translations of idioms

Hopping Mad

Instructions:
Place your answers to each challenge into a journal or folder

Challenge One:
Translate "Hopping Mad" **into your own words**.
(Comprehension)

Challenge Two:
Create two separate sentences using the idiom "Hopping Mad".(Application)

Challenge Three:
Identify another idiom that is similar to "Hopping Mad".(Analysis)

Challenge Four:
List **fictional** characters that were "Hopping Mad". Provide examples of their behavior. If possible, explain the reasoning for their behavior. Defend your answer through events from their fictional works. (Evaluation)

Challenge Five:
List historical figures that were known for becoming "Hopping Mad". Research, report and cite sources. (Evaluation)

Suggested Start:
Using an American English Idiom dictionary, define the figurative meaning of "Hopping Mad".

Potential Resources:
1.)Dictionary.reference.com/idioms

Challenge Six:

Create, draw or sketch three **individual** objects that represent the word "Conscious". Based on your images, explain the connection(s) to the subject.(Synthesis)

Example 1:
Humbled

Example 2:
Driven

Challenge Seven:

Create two or more images that express the feeling "Subconscious or Unconscious?" But, use as few images and letters as possible. Then, repeat this process with the thought, "They posed the question 'the subconscious or the unconscious, which do we value more?'". Explain and defend your artwork.(Synthesis)
Example One: *I dislike spiders.*

Example Two: *I love spiders.*

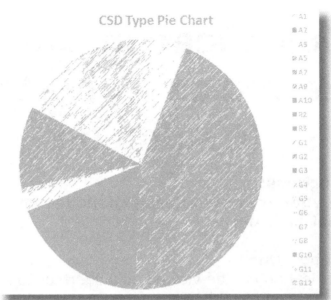

CSD Type Pie Chart

A1
A2
A3
A5
A7
A9
A10
R2
R3
G1
G2
G3
G4
G5
G6
G7
G8
G10
G11
G12

Chapter 22
Section 2

Perspectives on:
Visual Math

Common Core State Standards:
- CCSS.ELA-LITERACY.WHST.6-8.7
- CCSS.ELA-LITERACY.WHST.6-8.8
- CCSS.ELA-LITERACY.WHST.6-8.10
- CCSS.ELA-LITERACY.RST.6-8.1
- CCSS.ELA-LITERACY.RST.6-8.2

Learning Objectives:
- A. Gain perspective on vague writing
- B. Gain awareness of potential problems with "absolute" statements in writing
- C. Gain perspective on multiple answers

Multiplication can be Viewed as a Shortcut to Addition

Instructions:
Place your answers to each challenge into a journal or folder

Challenge One:
"Multiplication can be viewed as a shortcut to addition". Respond to this statement. (Analysis)

Challenge Two:
List real world examples where multiplication is described visually. Draw or collect images of real world examples.(Synthesis)

Here are recommendations to keep in mind when answering the above questions:
1. What is multiplication?
2. What is addition?
3. Start with small numbers, first.
3. Cite sources that defend your argument.

Suggested Start:
1. Pause before answering the question.
2. Using a dictionary, define "addition".
3. Using a dictionary, define "multiplication".

Potential Resources:
1.) Merriam-Webster.com
2.) Bartleby.com

Challenge Three:
Create a joke that you must answer in a figurative way and a literal way. Remember, keep it clean and respectful. NO PRACTICAL JOKES!(Analysis)

Example:
Joke(the setup):   *They say "failure is a part of learning".*
Figurative answer (punchline): *Could someone please explain that to my parents.*
Literal answer: *This quote translates more often into "We learn from our mistakes". Whether a person is completing a quiz or learning to ride a bike, mistakes may occur, and they have the option to grow from their small failures.*

The secret to creating jokes is to ask questions about the world. In other words, analyze the world around you. If it doesn't make sense, question it. Then, research it.

To help, start with a statement like:
   Why is it that...............
   Ever notice that...........
   Whose idea was it to make...
   One day, there was a.................
   Why does....
   Where's the......
   How is it that....

Don't forget to explore and explain the answer in a figurative and literal way. Creating jokes can be challenging. Worst case scenario, find and use a joke that you can answer in a figurative and literal way. Explain, why it is funny. Give credit to the comedian.

Challenge Four:

First, **define** the word, "Mercurial". Second, create a two column chart with a "negative factors" side and a "positive factors" side. Third, contrast the positive factors and negative issues of the word, "Mercurial". (Analysis)

Example:

According to _____'s dictionary, **failure** is....

Failure	
Negative Factors	**Positive Factors**
May spark negative emotions	Mistakes and failings are a part of the creation process
May affect interpersonal relationships	"When you quit that is true failure"
	Don't make failing a habit; however, if it happens, learn from your failure

Challenge Five:

Find an image. Then, create a chart that lists the directly observable features versus the not-visible, but inferable features of the image.(Analysis)

Example: Boxcar	
Observable and Visible	**Not Visible, but Inferable**
is a container	hold cargo
is on railroad tracks	

Chapter 22
Section 3

Exploring Quotations on: Failure

Common Core State Standards:
- CCSS.ELA-LITERACY.WHST.6-8.6
- CCSS.ELA-LITERACY.WHST.6-8.8
- CCSS.ELA-LITERACY.WHST.6-8.10
- CCSS.ELA-LITERACY.RH.6-8.1
- CCSS.ELA-LITERACY.RH.6-8.4
- CCSS.ELA-LITERACY.RH.6-8.7

Learning Objectives:
- A. Gain knowledge on the topic of "failure"
- B. Experience other perspectives on "failure"

Quotations on Failure

Instructions:
Place your answers to each challenge into a journal or folder

Challenge One:
Locate a quotation on the topic of "failure".(Knowl-edge)

Challenge Two:
Translate your selected quotation on "failure" into your own words.(Comprehension)

Challenge Three:
Compose a biographical statement using your chosen quotation on "failure".(Application)

Challenge Four:
Create your own quote on "failure".(Synthesis)

Challenge Five:
Choose or create a poem on "failure".(Synthesis)

Suggested Start:
1. Reflect on a "failed experience". Did you learn anything?
2. Quotation resources are available at your local library.

Potential Resources:
1.) Quoteland.com
2.) Brainyquote.com
3.) Quotationspage.com
4.) En.wikiquote.org

Challenge Six:

Using a quotation on "failure", discover a way to express the meaning through pictures and words. Then, create a comic strip that explains the quotation.(Synthesis)

Example:
"Hunger"
"Thou shouldst eat to live; not live to eat."
Socrates

Create a collection of images that relate to the quote. Then, add captions or messages that help express the quote. Lastly, connect images and create a comic strip.

Challenge Seven:
Complete the following sentence fragment with three or more separate statements. Figure out a way to incorporate a quotation, adage, or joke.(Application)

The orchard...

Example:

The last movie that I saw...
1.) ...caused my mind to reflect on the possibilities of humans having superpowers. For instance, by combining advanced nanotechnology with our understanding of genetics, we could modify ourselves into more supercharged people.

2.) ...agitated me because it depicted the cruelties of mankind. However, I then reflected on an anonymous quote that "Unfortunately, the road to progress can have various levels of bumpiness".

3.) ...frightened me because it was a creepy horror film. Now, I want to sleep with the lights on, but my parents disagree. Even though, I don't pay the electric bill. I feel that I should be able to make this decision!

Chapter 22
Section 4

Exploration of Adages, Aphorisms, Proverbs, and Maxims:

Common Core State Standards:
- CCSS.ELA-LITERACY.WHST.6-8.6
- CCSS.ELA-LITERACY.WHST.6-8.8
- CCSS.ELA-LITERACY.WHST.6-8.10
- CCSS.ELA-LITERACY.RH.6-8.4
- CCSS.ELA-LITERACY.RH.6-8.7

Learning Objectives:
- A. Experience perceptive sayings from various cultures
- B. Examine beliefs and understandings of various individuals and groups

Adages, Aphorisms, Proverbs, and Maxims

Instructions:
Place your answers to each challenge into a journal or folder

Challenge One:
Select an adage, aphorism, proverb, or maxim. Research the origin of the adage, aphorism, proverb, or maxim. Cite source(s).(Knowledge)

Challenge Two:
Translate your chosen adage, aphorism, proverb, or maxim into your own words.(Comprehension)

Challenge Three:
Compose a small paragraph or a short segment of dialogue that includes your chosen adage, aphorism, proverb, or maxim.(Application)

Challenge Four:
Do you agree or disagree with the message of your chosen adage, aphorism, proverb, or maxim. Defend your response. Cite sources.(Evaluation)

Suggested Start:
1. Reflect on your chosen adage, aphorism, proverb, or maxim.
2. Identify problems, if any.

Potential Resources:
1.) En.wikiquote.org
2.) Thinkexist.com

Challenge Five:
Select at least three pictures based on your selected adage, aphorism, proverb, or maxim. Next, build three posters by adding text to the chosen pictures. (Synthesis)

Suggested Start:
"Keep your Mouth Shut, and your Eyes Open"
1. Make sure you understand the adage, aphorism, proverb, or maxim.
2. Reflect on the meaning(s) of your chosen adage, aphorism, proverb, or maxim.
3. Search for images that symbolize or reflect the adage, aphorism, proverb, or maxim.
4. Construct posters.

Challenge Six:

Is it better to <u>ignore</u> or <u>explore</u>?

In this exercise, consider possible scenarios when it is better to do one or the other underlined options. Next, find scenarios that benefit from each underlined option. Then, try to find scenarios that do not benefit from each underlined option. Create a chart that represents your conclusions. Lastly, compose statements using historical examples or scientific data that validate each item inside your chart. (Evaluation)

Example: Is it better to <u>spark</u> or <u>spur</u>?

Neither	Spark	Spur	Both
malice	critical thoughts	truthfulness	healthy behavior
hatred	cooperation	obedience	innovations
ignorance	motivation	horse	inventions
	confidence		imagination
			students
			self-control

A. <u>Hatred</u> can <u>spark</u> destructive behavior such as... (insert historical example).
B. Although, at times effective, spurred obedience has a limited shelf life; eventually, the spurred will rebel or revolt such as a child or colony...
C. According to _____(author/researcher/expert), sparking confidence can boost students' comprehension.

Chapter 22
Section 5

Exploration of Business

Common Core State Standards:
- CCSS.ELA-LITERACY.WHST.6-8.6
- CCSS.ELA-LITERACY.WHST.6-8.7
- CCSS.ELA-LITERACY.WHST.6-8.8
- CCSS.ELA-LITERACY.WHST.6-8.9
- CCSS.ELA-LITERACY.WHST.6-8.10
- CCSS.ELA-LITERACY.RH.6-8.4
- CCSS.ELA-LITERACY.RH.6-8.7

Learning Objectives:
- A. Examine products and services from the view of an organizational entity such as a business
- B. Communicate information through graphics and text such as diagrams and charts

Product and Service Path

Instructions:
Place your answers to each challenge into a journal or folder

Challenge One:
Brainstorm a list of four products or services that are at least 75 years old. Select one of the products or services.(Knowledge)

Challenge Two:
Identify the type of companies that produce your chosen product or service. Classify their industry.(Comprehension)

Challenge Three:
Identify three direct competitors of your chosen product or service. Describe and chart the competition based on market share, business size (by employees), years available, marketing reach(local, regional, national, global), revenue and profits. Research and use industry averages if your chosen company or its competitors are not publicly traded.(Analysis)

Main Product (Web Browsers)				
	Market Share	Business Size	Marketing Reach	Years Available
Internet Explorer (product)	2	large enterprise	global	19
Chrome (competitor)	1	large enterprise	global	6
Firefox (competitor)	3	mid-size	global	12
Opera (competitor)	4	mid-size	global	18

Challenge four:

Create a diagram that displays the major parts or sequences of your chosen product or service. Next explain two of the product's major parts. For example, an Xbox 360 has multiple, specialized parts such as the central processing unit, the graphics processing unit and the hard drive. Use graphics. Cite sources. (Analysis)

Challenge Five:

Based on your chosen product or service, identify three influential people that had a major impact on this industry through improvements, innovations, or inventions. Describe their effects on the industry. Cite sources.(Analysis)

Industry: Telecommunications		
insert image	John Doe	was an inventor whose radical and unorthodox methods produced the first....
insert image	Jane Doe	was an amazing engineer who invented the first....
insert image	Dr. Cooper	was a well-known and well-respected physician that accidentally invented....

Challenge Six:

Create an organizational chart (unofficial) of a company that offers your chosen product or service. Next, pinpoint the areas where your three previously chosen influential people would work. For example, if one of your selected influential people is a visionary executive leader, then they would fit somewhere at the top of the organizational chart(org chart).(Synthesis)

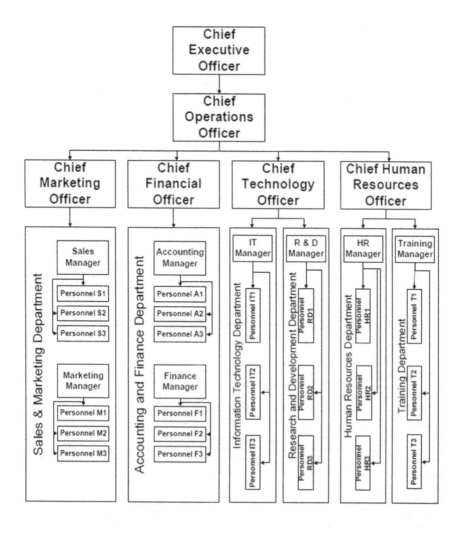

Challenge Seven:
Based on your gathered research and your product choice, create a visual flowchart or graphical diagram that demonstrates the interaction between human resources and non-human resources to produce the product or service. Start with the necessary (raw) materials required to produce the product or service. For example, an organic farmer needs supplies, materials, equipment, and workers. Then, your flowchart should display the interactions between the workforce and resources until the end-product reaches consumers. (Synthesis)

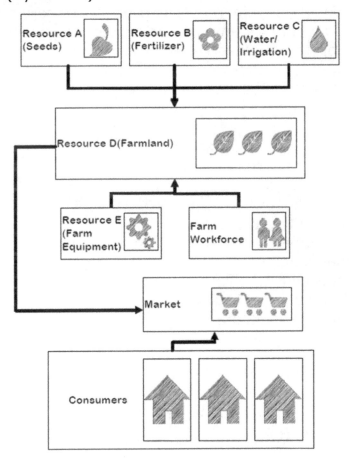

Challenge Eight:

Based on your product choice or service selection,
- Identify two supplemental/complementary products or services such as computer applications complement computer operating systems
- Identify two required/necessary products (computer operating system are necessary to operate computers)
- Identify two separate or indirectly connected products or services that the company produces(Xbox 360 or Zune)

Discover which product(s) is your strongest seller(s). Why? Would you eliminate any products or services from the company's product lineup? Explain. Which product or service deserves the most research and development? Elaborate. Lastly, which product or service deserves the most marketing. Explain. Cite sources.(Evaluation)

Potential Resources:
- www.bls.gov/ooh
- www.bls.gov/iag
- howstuffworks.com
- visual.merriam-webster.com
- finance.yahoo.com
- ehow.com
- sba.gov
- entrepreneur.com

Rubric for Chapter
See Appendix A

Reflective Questions for Chapter
See Appendix B

Chapter 23

Connections to
Common Core State Standards:

CCSS.ELA-LITERACY.WHST.6-8.6
Use technology, including the Internet, to produce and publish writing and present the relationships between information and ideas clearly and efficiently.(2010)

CCSS.ELA-LITERACY.WHST.6-8.7
Conduct short research projects to answer a question(including a self-generated question), drawing on several sources and generating additional related, focused questions that allow for multiple avenues of exploration.(2010)

CCSS.ELA-LITERACY.WHST.6-8.8
Gather relevant information from multiple print and digital sources, using search terms effectively; assess the credibility and accuracy of each source; and quote or paraphrase the data and conclusions of others while avoiding plagiarism and following a standard form of citation.(2010)

CCSS.ELA-LITERACY.WHST.6-8.9
Draw evidence from informational texts to support analysis, reflection, and research.(2010)

Connections to
Common Core State Standards:
(continued)

CCSS.ELA-LITERACY.WHST.6-8.10
Write routinely over extended time frames(time for revision and reflection) and shorter time frames(a single sitting or a day or two) for a range of discipline-specific tasks, purposes, and audiences.(2010)

CCSS.ELA-LITERACY.RH.6-8.1
Cite specific textual evidence to support analysis of primary and secondary sources.(2010)

CCSS.ELA-LITERACY.RH.6-8.4
Determine the meaning of words and phrases as they are used in a text, including vocabulary specific to domains related to history/social studies.(2010)

CCSS.ELA-LITERACY.RH.6-8.7
Integrate visual information(e.g., in charts, graphs, photographs, videos, or maps) with other information in print and digital text.(2010)

CCSS.ELA-LITERACY.RST.6-8.1
Cite specific textual evidence to support analysis of science and technical texts.(2010)

CCSS.ELA-LITERACY.RST.6-8.2
Determine the central ideas or conclusions of a text; provide an accurate summary of the text distinct from prior knowledge or opinions.(2010)

CCSS.ELA-LITERACY.RST.6-8.
Distinguish among facts, reasoned judgment based on research findings, and speculation in text.(2010)

Chapter 23
Section 1

Exploration of the Idiom:
Scratch the Surface

Common Core State Standards:
- CCSS.ELA-LITERACY.WHST.6-8.8
- CCSS.ELA-LITERACY.WHST.6-8.10
- CCSS.ELA-LITERACY.RH.6-8.4
- CCSS.ELA-LITERACY.RH.6-8.7

Learning Objectives:
- A. Understand the figurative meaning of idioms
- B. Comprehend the problematic issues with literal translations of idioms

Scratch the Surface

Instructions:
Place your answers to each challenge into a journal or folder

Challenge One:
Translate "Scratch the Surface" **into your own words**.(Comprehension)

Challenge Two:
Create two separate sentences using the idiom "Scratch the Surface".(Application)

Challenge Three:
Identify another idiom that is similar to "Scratch the surface".(Analysis)

Challenge Four:
Point out events that represented "Scratching the surface" of technological or scientific breakthroughs. Explain. Cite sources.(Analysis)

Suggested Start:
Using an American English Idiom dictionary, define the figurative meaning of "Scratch the Surface".

Potential Resources:
    1.) Idioms.thefreedictionary.com
    2.) Dictionary.reference.com/idioms

Challenge Five:

Create, draw or sketch three **individual** objects that represent the word "whimsical". Based on your images, explain the connection(s) to the subject.(Synthesis)

Example 1:
Humbled

Example 2:
Driven

Challenge Six:

Create two or more images that express the statement "He suffers from hydrophobia!" But, use as few images and letters as possible. Then, repeat this process with the thought, "The dog has hydrophobia." Communicate the subtle or overt meaning of the objects inside your images.(Synthesis)

Example One: *I dislike tigers.*

Example Two: *I love tigers.*

Chapter 23
Section 2

Perspectives on:
Viruses

Common Core State Standards:
- CCSS.ELA-LITERACY.WHST.6-8.7
- CCSS.ELA-LITERACY.WHST.6-8.8
- CCSS.ELA-LITERACY.WHST.6-8.10
- CCSS.ELA-LITERACY.RST.6-8.1
- CCSS.ELA-LITERACY.RST.6-8.2

Learning Objectives:
- A. Gain perspective on vague writing
- B. Gain awareness of potential problems with "absolute" statements in writing
- C. Gain perspective on multiple answers

All Biological Viruses are Unhealthy

Instructions:
Place your answers to each challenge into a journal or folder

Challenge One:
"All Biological Viruses are Unhealthy". Respond to this statement.(Analysis)

Challenge Two:
"Computer viruses and biological viruses operate in a similar way." Respond to this statement.(Analysis)

Here are recommendations to keep in mind when answering the above questions:
1. What is a virus?
2. How do viruses operate?
3. Can viruses mutate?
4. Cite sources that defend your argument.

Suggested Start:
   1. Pause before answering the question.
   2. Using a dictionary, define "virus".
   3. Using an encyclopedia, research "virus".

Potential Resources:
      1.) Merriam-Webster.com
      2.) Bartleby.com

Challenge Three:
Create a joke that you must answer in a figurative way and a literal way. Remember, keep it clean and respectful. NO PRACTICAL JOKES!(Analysis)

Example:
Joke(the setup): *They say "failure is a part of learning".*
Figurative answer (punchline): *Could someone please explain that to my parents.*
Literal answer: *This quote translates more often into "We learn from our mistakes". Whether a person is completing a quiz or learning to ride a bike, mistakes may occur, and they have the option to grow from their small failures.*

The secret to creating jokes is to ask questions about the world. In other words, analyze the world around you. If it doesn't make sense, question it. Then, research it.

To help, start with a statement like:
Why is it that..............
Ever notice that...........
Whose idea was it to make...
One day, there was a.................
Why does....
Where's the......
How is it that....

Don't forget to explore and explain the answer in a figurative and literal way. Creating jokes can be challenging. Worst case scenario, find and use a joke that you can answer in a figurative and literal way. Explain, why it is funny. Give credit to the comedian.

Challenge Four:
First, **define** the word, "Dependable". Second, create a two column chart with a "negative factors" side and a "positive factors" side. Third, contrast the positive factors and negative issues of the word, "Dependable".(Analysis)
Example:
According to _____'s dictionary, **failure** is....

Failure	
Negative Factors	**Positive Factors**
May spark negative emotions	Mistakes and failings are a part of the creation process
May affect interpersonal relationships	"When you quit that is true failure"
	Don't make failing a habit; however, if it happens, learn from your failure

Challenge Five:
Find an image. Then, create a chart that lists the directly observable features versus the not-visible, but inferable features of the image.(Analysis)

Example: Camel	
Observable and Visible	**Not Visible, but Inferable**
is a mammal	stores water
is on the ground	holds cargo
	contains biological organs

Chapter 23
Section 3

Exploring Quotations by: Presidents of the United States

Common Core State Standards:
- CCSS.ELA-LITERACY.WHST.6-8.6
- CCSS.ELA-LITERACY.WHST.6-8.8
- CCSS.ELA-LITERACY.WHST.6-8.10
- CCSS.ELA-LITERACY.RH.6-8.1
- CCSS.ELA-LITERACY.RH.6-8.4
- CCSS.ELA-LITERACY.RH.6-8.7

Learning Objectives:
- A. Gain knowledge on the topic of a U.S. President
- B. Experience historical perspectives

Quotations by U.S. Presidents

Instructions:
Place your answers to each challenge into a journal or folder

Challenge One:
Locate a quotation by a former U.S. President.(Knowledge)

Challenge Two:
Translate your chosen quotation into your own words. (Comprehension)

Challenge Three:
Locate another quote on the same subject as your chosen quotation by a different U.S. President. Compare and contrast both quotations.(Analysis)

Suggested Start:
1. Reflect on a President of the United States of America.
2. Quotation resources are available at your local library.

Potential Resources:
1.) Quoteland.com
2.) Brainyquote.com
3.) Quotationspage.com
4.) En.wikiquote.org

Challenge Four:
Using a quotation by a U.S. President, discover a way to express the meaning through pictures and words. Then, create a comic strip that explains the quotation. (Synthesis)

Example:
"Hunger"
"Thou shouldst eat to live; not live to eat."
Socrates

Create a collection of images that relate to the quote. Then, add captions or messages that help express the quote. Lastly, connect images and create a comic strip.

Challenge Five:

Complete the following sentence fragment with three or more separate statements. Figure out a way to incorporate a quotation, adage, or joke.(Application)

Political power...

Example:

The last movie that I saw...

1.) ...caused my mind to reflect on the possibilities of humans having superpowers. For instance, by combining advanced nanotechnology with our understanding of genetics, we could modify ourselves into more supercharged people.

2.) ...agitated me because it depicted the cruelties of mankind. However, I then reflected on an anonymous quote that "Unfortunately, the road to progress can have various levels of bumpiness".

3.) ...frightened me because it was a creepy horror film. Now, I want to sleep with the lights on, but my parents disagree. Even though, I don't pay the electric bill. I feel that I should be able to make this decision!

Chapter 23
Section 4

Exploration of Adages, Aphorisms, Proverbs, and Maxims:

Common Core State Standards:
- CCSS.ELA-LITERACY.WHST.6-8.6
- CCSS.ELA-LITERACY.WHST.6-8.8
- CCSS.ELA-LITERACY.WHST.6-8.10
- CCSS.ELA-LITERACY.RH.6-8.4
- CCSS.ELA-LITERACY.RH.6-8.7

Learning Objectives:
A. Experience perceptive sayings from various cultures
B. Examine beliefs and understandings of various individuals and groups

Adages, Aphorisms, Proverbs, and Maxims

Instructions:
Place your answers to each challenge into a journal or folder

Challenge One:
Select an adage, aphorism, proverb, or maxim. Research the origin of the adage, aphorism, proverb, or maxim. Cite source(s).(Knowledge)

Challenge Two:
Translate your chosen adage, aphorism, proverb, or maxim into your own words.(Comprehension)

Challenge Three:
Compose a small paragraph or a short segment of dialogue that includes your chosen adage, aphorism, proverb, or maxim.(Application)

Challenge Four:
Do you agree or disagree with the message of your chosen adage, aphorism, proverb, or maxim. Defend your response. Cite sources.(Evaluation)

Suggested Start:
   1. Reflect on your chosen adage, aphorism, proverb, or maxim.
   2. Identify problems, if any.

Potential Resources:
   1.) En.wikiquote.org
   2.) Thinkexist.com

Challenge Five:
Select at least three pictures based on your selected adage, aphorism, proverb, or maxim. Next, build three posters by adding text to the chosen pictures. (Synthesis)

Suggested Start:
"Keep your Mouth Shut, and your Eyes Open"
1. Make sure you understand the adage, aphorism, proverb, or maxim.
2. Reflect on the meaning(s) of your chosen adage, aphorism, proverb, or maxim.
3. Search for images that symbolize or reflect the adage, aphorism, proverb, or maxim.
4. Construct posters.

Challenge Six:

Is it better to <u>negate</u> or <u>undermine</u>?

In this exercise, consider possible scenarios when it is better to do one or the other underlined options. Next, find scenarios that benefit from each underlined option. Then, try to find scenarios that do not benefit from each underlined option. Create a chart that represents your conclusions. Lastly, compose statements using historical examples or scientific data that validate each item inside your chart. (Evaluation)

Example: Is it better to <u>spark</u> or <u>spur</u>?

Neither	Spark	Spur	Both
malice	critical thoughts	truthfulness	healthy behavior
hatred	cooperation	obedience	innovations
ignorance	motivation	horse	inventions
	confidence		imagination
			students
			self-control

A. <u>Hatred</u> can <u>spark</u> destructive behavior such as... (insert historical example).
B. Although, at times effective, spurred obedience has a limited shelf life; eventually, the spurred will rebel or revolt such as a child or colony...
C. According to _____(author/researcher/expert), sparking confidence can boost students' comprehension.

Chapter 23
Section 5

Exploration of Business

Common Core State Standards:
- CCSS.ELA-LITERACY.WHST.6-8.6
- CCSS.ELA-LITERACY.WHST.6-8.7
- CCSS.ELA-LITERACY.WHST.6-8.8
- CCSS.ELA-LITERACY.WHST.6-8.9
- CCSS.ELA-LITERACY.WHST.6-8.10
- CCSS.ELA-LITERACY.RH.6-8.4
- CCSS.ELA-LITERACY.RH.6-8.7

Learning Objectives:
A. Examine business costs and opportunities
B. Communicate information through graphics and text such as diagrams and charts

Organization Path

Instructions:
Place your answers to each challenge into a journal or folder

Challenge One:
Brainstorm a list of four businesses that have the best commercials. Choose one of the businesses. Then, classify the business by type. Identify its main product.(Knowledge)

Challenge Two:
Identify three competitors of this business.(Comprehension)

Challenge Three:
Identify three products or services of your chosen company. Create a chart that displays the relationship among the main product and the additional products. Determine if these products are:
- Integrated and necessary for the main product to operate such as gasoline or motor oil for cars
- Complementary to the product and enhances product like air conditioning and power windows for cars
- Vital to the business such as their brand brake pads and spark plugs for cars (Application)

Main Product(Windows Operating System)			
	Integrated and Necessary	Enhances Main Product	Vital to Business
Microsoft Office	No	Yes	Yes
Internet Explorer	Yes	Yes	Yes
Xbox 360	No	No	No

Challenge Four:

Categorize the four chosen products by popularity among consumers, history of the products, revenue, profit, target audience(name their main customers), and strongest direct competitor, quasi-competitor and indirect competitor. Use a scale from 4 to 1, 4 being highest, to grade each category. Then, based on your chart, describe the growth potential (or lack of future potential) of each product. Which product is the strongest? Which product would you focus more resources on for the future of the company. Defend your decision. Cite sources.(Analysis)

Strengths and Weaknesses				
	Windows OS	Microsoft Office	Internet Explorer	Xbox 360
Popularity	3	4	2	1
Revenue	3	4	2	1
Profitabil- ity	3	4	2	1

Strengths and Weaknesses by Details				
	Windows OS	Microsoft Office	Internet Explorer	Xbox 360
Years Available	28 yrs.	23 yrs.	19 yrs.	8 yrs.
Direct Competitor	Mac OS X	LibreOf- fice	Chrome	Playsta- tion 3
Quasi- Competitor	Android OS	QuickOf- fice	Smart- TVs	Gameboy Advance
Indirect Competitor	Pen and Paper	Typewriter	Library Card	Mobile Device
Rankings among direct Com- petitors	#1	#1	#2	#1

Challenge Five:

Choose one of your chosen company's most popular or well-known products or services. Research this product or service and build a diagram that displays the fabrication process of the product or service. Cite sources.(Synthesis)

Your diagram or chart should display the work that goes into producing a product or service.

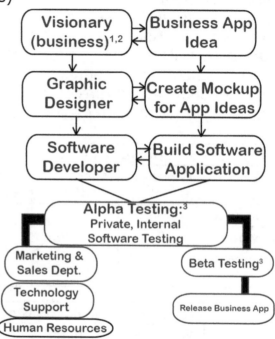

1 Does the app solve a problem?
2 Can it be profitable?
3 Testing may require restarts or revisions.

Challenge Six:

Create a chart that explains two of the chosen product's major features. For example, an alarm clock normally has a minimum of two features, the time display and the alarm function. Use graphics, if possible. Cite sources.(Analysis)

Alarm Radio	
Radio	converts radio waves...
Alarm Buzzer	is a feature of the...

Challenge Seven:
Based on your gathered research and your product choice, create a visual flowchart or graphical diagram that demonstrates the interaction between human resources and non-human resources to produce the product or service. Start with the necessary (raw) materials required to produce the product or service. For example, an organic farmer needs supplies, materials, equipment, and workers. Then, your flowchart should display the interactions between the workforce and resources until the end-product reaches consumers. (Synthesis)

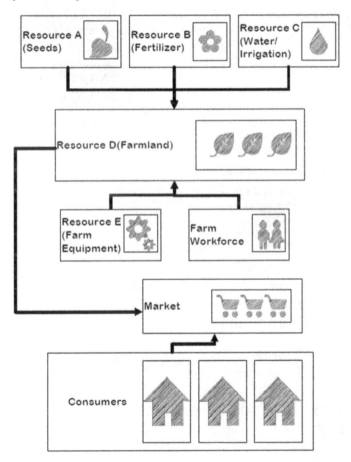

Challenge Eight:

Identify three individuals that had a major impact on your chosen company's industry. Create a multi-media chart to describe their impact. Based on your research of these three individuals, which individual had the biggest impact on their industry. Defend your argument. Cite sources.(Evaluation)

Industry: Telecommunications		
insert image	John Doe	was an inventor whose radical and unorthodox methods produced the first....
insert image	Jane Doe	was an amazing engineer who invented the first....
insert image	Dr. Cooper	was a well-known and well-respected physician that accidentally invented....

Potential Resources:
- www.bls.gov/ooh
- www.bls.gov/iag
- howstuffworks.com
- visual.merriam-webster.com
- finance.yahoo.com
- ehow.com
- sba.gov
- entrepreneur.com

Rubric for Chapter
See Appendix A

Reflective Questions for Chapter
See Appendix B

Chapter 24

Connections to
Common Core State Standards:

CCSS.ELA-LITERACY.WHST.6-8.6
Use technology, including the Internet, to produce and
publish writing and present the relationships between
information and ideas clearly and efficiently.(2010)

CCSS.ELA-LITERACY.WHST.6-8.7
Conduct short research projects to answer a
question(including a self-generated question), drawing
on several sources and generating additional related,
focused questions that allow for multiple avenues of exploration.(2010)

CCSS.ELA-LITERACY.WHST.6-8.8
Gather relevant information from multiple print and digital sources, using search terms effectively; assess the
credibility and accuracy of each source; and quote or
paraphrase the data and conclusions of others while
avoiding plagiarism and following a standard form of
citation.(2010)

CCSS.ELA-LITERACY.WHST.6-8.9
Draw evidence from informational texts to support analysis, reflection, and research.(2010)

Connections to
Common Core State Standards:
<u>(continued)</u>

CCSS.ELA-LITERACY.WHST.6-8.10
Write routinely over extended time frames(time for revision and reflection) and shorter time frames(a single sitting or a day or two) for a range of discipline-specific tasks, purposes, and audiences.(2010)

CCSS.ELA-LITERACY.RH.6-8.1
Cite specific textual evidence to support analysis of primary and secondary sources.(2010)

CCSS.ELA-LITERACY.RH.6-8.4
Determine the meaning of words and phrases as they are used in a text, including vocabulary specific to domains related to history/social studies.(2010)

CCSS.ELA-LITERACY.RH.6-8.7
Integrate visual information(e.g., in charts, graphs, photographs, videos, or maps) with other information in print and digital text.(2010)

CCSS.ELA-LITERACY.RST.6-8.1
Cite specific textual evidence to support analysis of science and technical texts.(2010)

CCSS.ELA-LITERACY.RST.6-8.2
Determine the central ideas or conclusions of a text; provide an accurate summary of the text distinct from prior knowledge or opinions.(2010)

CCSS.ELA-LITERACY.RST.6-8.
Distinguish among facts, reasoned judgment based on research findings, and speculation in text.(2010)

Chapter 24
Section 1

Exploration of the Idiom:
As the Story Goes

Common Core State Standards:
- CCSS.ELA-LITERACY.WHST.6-8.8
- CCSS.ELA-LITERACY.WHST.6-8.10
- CCSS.ELA-LITERACY.RH.6-8.4
- CCSS.ELA-LITERACY.RH.6-8.7

Learning Objectives:
- A. Understand the figurative meaning of idioms
- B. Comprehend the problematic issues with literal translations of idioms

As the Story Goes

Instructions:
Place your answers to each challenge into a journal or folder

Challenge One:
Translate "As the Story Goes" **into your own words**. (Comprehension)

Challenge Two:
Create two separate sentences using the idiom "As the Story Goes".(Application)

Challenge Three:
Identify another idiom that is similar to "As the Story Goes".(Analysis)

Challenge Four:
List creative works that revolve around the concept "As the Story Goes". Explain.(Analysis)

Suggested Start:
Using an American English Idiom dictionary, define the figurative meaning of "As the Story Goes".

Potential Resources:
     1.) Idioms.thefreedictionary.com
     2.) Dictionary.reference.com/idioms

Challenge Five:

Create, draw or sketch three **individual** objects that represent the word "trailblazer". Based on your images, explain the connection(s) to the subject.(Synthesis)

Example 1:
Humbled

Example 2:
Driven

Challenge Six:

Create two or more images that express the question "Life on Mars?" But, use as few images and letters as possible. Then, repeat this process with the thought, "Life on Earth". Communicate the subtle or overt meaning of the objects inside your images.(Synthesis)

Example One: *I dislike turtles.*

Example Two: *I love turtles.*

Chapter 24
Section 2

Perspectives on:
Differentiation

Common Core State Standards:
- CCSS.ELA-LITERACY.WHST.6-8.7
- CCSS.ELA-LITERACY.WHST.6-8.8
- CCSS.ELA-LITERACY.WHST.6-8.10
- CCSS.ELA-LITERACY.RST.6-8.1
- CCSS.ELA-LITERACY.RST.6-8.2

Learning Objectives:
- A. Gain perspective on vague writing
- B. Gain awareness of potential problems with "absolute" statements in writing
- C. Gain perspective on multiple answers

Consonants and Vowels are the same

Instructions:
Place your answers to each challenge into a journal or folder

Challenge One:
"Vowels and consonants are the same." Respond to the statement. Explain.(Analysis)

Challenge Two:
"Vowels and consonants are different". Respond to the statement.   Explain.(Analysis)

Here are recommendations to keep in mind when answering the above questions:
1. Operationalize the word "same".
2. Operationalize the word "vowel".
3. Operationalize the word "consonant".
4. Cite sources that defend your argument.

Suggested Start:
   1. Pause before answering the question.
   2. Using a dictionary, define "vowel".
   3. Using a dictionary, define "consonant".

Potential Resources:
   1.) Merriam-Webster.com
   2.) Bartleby.com

Challenge Three:
Create a joke that you must answer in a figurative way and a literal way. Remember, keep it clean and respectful. NO PRACTICAL JOKES!(Analysis)

Example:
Joke(the setup): *They say "failure is a part of learning".*
Figurative answer (punchline): *Could someone please explain that to my parents.*
Literal answer: *This quote translates more often into "We learn from our mistakes". Whether a person is completing a quiz or learning to ride a bike, mistakes may occur, and they have the option to grow from their small failures.*

The secret to creating jokes is to ask questions about the world. In other words, analyze the world around you. If it doesn't make sense, question it. Then, research it.

To help, start with a statement like:
Why is it that...............
Ever notice that...........
Whose idea was it to make...
One day, there was a..................
Why does....
Where's the......
How is it that....

Don't forget to explore and explain the answer in a figurative and literal way. Creating jokes can be challenging. Worst case scenario, find and use a joke that you can answer in a figurative and literal way. Explain, why it is funny. Give credit to the comedian.

Challenge Four:
First, **define** the word, "Independent". Second, create a two column chart with a "negative factors" side and a "positive factors" side. Third, contrast the positive factors and negative issues of the word, "Independent".(Analysis)

Example:

According to _____'s dictionary, **failure** is....

Failure	
Negative Factors	**Positive Factors**
May spark negative emotions	Mistakes and failings are a part of the creation process
May affect interpersonal relationships	"When you quit that is true failure"
	Don't make failing a habit; however, if it happens, learn from your failure

Challenge Five:
Find an image. Then, create a chart that lists the directly observable features versus the not-visible, but inferable features of the image.(Analysis)

Example: Elephants	
Observable and Visible	**Not Visible, but Inferable**
are mammals	have teeth
cannot fly (without help)	have tails

Chapter 24
Section 3

Exploring Quotations by:
an inventor

Common Core State Standards:
- CCSS.ELA-LITERACY.WHST.6-8.6
- CCSS.ELA-LITERACY.WHST.6-8.8
- CCSS.ELA-LITERACY.WHST.6-8.10
- CCSS.ELA-LITERACY.RH.6-8.1
- CCSS.ELA-LITERACY.RH.6-8.4
- CCSS.ELA-LITERACY.RH.6-8.7

Learning Objectives:
A. Gain knowledge from your chosen inventor
B. Experience historical perspectives

Quotations by an Inventor

Instructions:
Place your answers to each challenge into a journal or folder

Challenge One:
Locate a quotation by an inventor.(Knowledge)

Challenge Two:
Translate your selected quotation into your own words.(Comprehension)

Challenge Three:
Compose a biographical statement using your chosen quotation by an inventor.(Application)

Challenge Four:
Locate another quote on the same subject as your chosen quotation by a different inventor. Compare and contrast both quotations.(Analysis)

Suggested Start:
1. Reflect on "inventions".
2. Quotation resources are available at your local library.

Potential Resources:
1.) Quoteland.com
2.) Brainyquote.com
3.) Quotationspage.com
4.) En.wikiquote.org

Challenge Five:
Using a quotation by an inventor, discover a way to express the meaning through pictures and words. Then, create a comic strip that explains the quotation. (Synthesis)

Example:
"Hunger"
"Thou shouldst eat to live; not live to eat."
Socrates

Create a collection of images that relate to the quote. Then, add captions or messages that help express the quote. Lastly, connect images and create a comic strip.

Challenge Six:
Complete the following sentence fragment with three
or more separate statements. Figure out a way to incorporate a quotation, adage, or joke.(Application)

Problem Solving...

Example:

The last movie that I saw...
1.) ...caused my mind to reflect on the possibilities of humans having superpowers. For
instance, by combining advanced nanotechnology with our understanding of genetics, we
could modify ourselves into more supercharged
people.

2.) ...agitated me because it depicted the cruelties of mankind. However, I then reflected on an
anonymous quote that "Unfortunately, the road
to progress can have various levels of bumpiness".

3.) ...frightened me because it was a creepy
horror film. Now, I want to sleep with the lights
on, but my parents disagree. Even though, I
don't pay the electric bill. I feel that I should be
able to make this decision!

Chapter 24
Section 4

Exploration of Adages,
Aphorisms, Proverbs, and Maxims:

Common Core State Standards:
- CCSS.ELA-LITERACY.WHST.6-8.6
- CCSS.ELA-LITERACY.WHST.6-8.8
- CCSS.ELA-LITERACY.WHST.6-8.10
- CCSS.ELA-LITERACY.RH.6-8.4
- CCSS.ELA-LITERACY.RH.6-8.7

Learning Objectives:
  A. Experience perceptive sayings from various cultures
  B. Examine beliefs and understandings of various individuals and groups

Adages, Aphorisms, Proverbs, and Maxims

Instructions:
Place your answers to each challenge into a journal or folder

Challenge One:
Select an adage, aphorism, proverb, or maxim. Research the origin of the adage, aphorism, proverb, or maxim. Cite source(s).(Knowledge)

Challenge Two:
Translate your chosen adage, aphorism, proverb, or maxim into your own words.(Comprehension)

Challenge Three:
Compose a small paragraph or a short segment of dialogue that includes your chosen adage, aphorism, proverb, or maxim.(Application)

Challenge Four:
Do you agree or disagree with the message of your chosen adage, aphorism, proverb, or maxim. Defend your response. Cite sources.(Evaluation)

Suggested Start:
1. Reflect on your chosen adage, aphorism, proverb, or maxim.
2. Identify problems, if any.

Potential Resources:
1.) En.wikiquote.org
2.) Thinkexist.com

Challenge Five:

Select at least three pictures based on your selected adage, aphorism, proverb, or maxim. Next, build three posters by adding text to the chosen pictures. (Synthesis)

Suggested Start:
"Keep your Mouth Shut, and your Eyes Open"

1. Make sure you understand the adage, aphorism, proverb, or maxim.
2. Reflect on the meaning(s) of your chosen adage, aphorism, proverb, or maxim.
3. Search for images that symbolize or reflect the adage, aphorism, proverb, or maxim.
4. Construct posters.

Think Before You Speak

Keep your Mouth Shut and your Eyes Open.

Challenge Six:

Is it better to <u>demand</u> or <u>request</u>?

In this exercise, consider possible scenarios when it is better to do one or the other underlined options. Next, find scenarios that benefit from each underlined option. Then, try to find scenarios that do not benefit from each underlined option. Create a chart that represents your conclusions. Lastly, compose statements using historical examples or scientific data that validate each item inside your chart. (Evaluation)

Example: Is it better to <u>spark</u> or <u>spur</u>?

Neither	Spark	Spur	Both
malice	critical thoughts	truthfulness	healthy behavior
hatred	cooperation	obedience	innovations
ignorance	motivation	horse	inventions
	confidence		imagination
			students
			self-control

   A. <u>Hatred</u> can <u>spark</u> destructive behavior such as... (insert historical example).
   B. Although, at times effective, spurred obedience has a limited shelf life; eventually, the spurred will rebel or revolt such as a child or colony...
   C. According to _____(author/researcher/expert), sparking confidence can boost students' comprehension.

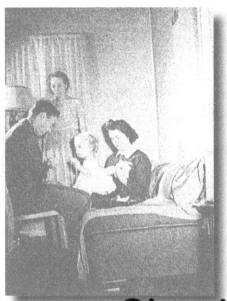

Chapter 24
Section 5

Exploration of Business

Common Core State Standards:
- CCSS.ELA-LITERACY.WHST.6-8.6
- CCSS.ELA-LITERACY.WHST.6-8.7
- CCSS.ELA-LITERACY.WHST.6-8.8
- CCSS.ELA-LITERACY.WHST.6-8.9
- CCSS.ELA-LITERACY.WHST.6-8.10
- CCSS.ELA-LITERACY.RH.6-8.4
- CCSS.ELA-LITERACY.RH.6-8.7

Learning Objectives:
- A. Examine products and services from the view of an organizational entity such as a business
- B. Communicate information through graphics and text such as diagrams and charts

Product and Service Path

Instructions:
Place your answers to each challenge into a journal or folder

Challenge One:
Brainstorm a list of four new products or services that are less than 3 years old. Select one of the products or services.(Knowledge)

Challenge Two:
Identify the type of companies that produce your chosen product or service. Classify their industry.(Comprehension)

Challenge Three:
Identify three direct competitors of your chosen product or service. Describe and chart the competition based on market share, business size (by employees), years available, marketing reach(local, regional, national, global), revenue and profits. Research and use industry averages if your chosen company or its competitors are not publicly traded.(Analysis)

Main Product (Web Browsers)				
	Market Share	**Business Size**	**Marketing Reach**	**Years Available**
Internet Explorer (product)	2	large enterprise	global	19
Chrome (competitor)	1	large enterprise	global	6
Firefox (competitor)	3	mid-size	global	12
Opera (competitor)	4	mid-size	global	18

Challenge four:

Create a diagram that displays the major parts or sequences of your chosen product or service. Next explain two of the product's major parts. For example, an Xbox 360 has multiple, specialized parts such as the central processing unit, the graphics processing unit and the hard drive. Use graphics. Cite sources. (Analysis)

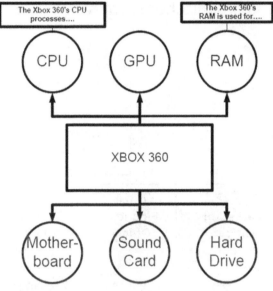

Challenge Five:

Based on your chosen product or service, identify three influential people that had a major impact on this industry through improvements, innovations, or inventions. Describe their effects on the industry. Cite sources.(Analysis)

Industry: Telecommunications		
insert image	John Doe	was an inventor whose radical and unorthodox methods produced the first....
insert image	Jane Doe	was an amazing engineer who invented the first....
insert image	Dr. Cooper	was a well-known and well-respected physician that accidentally invented....

Challenge Six:
Create an organizational chart (unofficial) of a company that offers your chosen product or service. Next, pinpoint the areas where your three previously chosen influential people would work. For example, if one of your selected influential people is a visionary executive leader, then they would fit somewhere at the top of the organizational chart(org chart).(Synthesis)

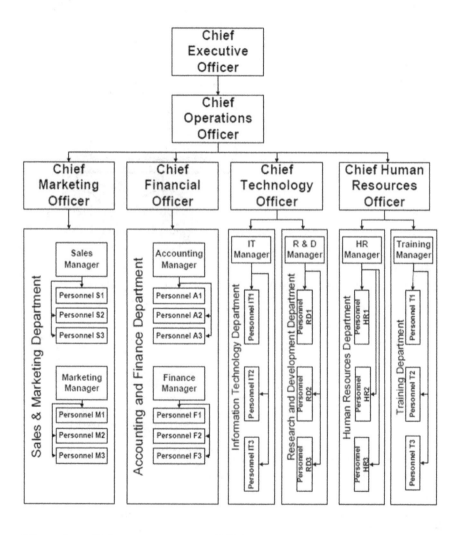

Challenge Seven:
Based on your gathered research and your product choice, create a visual flowchart or graphical diagram that demonstrates the interaction between human resources and non-human resources to produce the product or service. Start with the necessary (raw) materials required to produce the product or service. For example, an organic farmer needs supplies, materials, equipment, and workers. Then, your flowchart should display the interactions between the workforce and resources until the end-product reaches consumers. (Synthesis)

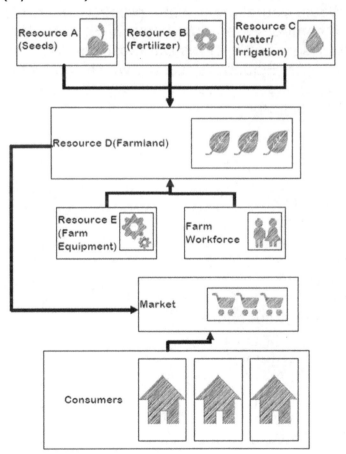

Challenge Eight:

Based on your product choice or service selection,
- Identify two supplemental/complementary products or services such as computer applications complement computer operating systems
- Identify two required/necessary products (computer operating system are necessary to operate computers)
- Identify two separate or indirectly connected products or services that the company produces(Xbox 360 or Zune)

Discover which product(s) is your strongest seller(s). Why? Would you eliminate any products or services from the company's product lineup? Explain. Which product or service deserves the most research and development? Elaborate. Lastly, which product or service deserves the most marketing. Explain. Cite sources.(Evaluation)

Potential Resources:
- www.bls.gov/ooh
- www.bls.gov/iag
- howstuffworks.com
- visual.merriam-webster.com
- finance.yahoo.com
- ehow.com
- sba.gov
- entrepreneur.com

Rubric for Chapter
See Appendix A

Reflective Questions for Chapter
See Appendix B

Chapter 25

Connections to
Common Core State Standards:

CCSS.ELA-LITERACY.WHST.6-8.6
Use technology, including the Internet, to produce and publish writing and present the relationships between information and ideas clearly and efficiently.(2010)

CCSS.ELA-LITERACY.WHST.6-8.7
Conduct short research projects to answer a question(including a self-generated question), drawing on several sources and generating additional related, focused questions that allow for multiple avenues of exploration.(2010)

CCSS.ELA-LITERACY.WHST.6-8.8
Gather relevant information from multiple print and digital sources, using search terms effectively; assess the credibility and accuracy of each source; and quote or paraphrase the data and conclusions of others while avoiding plagiarism and following a standard form of citation.(2010)

CCSS.ELA-LITERACY.WHST.6-8.9
Draw evidence from informational texts to support analysis, reflection, and research.(2010)

Connections to
Common Core State Standards:

CCSS.ELA-LITERACY.WHST.6-8.10
Write routinely over extended time frames(time for revision and reflection) and shorter time frames(a single sitting or a day or two) for a range of discipline-specific tasks, purposes, and audiences.(2010)

CCSS.ELA-LITERACY.RH.6-8.1
Cite specific textual evidence to support analysis of primary and secondary sources.(2010)

CCSS.ELA-LITERACY.RH.6-8.4
Determine the meaning of words and phrases as they are used in a text, including vocabulary specific to domains related to history/social studies.(2010)

CCSS.ELA-LITERACY.RH.6-8.7
Integrate visual information(e.g., in charts, graphs, photographs, videos, or maps) with other information in print and digital text.(2010)

CCSS.ELA-LITERACY.RST.6-8.1
Cite specific textual evidence to support analysis of science and technical texts.(2010)

CCSS.ELA-LITERACY.RST.6-8.2
Determine the central ideas or conclusions of a text; provide an accurate summary of the text distinct from prior knowledge or opinions.(2010)

CCSS.ELA-LITERACY.RST.6-8.
Distinguish among facts, reasoned judgment based on research findings, and speculation in text.(2010)

Chapter 25
Section 1

Exploration of the Idiom:
Cat Got Your Tongue

Common Core State Standards:
- CCSS.ELA-LITERACY.WHST.6-8.8
- CCSS.ELA-LITERACY.WHST.6-8.10
- CCSS.ELA-LITERACY.RH.6-8.4
- CCSS.ELA-LITERACY.RH.6-8.7

Learning Objectives:
- A. Understand the figurative meaning of idioms
- B. Comprehend the problematic issues with literal translations of idioms

Cat Got Your Tongue

Instructions:
Place your answers to each challenge into a journal or folder

Challenge One:
Translate "Cat Got Your Tongue" **into your own words**.(Comprehension)

Challenge Two:
Create two separate sentences using the idiom "Cat Got Your Tongue".(Application)

Challenge Three:
Identify another idiom that is similar to "Cat Got Your Tongue".(Analysis)

Challenge Four:
Recall and list **fictional** characters that exhibited or symbolized this idiomatic expression. Provide examples of their behavior.(Analysis)

Challenge Five:
List words that can be associated with the idiomatic expression, "Cat got your Tongue". Explain each word association.(Evaluation)

Suggested Start:
Using an American English Idiom dictionary, define the figurative meaning of "Cat got your tongue".

Potential Resources:
      1.) Idioms.thefreedictionary.com
      2.) Dictionary.reference.com/idioms

Challenge Six:

Create, draw or sketch three **individual** objects that represent the word "Inflated". Based on your images, explain the connection(s) to the subject.(Synthesis)

Example 1:
Humbled

Example 2:
Driven

Challenge Seven:

Create two or more images that express the statement "That's an ebullient attitude!" But, use as few images and letters as possible. Then, repeat this process with the thought, "It is hard to argue with their polemic statements!" Explain and defend your artwork.(Synthesis)

Example One: *I dislike wasps.*

Example Two: *I love wasps.*

Chapter 25
Section 2

Perspectives on:
Necessities

Common Core State Standards:
- CCSS.ELA-LITERACY.WHST.6-8.7
- CCSS.ELA-LITERACY.WHST.6-8.8
- CCSS.ELA-LITERACY.WHST.6-8.10
- CCSS.ELA-LITERACY.RST.6-8.1
- CCSS.ELA-LITERACY.RST.6-8.2

Learning Objectives:
A. Gain perspective on vague writing
B. Gain awareness of potential problems with "absolute" statements in writing
C. Gain perspective on multiple answers

Electricity is a Necessity

Instructions:
Place your answers to each challenge into a journal or folder

Challenge One:
"Electricity is a necessity." Respond to this statement. Defend your response.(Analysis)

Challenge Two:
"Humans cannot exist without electricity." Respond to this statement. Defend your response.(Analysis)

Challenge Three:
"Electricity has always been a necessity." Respond to this statement. Defend your response.(Analysis)

Here are recommendations to keep in mind when answering the above questions:
1. What is a necessity?
2. Is there more than one type of electricity?
3. Cite sources that defend your argument.

Suggested Start:
1. Pause before answering the question.
2. Using a dictionary, define "Electricity".
3. Using an encyclopedia, research "Electricity".

Potential Resources:
1.) Merriam-Webster.com
2.) Bartleby.com

Challenge Four:
Create a joke that you must answer in a figurative way and a literal way. Remember, keep it clean and respectful. NO PRACTICAL JOKES!

Example:
Joke(setup): *They say "failure is a part of learning".*
Figurative answer (punchline): *Could someone please explain that to my parents.*
Literal answer: *This quote translates more often into "We learn from our mistakes". Whether a person is completing a quiz or learning to ride a bike, mistakes may occur, and they have the option to grow from their small failures.*

The secret to creating jokes is to ask questions about the world. In other words, analyze the world around you. If it doesn't make sense, question it. Then, research it.

To help, start with a statement like:
Why is it that..............
Ever notice that...........
Whose idea was it to make...
One day, there was a.................
Why does....
Where's the......
How is it that....

Don't forget to explore and explain the answer in a figurative and literal way. Creating jokes can be challenging. Worst case scenario, find and use a joke that you can answer in a figurative and literal way. Explain, why it is funny. Give credit to the comedian.

Challenge Five:
First, **define** the word, "Success". Second, create a two column chart with a "negative factors" side and a "positive factors" side. Third, contrast the positive factors and negative issues of the word, "Success". (Analysis)

Example:
According to _____'s dictionary, **failure** is....

Failure	
Negative Factors	**Positive Factors**
May spark negative emotions	Mistakes and failings are a part of the creation process
May affect interpersonal relationships	"When you quit that is true failure"
	Don't make failing a habit; however, if it happens, learn from your failure

Challenge Six:
Find an image. Then, create a chart that lists the directly observable features versus the not-visible, but inferable features of the image.(Analysis)

Example: Horse	
Observable and Visible	**Not Visible, but Inferable**
is a mammal	has teeth
has tail	likes carrots

Chapter 25
Section 3

Exploring Quotations by:
a Historical Figure

Common Core State Standards:
- CCSS.ELA-LITERACY.WHST.6-8.6
- CCSS.ELA-LITERACY.WHST.6-8.8
- CCSS.ELA-LITERACY.WHST.6-8.10
- CCSS.ELA-LITERACY.RH.6-8.1
- CCSS.ELA-LITERACY.RH.6-8.4
- CCSS.ELA-LITERACY.RH.6-8.7

Learning Objectives:
- A. Gain knowledge on the topic of a famous histori-cal figure
- B. Experience historical perspectives

Quotations by a Famous Historical Figure

Instructions:
Place your answers to each challenge into a journal or folder

Challenge One:
Locate a quotation by a famous historical figure. (Knowledge)

Challenge Two:
Translate your chosen quotation into your own words. (Comprehension)

Challenge Three:
Compose a biographical statement using your chosen quotation.(Application)

Challenge Four:
Locate another quote on the same subject as your chosen quotation by a different historical figure. Compare and contrast both quotations.(Analysis)

Suggested Start:
1. Reflect on famous contributors to an area of interest.
2. Quotation resources are available at your local library.

Potential Resource:
1.) En.wikiquote.org

Challenge Five:
Using a quotation from a historical figure, discover a way to express the meaning through pictures and words. Then, create a comic strip that explains the quotation.(Synthesis)

Example:
"Hunger"
"Thou shouldst eat to live; not live to eat."
Socrates

Create a collection of images that relate to the quote. Then, add captions or messages that help express the quote. Lastly, connect images and create a comic strip.

Challenge Six:
Complete the following sentence fragment with three
or more separate statements. Figure out a way to incorporate a quotation, adage, or joke.(Application)

Historical wisdom...

Example:

The last movie that I saw...
1.) ...caused my mind to reflect on the possibilities of humans having superpowers. For
instance, by combining advanced nanotechnology with our understanding of genetics, we
could modify ourselves into more supercharged
people.

2.) ...agitated me because it depicted the cruelties of mankind. However, I then reflected on an
anonymous quote that "Unfortunately, the road
to progress can have various levels of bumpiness".

3.) ...frightened me because it was a creepy
horror film. Now, I want to sleep with the lights
on, but my parents disagree. Even though, I
don't pay the electric bill. I feel that I should be
able to make this decision!

Chapter 25
Section 4

Exploration of Adages, Aphorisms, Proverbs, and Maxims:

Common Core State Standards:
- CCSS.ELA-LITERACY.WHST.6-8.6
- CCSS.ELA-LITERACY.WHST.6-8.8
- CCSS.ELA-LITERACY.WHST.6-8.10
- CCSS.ELA-LITERACY.RH.6-8.4
- CCSS.ELA-LITERACY.RH.6-8.7

Learning Objectives:
- A. Experience perceptive sayings from various cultures
- B. Examine beliefs and understandings of various individuals and groups

Adages, Aphorisms, Proverbs, and Maxims

Instructions:
Place your answers to each challenge into a journal or folder

Challenge One:
Select an adage, aphorism, proverb, or maxim. Research the origin of the adage, aphorism, proverb, or maxim. Cite source(s).(Knowledge)

Challenge Two:
Translate your chosen adage, aphorism, proverb, or maxim into your own words.(Comprehension)

Challenge Three:
Compose a small paragraph or a short segment of dialogue that includes your chosen adage, aphorism, proverb, or maxim.(Application)

Challenge Four:
Do you agree or disagree with the message of your chosen adage, aphorism, proverb, or maxim. Defend your response. Cite sources.(Evaluation)

Suggested Start:
1. Reflect on your chosen adage, aphorism, proverb, or maxim.
2. Identify problems, if any.

Potential Resources:
   1.) En.wikiquote.org
   2.) Thinkexist.com

Challenge Five:
Select at least three pictures based on your selected adage, aphorism, proverb, or maxim. Next, build three posters by adding text to the chosen pictures. (Synthesis)

Suggested Start:
"Keep your Mouth Shut, and your Eyes Open"
1. Make sure you understand the adage, aphorism, proverb, or maxim.
2. Reflect on the meaning(s) of your chosen adage, aphorism, proverb, or maxim.
3. Search for images that symbolize or reflect the adage, aphorism, proverb, or maxim.
4. Construct posters.

Challenge Six:

Is it better to <u>act</u> or <u>react</u>?

In this exercise, consider possible scenarios when it is better to do one or the other underlined options. Next, find scenarios that benefit from each underlined option. Then, try to find scenarios that do not benefit from each underlined option. Create a chart that represents your conclusions. Lastly, compose statements using historical examples or scientific data that validate each item inside your chart. (Evaluation)

Example: Is it better to <u>spark</u> or <u>spur</u>?

Neither	Spark	Spur	Both
malice	critical thoughts	truthfulness	healthy behavior
hatred	cooperation	obedience	innovations
ignorance	motivation	horse	inventions
	confidence		imagination
			students
			self-control

A. <u>Hatred</u> can <u>spark</u> destructive behavior such as... (insert historical example).
B. Although, at times effective, spurred obedience has a limited shelf life; eventually, the spurred will rebel or revolt such as a child or colony...
C. According to _____(author/researcher/expert), sparking confidence can boost students' comprehension.

Chapter 25
Section 5

Exploration of Business

Common Core State Standards:
- CCSS.ELA-LITERACY.WHST.6-8.6
- CCSS.ELA-LITERACY.WHST.6-8.7
- CCSS.ELA-LITERACY.WHST.6-8.8
- CCSS.ELA-LITERACY.WHST.6-8.9
- CCSS.ELA-LITERACY.WHST.6-8.10
- CCSS.ELA-LITERACY.RH.6-8.4
- CCSS.ELA-LITERACY.RH.6-8.7

Learning Objectives:
- A. Examine business costs and opportunities
- B. Communicate information through graphics and text such as diagrams and charts

Organization Path

Instructions:
Place your answers to each challenge into a journal or folder

Challenge One:
Discover four businesses that are at least 100 years old. Choose one of the businesses. Then, classify the business by type. Identify its main product.(Knowledge)

Challenge Two:
Identify three competitors of this business.(Comprehension)

Challenge Three:
Identify three products or services of your chosen company. Create a chart that displays the relationship among the main product and the additional products. Determine if these products are:
- Integrated and necessary for the main product to operate such as gasoline or motor oil for cars
- Complementary to the product and enhances product like air conditioning and power windows for cars
- Vital to the business such as their brand brake pads and spark plugs for their car brand (Application)

Main Product(Windows Operating System)			
	Integrated and Necessary	Enhances Main Product	Vital to Business
Microsoft Office	No	Yes	Yes
Internet Explorer	Yes	Yes	Yes
Xbox 360	No	No	No

Challenge Four:

Categorize the four chosen products by popularity among consumers, history of the products, revenue, profit, target audience(name their main customers), and strongest direct competitor, quasi-competitor and indirect competitor. Use a scale from 4 to 1, 4 being highest, to grade each category. Then, based on your chart, describe the growth potential (or lack of future potential) of each product. Which product is the strongest? Which product would you focus more resources on for the future of the company. Defend your decision. Cite sources.(Analysis)

Strengths and Weaknesses				
	Windows OS	Microsoft Office	Internet Explorer	Xbox 360
Popularity	3	4	2	1
Revenue	3	4	2	1
Profitabil- ity	3	4	2	1

Strengths and Weaknesses by Details				
	Windows OS	Microsoft Office	Internet Explorer	Xbox 360
Years Available	28 yrs.	23 yrs.	19 yrs.	8 yrs.
Direct Competitor	Mac OS X	LibreOf- fice	Chrome	Playsta- tion 3
Quasi- Competitor	Android OS	QuickOf- fice	Smart- TVs	Gameboy Advance
Indirect Competitor	Pen and Paper	Typewriter	Library Card	Mobile Device
Rankings among direct Com- petitors	#1	#1	#2	#1

Challenge Five:

Choose one of your chosen company's most popular or well-known products or services. Research this product or service and build a diagram that displays the fabrication process of the product or service. Cite sources.(Synthesis)

Your diagram or chart should display the work that goes into producing a product or service.

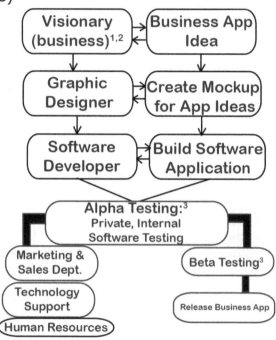

1 Does the app solve a problem?
2 Can it be profitable?
3 Testing may require restarts or revisions.

Challenge Six:

Create a chart that explains two of the chosen product's major features. For example, an alarm clock normally has a minimum of two features, the time display and the alarm function. Use graphics, if possible. Cite sources.(Analysis)

Alarm Radio	
Radio	converts radio waves...
Alarm Buzzer	is a feature of the...

Challenge Seven:

Based on your gathered research and your product choice, create a visual flowchart or graphical diagram that demonstrates the interaction between human resources and non-human resources to produce the product or service. Start with the necessary (raw) materials required to produce the product or service. For example, an organic farmer needs supplies, materials, equipment, and workers. Then, your flowchart should display the interactions between the workforce and resources until the end-product reaches consumers. (Synthesis)

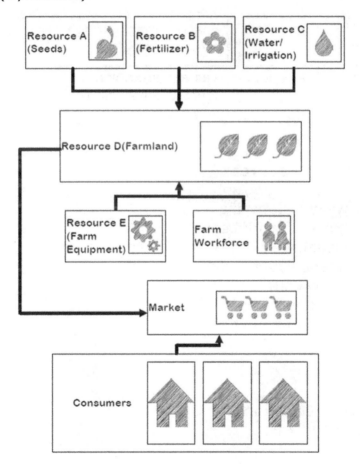

Challenge Eight:
Identify three individuals that had a major impact on your chosen company's industry. Create a multimedia chart to describe their impact. Based on your research of these three individuals, which individual had the biggest impact on their industry. Defend your argument. Cite sources.(Evaluation)

Industry: Telecommunications		
insert image	John Doe	was an inventor whose radical and unorthodox methods produced the first....
insert image	Jane Doe	was an amazing engineer who invented the first....
insert image	Dr. Cooper	was a well-known and well-respected physician that accidentally invented....

Potential Resources:
- www.bls.gov/ooh
- www.bls.gov/iag
- howstuffworks.com
- visual.merriam-webster.com
- finance.yahoo.com
- ehow.com
- sba.gov
- entrepreneur.com

Rubric for Chapter
See Appendix A

Reflective Questions for Chapter
See Appendix B

Appendix A

Rubric for Research Prompts

Rubric for Research Prompts:				
	Excellent [4 points]	Good [3 points]	Incomplete [2 points]	Points
Demonstration of Discovery	Student shows evidence of gathering information to defend their responses for challenges.	Student shows evidence of gathering information, but also relies on assumptions.	Shows lack of evidence of gathering information or data and strongly relies on assumptions to complete work.	
Demonstration of Expression	Student finishes visual and textual compositions such as a thought-provoking joke, comic strip, or other artwork based on the challenge.	Student nearly finishes visual and textual compositions such as a joke, comic strip, poster or other artwork based on the challenge.	Incomplete or lack of visual and textual compositions such as a joke, comic strip, poster or other artwork based on the challenge.	
Exhibition of Reflective Thinking	Student answers each question on the Reflection Checklist.	Student answers the majority of questions on the Reflection Checklist.	Student answers a few questions on the Reflection Checklist.	
			Subtotal:	/12

	Excellent [4 points]	Good [3 points]	Incomplete [2 points]	Points
Rubric for Research Prompts(continued)				
Quality of Arguments	Student presents arguments to defend their creations and evaluations. Arguments thoroughly defends their position and reasoning through examples, scenarios, and other forms of evidence.	Student delivers arguments that partially defend their position and reasoning. Some arguments may lack sufficient examples, scenarios, and other types of evidence.	Student's visual works and textual compositions lack arguments that defend their position and reasoning. Student's work lacks examples, scenarios, and other types of evidence.	
Grammar and Punctuation	Student's work has no more than two grammar or punctuation errors.	Student's work has between three and five grammar and punctuation errors.	More than five grammar or punctuation errors.	
Citations of References / Resources	Cite all sources in preferred format.	Cites most sources; however, some are not formatted correctly. Citations are not uniform.	Citations are missing from work.	
			Total Points:	/24

Appendix B

Reflective Questioning Checklist for Research Prompts

Checklist for Section 1:

Knowledge: Were you able to define the idiom?

Comprehension: Were you able to describe the idiom in your own words?

Application: Were you able to apply your understanding of the idiom and write two sentences using this idiomatic expression?

Analysis: Were you able to find a similar idiom to the assigned idiom? Did you discover a new understanding about the idiom? If so, what?

Synthesis: Were you able to transform the vocabulary into images? Were you able to create images that express a sentiment? What type of strategy did you use?

Evaluation: Were you able to compare various fictional characters to the idiom? Can you defend your responses to each challenge?

Final question: Upon reflection, did you discover anything new, interesting, useful, or strange?
Explain, why or why not.

Checklist for Section 2:

Knowledge: Were you able to locate the answer? Or, were you able to find answers to the problem? Was your first thought correct? After doing research, was your first educated guess or hypothesis correct?

Comprehension: Does perspective affect the outcome of the question? Does context matter with the current questions? Were there any statements using absolutes? Did any of the questions make you curious?

Application: Can perspective assist with finding alternative answers? How?

Analysis: If you created a joke, did it give you a wider perspective or narrower perspective on your topic? Were you able to explain your joke in a literal way? Were you able to explain your joke in a figurative manner? If you found a joke, did it give you a wider perspective or narrower perspective on your topic? Were you able to explain the joke in a figurative and literal way? After defining the topic, were you able to contrast the positives and negatives of the topic? After finding an image, were you able to visualize the visible and non-visual parts of an object?

Synthesis: Were you able to create a joke that highlights the truth in a funny way? Were you able to create a joke that demonstrates a peculiar reality of the universe in a humorous way? Were you able to create a joke that references a point of view that doesn't make sense to you? Is your joke original or a variation on a theme?

Evaluation: Are you able to defend your answer or answers per challenge?

Final question: Upon reflection, did you discover anything new, interesting, useful, or strange? Explain, why or why not.

Checklist for Section 3:

Knowledge: Were you able to find a quotation on the provided topic?

Comprehension: Were you able to translate your selected quotation into your own words?

Application: Were you able to compose a biographical statement using your chosen quotation? Were you able to compose three separate statements that incorporate a quotation, adage, or joke?

Analysis: Based on the chosen topic, which was more difficult to create a quote or a poem? Why?

Synthesis: Were you able to produce your own quote on the provided topic? Were you able to produce your own poem on the provided topic? Were you able to create a comic strip that relates to your chosen quotation?

Evaluation: Can you defend your responses to each challenge?

Final Checklist Question: Upon reflection, did you discover anything new, interesting, useful, or strange? Explain, why or why not.

Checklist for Section 4:

Knowledge: Were you able to gather an aphorism, proverb, adage, or maxim?

Comprehension: Were you able to express your chosen adage, proverb, aphorism, or maxim into your own words?

Application: Were you able to compose a small paragraph or short segment of dialogue that includes your chosen adage, proverb, aphorism, or maxim?

Analysis: Do you disagree or agree with your chosen adage, proverb, aphorism, or maxim? Why?

Synthesis: Were you able to create posters that symbolically represent your chosen adage, proverb, aphorism, or maxim?

Evaluation: Were you able to examine multiple possibilities and perspectives between two separate words, such as spark or spur? Can you defend your responses to each challenge?

Final Checklist Question: Upon reflection, did you discover anything new, interesting, useful, or strange? Explain, why or why not.

Checklist for Section 5	
Organization Path	
Knowledge	Based on your objectives, were you able to select a business?
Comprehension	Based on your objectives, were you able to identify three competing businesses?
Application	Based on your objectives, were you able to illustrate various criteria such as enhancements to main product or vital to main service?
Analysis	Were you able to make informed business decisions about these products or services? Were you able to identify major features of a product? Based on your research, were you able to compare three influential individuals in their industry. Were you able to determine which one of the three was the most influential?
Synthesis	Based on your research, were you able to build a step-by-step diagram that demonstrates the potential effort required to create a product or service? Were you able to design a chart that demonstrates the necessary resources required to produce a product or service?
Evaluation	Were you able to categorize your chosen products or services by criteria such as age of product and popularity of service? How do you feel about your business decisions based on your knowledge and understanding of your chosen product or service? Explain.
Upon reflection, did you discover anything new, interesting, useful or strange? Explain, why or why not.	

Checklist for Section 5	
Product and Service Path	
Knowledge	Based on your objectives, were you able to identify the required product or service?
Comprehension	Based on your objectives, were you able to identify competing products or services?
Application	Based on your objectives, were you able to illustrate business information about your identified products and services through charts? Were you able to produce a graphic that explains two functions of your chosen product or service?
Analysis	Were you able to determine upon analysis an influential person who had the greatest impact on their industry?
Synthesis	Were you able to create an organizational chart and insert an influential person into the chart? Were you able to design a chart that demonstrates the necessary connections required to produce a product or service?
Evaluation	How do you feel about your business decisions based on your knowledge and understanding of your chosen product or service? Explain.
Upon reflection, did you discover anything new, interesting, useful or strange? Explain, why or why not.	

Appendix B   612

Index

615

U

V

W

X

Y

Z

Reference List

National Governors Association Center for Best Practices., & Council of Chief State Officers(2010). Common Core State Standards Initiative English Language Arts Standards >> Writing >> Grade 6-8. Retrieved from http://www.corestandards.org/ ELA-Literacy/WHST/6-8/

National Governors Association Center for Best Practices., & Council of Chief State Officers(2010). Common Core State Standards Initiative English Language Arts Standards>>History/Social Studies>>Grade 6-8. Retrieved from http://www.corestandards. org/ELA-Literacy/RH/6-8/

National Governors Association Center for Best Practices., & Council of Chief State Officers(2010). Common Core State Standards Initiative English Language Arts Standards>>Science & Technical Subjects>>Grade 6-8. Retrieved from http:/www. corestandards.org/ELA-Literacy/RST/6-8/